P9-CAY-008

The New Americans
Recent Immigration and American Society

Edited by
Steven J. Gold and Rubén G. Rumbaut

A Series from LFB Scholarly

Economic Mobility and Cultural Assimilation among Children of Immigrants

Caroline L. Faulkner

LFB Scholarly Publishing LLC
El Paso 2011

Copyright © 2011 by LFB Scholarly Publishing LLC

All rights reserved.

Library of Congress Cataloging-in-Publication Data

Faulkner, Caroline L., 1976-
  Economic mobility and cultural assimilation among children of
immigrants / Caroline L. Faulkner.
      p. cm. -- (The new Americans: recent immigration and American
society)
  Includes bibliographical references and index.
  ISBN 978-1-59332-472-8 (hbk. : alk. paper)
  1. Immigrants--Cultural assimilation--United States. 2. Children of
immigrants--United States--Longitudinal studies. 3. Social mobility--
United States. I. Title.
  JV6475.F38 2011
  305.9'069120973--dc23
                                    2011021152

ISBN 978-1-59332-472-8

Printed on acid-free 250-year-life paper.

Manufactured in the United States of America.

Contents

Tables

Acknowledgments

Many people helped and guided me through the process of writing this book, and I am extremely grateful to them. I am especially grateful to Gary Sandefur who guided and encouraged me throughout this process. Ruth López Turley and Jeremy Freese also offered indispensable feedback and lots of support. This book benefited from the useful comments and suggestions of Mara Loveman and Thomas Archdeacon. Others, including Shawn Kanaiaupuni, Katharine Donato, Lincoln Quillian, Betty Thomson, and John Iceland, have shaped my interest in immigration and encouraged me both before and during this project, and I am thankful for their guidance. I would also like to thank Rubén Rumbaut for his insight, encouragement, and direction at various stages during this project. Carol Auster and Katherine McClelland have also supported and assisted me during this process. I owe them my sincere gratitude. Finally, I am grateful for the editorial assistance of Delphine Martin and Claire Mansbach.

CHAPTER 1

Introduction

Sociologists have long used the term "assimilation" to describe the incorporation of immigrants into American society (see, for example, Simons 1901; Park and Burgess 1924; Park 1928; Gordon 1964). In recent years, there has been much discussion about the meaning of assimilation and its applicability to the most recent waves of immigrants to the United States. Portes and Zhou (1993) developed segmented assimilation theory as a response to some of the critiques of earlier assimilation definitions. They suggest that immigrants who enter a stratified society will experience stratified, or segmented, outcomes of incorporation.

While this theoretical framework has been highly influential and has added much to the discussion of immigrant incorporation—most importantly, the idea that there are multiple ways of being "American"—it has consistently overlooked several factors critical to understanding the immigrant experience. First, segmented assimilation theory conflates paths, trajectories of change, with segments, outcomes of assimilation or mobility.[1] Second, segmented assimilation theory and research have often failed to fully consider how immigrants' initial values of assimilation indicators, or "starting points,"[2] are associated with directions of assimilation and their meaning. Third, despite the fact that generational change is the driving force behind assimilation, segmented assimilation theory and research lack a true intergenerational focus, from parents to their own children. Instead, they often infer generational change through a comparison, during the same time period, of individuals of the same age cohort who belong to different generations-since-immigration. Fourth, segmented assimilation theory and research typically overlook gender, considering it only as a variable to control and not an integral part of the assimilation experience. Fifth, much segmented assimilation research uses data on children of immigrants alone and often fails to consider the extent to which some indicators of adaptation, specifically economic mobility, are relevant to the non-immigrant population as well.[3] Finally, segmented assimilation theory and research have rarely considered assimilation or mobility experiences from a life course perspective, i.e., how patterns of assimilation differ depending on one's stage in life.

This book begins to address each of these gaps in the literature. I focus solely on *paths* of mobility and assimilation, examining the direction of change, or lack thereof, for various indicators. I do not make claims about ultimate outcomes of assimilation. I also analyze these paths by individuals' initial characteristics for each mobility or assimilation indicator, which allows me to investigate how individuals experience assimilation differently depending on their starting points. I study both inter- and intragenerational assimilation, incorporating a life course perspective for the latter. In addition, where possible, I consider differences in mobility and assimilation patterns by gender. Finally, I perform an analysis of economic mobility using data on children of immigrants and a comparable nationally representative sample to determine if patterns of mobility among children of immigrants are common to the third and later generation U.S. youth population.[4] This research permits me to examine the prevalence of various paths of assimilation and analyze how they differ across key social structural characteristics.

Classical Assimilation

Sociologists began examining the waves of European immigration in the early twentieth century. Based on these waves of immigrants, a classical description of assimilation emerged suggesting that immigrants followed a somewhat straightforward process— economically, socially, and culturally—into the American mainstream, or middle class. Some theorists associated assimilation with the advancement of immigrant groups and the loss of their "inferior" traits (Warner and Srole 1945). Other definitions of assimilation did not include such value judgments. For example, Park and Burgess, in their canonical work, described assimilation as "...a process of interpenetration and fusion in which persons and groups acquire the memories, sentiments, and attitudes of other persons or groups, and, by sharing their experience and history, are incorporated with them in a common cultural life" (1924: 735). Most classical assimilation theorists suggested that the process of assimilation was likely to take several generations and might differ in speed depending on the immigrant group and its circumstances (Gordon 1964; Park 1950; Warner and Srole 1945; Park and Burgess 1924). For example, Warner and Srole (1945) claimed that groups that were more far removed from the American mainstream—racially, economically, socially, and culturally—were likely to assimilate more slowly than groups whose characteristics upon arrival were more similar to the (white) middle class.

Later theoretical formulations added depth to the concept of assimilation. In particular, Gordon (1964) identified multiple dimensions of assimilation, including cultural, structural, and "identificational" (shifts in ethnic identification) assimilation. Immigrants' incorporation experiences were likely to vary across these different dimensions, particularly in terms of rates of change. Although Gordon presented three theories of assimilation, his illustrations of assimilation dimensions were most closely aligned with the Anglo conformity model, involving the entry of immigrant groups into the white Anglo Saxon mainstream social and cultural realm, rather than the melting pot or cultural pluralism models.[5]

Empirical research on the incorporation of late nineteenth and early twentieth century European immigrants and their descendants generally supports claims of classical assimilation theory. For example, over several generations, waves of European immigrants and their descendants experienced economic advancement, loss of non-English language, and increasing levels of intermarriage (Lieberson 1980; Alba and Golden 1986; Lieberson and Waters 1988; Hirschman and Kraly 1988, 1990; Jacobs and Greene 1994). Some researchers, nevertheless, suggest that these European immigrants' paths of assimilation were not completely unproblematic straight-line marches into the white, Anglo Saxon middle class (Perlmann and Waldinger 1997; Foner 2000; Alba and Nee 2003). Experiences of immigrants since the 1960s also call into question classical assimilation's basic claims.

The Downfall of Classical Assimilation

There have been remarkable shifts in the immigrant experience over the last one-and-a-half centuries. The ethnic and demographic composition of the recent immigrant flow to the United States and the social structure that they encounter differ dramatically from previous waves of immigration. Portes and Zhou (1993) argue that the conditions under which the recent immigration has occurred—particularly the racial backgrounds of immigrants and the current U.S. economic structure—are so different from those of the "old" immigration that classical forms of assimilation will not hold for them.

Portes and Zhou (1993) claim that today's immigrants are more easily kept apart from more mainstream (white) society today because of their non-white racial origins. They argue that, "Even if of a somewhat darker hue than the natives, [European immigrants'] skin color reduced a major barrier to entry into the American mainstream" (76). Non-white skin marks the majority of today's immigrants as "other"; therefore, they do not have the option of blending as seamlessly into white middle-class society (Waters 1990, 1999).[6]

Portes and Zhou (1993) further argue that the economic structure more recent immigrants have encountered presents serious obstacles to economic advancement over the generations for many immigrants. According to segmented assimilation theorists, European second and later generations entered a labor market brimming with diverse job opportunities. These opportunities provided a ladder for economic advancement over the course of individuals' own lives as well as across generations. In contrast, Portes and colleagues (Portes and Zhou 1993; Portes 1995; Zhou 1997; Portes and Rumbaut 2001a; Portes and Rumbaut 2001b; Portes and Fernández-Kelly 2008; Portes, Fernández-Kelly, and Haller 2009; hereafter not cited) claim that today's immigrants encounter an "hourglass" economy, marked by a large supply of jobs at the bottom and the top but few jobs in between. Under these circumstances, economic advancement requires large gains—particularly in educational attainment—in order to make it to the higher rungs of the ladder.[7] Portes and colleagues suggest that many immigrant offspring will fail to overcome this obstacle to advancement and will be trapped at the bottom of the economic hierarchy.

Along with immigrants' non-white racial status and the "hourglass" economy, Portes and colleagues, as well as other researchers, have uncovered two general patterns among children of immigrants that they believe challenge classical assimilation theory. First, for certain characteristics, some second generation immigrants experience changes opposite of the expected classical assimilation outcomes. Portes and Rumbaut (2001a) have found this pattern for ethnic self-identification, in particular. In this case, more second generation youths identify by their national origin groups rather than as "American" or hyphenated American over time in the United States. Second, there is evidence that assimilation can yield a number of negative consequences. For example, there is evidence that assimilation is hazardous, literally, to immigrants' health, as their health risk behaviors become more like their native-born counterparts (Harris 1999). In other words, becoming American involves some unexpected outcomes—some of which have negative repercussions.

Segmented Assimilation

Findings such as these led Portes and Zhou (1993) to propose a new theory of assimilation: segmented assimilation theory.[8] Its most basic premise is that as immigrants enter a stratified society, the outcomes of their incorporation into that society will also be stratified. In other words, experiences of assimilation will not be the same for all immigrants. The question segmented assimilation theorists propose is not whether immigrants assimilate into American society but rather into which *segment* of American society they assimilate.

Portes and Zhou (1993) reveal that there are *at least* three paths of assimilation, involving cultural and economic elements, which lead into different segments of American society. "One of them replicates the time-honored portrayal of growing acculturation and parallel integration into the white middle class; a second leads straight in the opposite direction to permanent poverty and assimilation into the underclass; still a third associates rapid economic advancement with deliberate preservation of the immigrant community's values and tight solidarity" (Portes and Zhou 1993: 82). Zhou (1997) describes the first and third patterns explicitly as involving upward mobility into the middle class. Portes and colleagues assert that the first path represents the classical form of assimilation; the second path involves economic and cultural incorporation into the very bottom of American society; and the third path involves classical economic mobility but only partial classical acculturation. Although they allow that there may be other paths and segments, segmented assimilation theorists do not describe any.

Portes and his colleagues provide little additional theoretical explication on the patterns of assimilation. Most segmented assimilation writings focus on the factors that influence assimilation outcomes—while not always specifically referencing these three patterns. Many of the factors that Portes and Zhou highlight as important in determining these outcomes are also considered important in other theories of assimilation. What is new in segmented assimilation is the focus on the *interaction* of these individual and structural factors as the determinant of the path and the segment of assimilation.

Factors Associated with Paths of Assimilation

Modes of Incorporation

Portes and colleagues suggest that "modes of incorporation," "downward leveling factors," and protective factors influence mobility and assimilation outcomes.[9] Modes of incorporation relate to how immigrants' own characteristics influence their incorporation experiences. These characteristics comprise immigrant human capital, including occupational, familial, financial, linguistic and other resources that immigrant parents bring along with them to their new home countries, as well as "context of reception," or government-, society-, and community-level responses to immigrant groups.

Portes and colleagues assert that, generally, immigrants with more human capital are more likely to succeed economically than other immigrants. They also are able to provide more resources for their own children's success. However, other factors, such as a negative context of reception, which I discuss below, can lessen those associations.

Portes and colleagues do not explicitly discuss how parental or family human capital is likely to influence cultural assimilation. They suggest that youths whose parents have greater resources may experience greater inclusion in American society; that is, they have resources that allow them to participate more fully in mainstream schools and institutions. This greater participation may yield more classical forms of acculturation. However, they also suggest that parents with greater resources may be more able and willing to involve their children in activities that maintain their cultural ties. For example, well-off Cuban parents in Miami often send their children to bilingual private Cuban schools, thereby reinforcing their children's Cuban cultural attachment (Portes and Rumbaut 2001a). Portes and colleagues also imply that those parents who can afford to send their own children back to their countries of origin may help slow more classical forms of assimilation.

Modes of incorporation also include immigrants' context of reception—the governmental, societal, and communal environments that immigrants encounter upon their arrival and during their settlement in the United States. The level of warmth or hostility of this reception is directly tied to immigrants' ethnic origin and the circumstances of their migration. Segmented assimilation theorists and researchers often have used ethnic origin to represent these factors. Rumbaut (2008), for example, outlines three different modes of incorporation associated with various national origin groups. Mode I includes groups characterized by a high proportion of unauthorized immigrants and low levels of education, such as Mexicans, Salvadorans, and Guatemalans. These groups tend to experience hostile governmental reception. Mode II groups are largely legal permanent residents with higher levels of education, including Filipinos, Chinese, Koreans, and Indians. Portes and Rumbaut (2001a) describe their governmental reception as neutral. Mode III includes groups characterized by refugee status and somewhat more mixed human capital (Vietnamese, Cambodians, and Laotians). These groups receive legal protections, resources, and services to which other immigrants are not entitled and, therefore, encounter a more favorable context of reception.

Along with governmental reception, societal reception differs across immigrant groups. Portes and Rumbaut suggest that this reception ranges from favorable to prejudiced. In their book, they suggest that the bulk of recent immigrants—because of their non-white status and/or the perception that they are involved in the drug trade—experience a prejudiced reception. Finally, communal reception refers to the immigrant community in the place of settlement, particularly its socioeconomic status, size, and concentration. It is related to the kinds of resources immigrants can provide to each other.[10] Depending on one's group's resources and level of dispersion, immigrants can (or cannot) count on their co-ethnic counterparts for information and aid. For example, according to Portes and Rumbaut (2001a), the Mexican ethnic community is generally concentrated but of working class status. The kinds of financial resources that members can provide to one another are, therefore, limited. Other groups may be well off but dispersed, such as Filipinos. These groups may have the financial resources to aid their co-ethnic members, but their dispersion makes their community less cohesive and the members' needs are less likely to be met within the community.

The structural conditions that immigrants encounter shape their incorporation experiences. Groups that experience more favorable contexts of reception have higher odds of upward economic mobility. Those that experience favorable governmental and societal reception are also more likely to acculturate in a more classical form. However, those who have more favorable communal reception may be more likely to hold on to (at least some) of their own cultural values and attributes. Segmented assimilation theory predicts that those who experience more negative contexts of reception are at greater risk of downward mobility and acculturation into "underclass" forms.

Downward Leveling Factors

Along with these modes of incorporation, Portes and his collaborators (Portes and Rumbaut 2001a; Portes, Fernández-Kelly, and Haller 2005) describe three obstacles to children of immigrants' incorporation, which they term "downward leveling factors": racial discrimination, the hourglass economy and growing inequality, and inner-city subcultures. First, Portes and colleagues argue that, even among the most "assimilated," many immigrants' skin color sets them apart from a large segment of American society. Racial discrimination "throws a barrier in the path of occupational mobility and social acceptance" for non-whites—whether of immigrant origin or not (Portes and Rumbaut 2001a: 56). Racial discrimination, then, is likely to limit many immigrants' economic success. Moreover, it is likely to increase their odds of rejecting mainstream cultural norms and taking on more "underclass" cultural forms. I discuss adoption of subcultural forms further below.

Second, because the hourglass economy makes it more difficult for children of immigrants to move up the occupational ladder,[11] occupational advancement requires significant gains in educational attainment—gains that took previous immigrants many generations to make (Portes and Rumbaut 2001a). Segmented assimilation theory predicts that the hourglass economy will reduce economic success for children of immigrants, but less so when their parents have more resources.

The third obstacle, countercultures, relates to the social context that individuals encounter. Poor individuals, particularly non-whites, are concentrated geographically in inner-city neighborhoods. In these neighborhoods, behaviors and values antithetical to the mainstream are also concentrated, including low labor force attachment, welfare use, and crime. Immigrants, particularly poor, non-white immigrants, often settle in these areas. Here, they and their children are exposed to these behaviors and values, often from later-generation members of their own racial-ethnic groups. According to segmented assimilation theory, their children see that racial discrimination limits their chances for mainstream success, so they reject these modes of advancement and adopt norms and behaviors in opposition to the mainstream. As Portes and Rumbaut (2001a: 60) claim, "A crucial consequence of social and economic marginalization is the emergence of a measure of solidarity in opposition to external discrimination, based on the central notion that the plight of the minority is due to the hostility of mainstream institutions." Segmented assimilation theorists suggest that Mexican, Puerto Rican, and black immigrants are most at risk because these groups have sizeable dispossessed third and later generation co-ethnics (or individuals of similar racial background) exhibiting these countercultural traits and experiencing the associated downward assimilation.

Protective Factors

Segmented assimilation theory refers specifically to two kinds of protective factors: parent-child acculturation[12] and social capital. Portes and colleagues argue that problems are likely when children adopt American cultural characteristics at a faster rate than their parents. Under these conditions, children encounter American society in isolation from their parents and often experience role reversal, becoming sources of outside information and taking on responsibility for important family decisions. According to segmented assimilation theory, this dissonant form of parent-child acculturation is likely to result in children's loss of parental language and cultural ties and "does not necessarily lead to downward assimilation but...places children at risk" (Portes and Rumbaut 2001a: 54), particularly because these families often lack economic resources as well. When parents and children acculturate at the same rate, however, parents maintain their authority and youths are more protected from negative outside influences—particularly if the rate of acculturation is slow for both.

Portes and colleagues also focus on social capital as a predictor of assimilation experiences. They define it as "the ability to gain access to resources by virtue of membership in social networks and other social structures" (Portes and Rumbaut 2001a: 353). According to Coleman (1988: S95), social capital includes "obligations and expectations, information channels, and social norms."

Portes and Rumbaut (2001a) include parental status, family structure,[13] and gender as forms of social capital. As Portes and Rumbaut (2001a: 64) assert, families of higher socioeconomic status are likely to have "greater information about opportunities and pitfalls in the surrounding environment... [and] they can earn higher incomes giving them access to strategic goods." Researchers have more commonly used family structure as an indicator of social capital than parental economic status (see Coleman 1988; Astone and McLanahan 1991; Teachman, Paasch, and Carver 1997).[14] At the most basic level, two parents are likely to have more time and energy to devote to their children and the maintenance of good relations between them (Coleman 1988). Moreover, two-parent families are likely to have more ties outside of their immediate families providing information or resources than single parents.[15] Portes and Rumbaut (2001a) suggest that having greater economic resources and being in a two-parent family supports positive economic consequences for youths. They make no claims about associations between these forms of social capital and acculturation.

Portes and Rumbaut (2001a) also include gender under the social capital banner, although the association with social capital is unclear. They assert that "females tend to be more under the influence of their parents because of the less autonomous and more protective character of their upbringing" (Portes and Rumbaut 2001a: 64). Thus, females are purportedly more influenced by social capital within the family than males. Although they claim that gender differences will affect both cultural and economic adaptation outcomes, they do not elaborate on how assimilation will differ by gender.

Finally, segmented assimilation theorists focus on social capital within the co-ethnic immigrant community. Immigrant social networks not only increase economic opportunities for immigrant parents and their children but also "directly reinforce parental authority" (65). For immigrant families, they are networks of support and control (Zhou 1997) that promote economic success through partial or selective acculturation. Within these networks, the density of ties—rather than the socioeconomic status of the members—is most important.[16] Lower economic status immigrants can benefit from the social support they receive from closely knit co-ethnic communities. Segmented assimilation theorists typically describe some Asian groups and Cubans as having greater levels of this protective social capital than other groups (see, for example, Portes and Rumbaut 2001a). However, as Portes (1998) points out in his review of the social capital literature, social capital can have negative consequences for network members, although in their segmented assimilation writings, Portes and colleagues rarely discuss them. Social capital's negative consequences result from networks' possible "excess claims on group members, restrictions on individual freedoms, and downward leveling norms" (Portes 1998: 15).

Support for Segmented Assimilation

Portes, Fernández-Kelly, and Haller (2005: 1019) claim that one could disprove segmented assimilation theory by demonstrating that: (1) downward assimilation does not exist or affects a very small number of individuals or (2) "differences between immigrant nationalities are random so that, regardless of the average human capital and mode of incorporation of different groups, they will have about the same number of 'success stories' and failures in the second generation." However, as Gratton (2002) asserts, the tenets of segmented assimilation theory are so broad and imprecise that "[t]here appears to be no outcome that some aspect of segmented assimilation theory cannot explain" (81).[17]

As such, many researchers have claimed some support for segmented assimilation theory in a variety of qualitative and quantitative studies focusing on the children of immigrants. Some of these studies have focused on the factors associated with greater or lesser levels of particular characteristics—such as grades, English ability, English use, and health status—or on specific outcomes—such as ethnic identity, family structure, or language preference—rather than trajectories of change over time (e.g., Gibson 1988; Fernández-Kelly and Schauffler 1994; Hirschman 1994, 2001; Bankston and Zhou 1995; Zhou and Bankston 1998; Harris 1999; Waters 1999; Pérez 2001;

Portes and Rumbaut 2001a, 2001b, Brandon 2002; Portes, Fernández-Kelly, and Haller 2005; Kroneberg 2008). Many researchers also claim support for segmented assimilation theory when they find evidence that some immigrant groups do less well over generations than others (Portes and Zhou 1993; Hirschman 1994, 2001; Harris 1999, Kao 1999; Pérez 2001; Portes and Rumbaut 2001a; Stepick et al. 2001; St-Hilaire 2002; Van Hook and Balistreri 2002; Perreira, Harris, and Lee 2006; Telles and Ortiz 2008). These groups seem to experience downward assimilation. Other researchers have included more of a focus on the positive effects on economic achievement that children of immigrants experience from maintaining their cultural and other attachments from their places of origin (Gibson 1988, Matute-Bianchi 1986; Portes and Zhou 1993; Zhou and Bankston 1994; Bankston and Zhou 1995; Waters 1999; Portes and Rumbaut 2001a; St-Hilaire 2002; Fernández-Kelly 2008; Portes and Fernández-Kelly 2008). For example, a number of researchers have found more positive educational and mental health outcomes among youths who were fluent in both English and their native language (Portes and Schauffler 1994; Rumbaut 1994, 1995; Zhou and Bankston 1994; Bankston and Zhou 1995; García-Vázquez et al. 1997; Portes and Rumbaut 2001a; Portes and Hao 2002).[18]

Problems of Segmented Assimilation

The idea that there are multiple paths of assimilation—and multiple ways to be American—has added much to our consideration of the immigrant experience and immigrant incorporation. While many researchers have found support for segmented assimilation theory, a number of problems exist. The specific forms of assimilation outlined by this theoretical framework and the empirical research used to examine it lack clarity and precision. Moreover, segmented assimilation theory does not answer all of the critiques it makes of classical forms of assimilation.

Pathways of Mobility and Assimilation

Segmented assimilation theory conflates two different concepts: (1) segments and (2) paths of assimilation. Segments are outcomes or ultimate destinations of assimilation, while paths represent, at the very least, a direction of change between two points in time. Assimilation is generally about change over time; however, segmented assimilation theory's focus on the endpoint or segment of assimilation clouds understandings of assimilation paths. The three patterns of assimilation that Portes and colleagues describe in their theory are (1) upward mobility and acculturation into the middle class, (2) downward mobility and acculturation into the underclass, and (3) upward economic mobility (into the middle class) with partial acculturation. These patterns refer to upward and downward mobility or paths of change, and they also refer to endpoints, specifically, the middle class and the underclass. More recently, Portes, Fernández-Kelly, and Haller (2005; Portes and Fernández-Kelly 2008) replaced "middle class" with the term "mainstream," taking into considerations Alba and Nee's (2003) theoretical contribution, and described the second pattern as involving downward assimilation into the underclass *or* "stagnation into the working class" (Portes, Fernández-Kelly, and Haller 2008: 1083).

Even with these changes, the particular directions of mobility or assimilation, however, do not necessarily lead to integration into a particular segment of American society. Those familiar with Alba and Nee's (2003) conception of the "mainstream" are likely to conceive of it as including socioeconomic positions from working class to affluent. But Portes, Fernández-Kelly, and Haller (2008) have replaced the "middle class" designation with "mainstream" without changing the ideas behind it: They explicitly equate mainstream economic integration with professional and entrepreneurial occupations, middle to upper-middle class occupations. For some, upward economic mobility may not be substantial enough for them to quite reach this version of "mainstream" status. For others, upward economic mobility is not required to attain mainstream ,or middle-class status. Portes, Fernández-Kelly, and Haller (2005) reveal that the children of immigrants who follow this pattern often have parents who arrive with high levels of human capital with which they achieve middle-class status. As Vermeulen (2010) points out, this pattern, often equated with the classical assimilation model, actually stands in sharp contrast to the generations required by previous waves of European immigrants to achieve middle-class membership.

Similarly, a downward economic trajectory does not automatically indicate integration into the underclass nor is stagnation only an option for members of the working class. Stagnation, or horizontal mobility, is possible at every level of the socioeconomic ladder. The underclass segment is even more problematic. Although segmented assimilation theorists have not carefully explained their understanding of the underclass (Jung 2009), there is no consensus about the definition of the underclass and who exactly should be included in this segment of society, although poverty, work status, area of residence, and some additional indicators of "deviance" usually come into play (see, for example, Gans 1990; Jencks 1992; Katz 1993; Alba and Nee 2003; Waldinger and Feliciano 2004).[19] The underclass segment, particularly as defined by Portes and colleagues, seems to involve those at the very bottom of the economic ladder who also participate in "deviant lifestyles" (Portes, Fernández-Kelly, and Haller 2005: 1080). Not all downward mobility, then, will result in economic and/or cultural incorporation into the underclass segment.

Portes and colleagues also conflate direction and segment of acculturation; however, the direction of change for cultural factors also should not be associated with particular segments of American society in many cases. Acquisition of more American cultural traits (classical acculturation), while in the direction of the mainstream American culture, cannot be equated with full entry and integration into that culture. English language ability and use, for example, can be associated with entrance into mainstream, middle-class (white) American culture, working class culture, many minority cultures, and even underclass culture.

A similar problem exists for downward acculturation into the underclass. According to Portes and colleagues, underclass culture is an oppositional or adversarial subculture that includes norms and behaviors antithetical to the middle class, such as denigration of education, involvement in crime, drugs, and/or gangs, and teen pregnancy.[20] This conception of oppositional subculture came out of Ogbu's (1978) work on African Americans' academic achievement. However, many researchers (Cook and Ludwig 1998; Ainsworth-Darnell and Downey 1998; Waldinger and Feliciano 2004; Carter 2005; Tyson, Darity, and Castellino 2005; Kasinitz et al. 2008; Kroneberg 2008) have challenged the extent to which oppositional cultural values and behaviors help explain negative outcomes among youths. Waldinger and Feliciano (2004: 381) point out that "...far more persons subscribe to some aspect of an 'oppositional culture' than ever fall into an 'underclass.'" Individuals with one or more of these characteristics may be more likely to have negative outcomes and limited life chances in some respects, but it is not certain that the path they are following leads to underclass membership. Moreover, segmented assimilation theorists' discussions of the underclass and oppositional culture suggest that the influence of native minority groups, particularly inner-city African Americans, are primarily economically and culturally deleterious. These theorists discount possible positive contributions of minority cultures of mobility (Neckerman, Carter, and Lee 1999) and even possible positive contributions of oppositional cultures (Jung 2009).

This conflation of path and segment plays out in the empirical research as well. Investigators have mostly failed to examine pathways of change (or lack thereof) over time. Much segmented assimilation research focuses on a particular characteristic—such as grades, language ability and use, or health status—and examines the factors that are associated with a greater or lesser level of that characteristic (see, for example, Bankston and Zhou 1995; Harris 1999; Hirschman 2001; Portes and Rumbaut 2001a; Brandon 2002; Rumbaut 2005; Portes, Fernández-Kelly, and Haller 2005; Kroneberg 2008). This form of analysis explores only static characteristics, but inherent in the concept of assimilation is the idea of change. Therefore, one does not learn about assimilation by examining a characteristic at one point in time. Such an analysis only reveals something about that particular characteristic—such as grades or English ability—and does not provide information about how that characteristic changes over time.

Some researchers working within the segmented assimilation framework (Portes and Rumbaut 2001a; Glick and White 2003) included an auto-regressor in their analyses, thereby examining change in an indicator of assimilation or mobility (for example, grades or test scores), but this form of analysis is rare and only suitable for examining certain kinds of outcomes. Feliciano and Rumbaut (2005) also examine intragenerational mobility by examining individuals' educational trajectories over time; however, they only perform descriptive analyses and do not examine these trajectories with a multivariate analysis. Similarly, with their rich, multigenerational data on individuals of Mexican origin, Telles and Ortiz (2008) examine intergenerational pathways of change in education, economic status, and other characteristics at the descriptive level, but their multivariate analyses examine the factors that influence these characteristics at one point in time—not the changes from one generation to the next. In all of these studies, researchers have not analyzed how trajectories and the factors associated with them differ depending on immigrants' initial level of the particular characteristic, or "starting point." I discuss this matter further below.

The Starting Points of Mobility and Assimilation

In his article critiquing classical assimilation theory, Rumbaut (1997a: 946) argues that classical assimilation fails to take into account the idea that "origins shape destinies." According to Rumbaut, classical assimilation theories assume that all immigrants start off at some kind of American "ground zero," at a low rung on the economic ladder and with little American cultural knowledge or skills. From this point, immigrants experience upward economic mobility and a path of acculturation into the white middle class over time until they achieve some kind of "'parity' with the native majority" (Rumbaut 1997a: 946).

As Rumbaut points out, however, these assumptions are unrealistic. Immigrants entering the United States in the last 40 years actually have had a wide range of economic statuses, American cultural exposure, and English language ability. This diversity leads Rumbaut (1997a: 946; 1997b: 499) to ask, "[W]hat does the concept of 'socioeconomic assimilation' mean for immigrant groups who arrive in the United States already well above (let alone at 'parity' with) the educational and occupational medians of the native majority population...?" He also poses a similar question regarding acculturation for immigrants who come to the United States with high levels of exposure to "American consumption patterns, lifestyles, and popular culture" (948). In answer to both of these questions, Rumbaut asserts that those starting out from different socioeconomic and cultural positions will have different experiences of incorporation; therefore, to understand the great variety of assimilation experiences, one must consider this origin, or starting point.

The segmented assimilation framework suggests that immigrant parents' economic statuses and levels of acculturation shape the patterns of assimilation for themselves and their children. For example, Portes and colleagues indicate that youths whose parents have high socioeconomic status will be more likely to experience positive economic outcomes than youths from lower status backgrounds. However, Rumbaut's (1997a,b) point is not that those immigrants with higher socioeconomic status are more likely to have children with higher socioeconomic status or that individuals' levels of acculturation influence their assimilation outcomes. Instead, he suggests that the very meaning and experience of assimilation differ depending on one's rung on the economic ladder or position along the cultural continuum.

Portes and colleagues focus less on economic and cultural starting points than on how modes of incorporation—governmental, societal, and communal reception—shape experiences of incorporation. Portes, Fernández-Kelly and Haller (2005; Portes and Fernández-Kelly 2008), for example, argue that the effects of human capital on immigrants' incorporation experiences depend upon their context of reception. Immigrants with higher levels of education and skills will have more difficulty putting them to use if they are unauthorized or experience high levels of discrimination. Segmented assimilation theorists have considered somewhat less how economic starting points may shape experiences of particular contexts of reception. Immigrants from high economic starting points may have the resources to make up for some of the negative consequences of a hostile context of reception, while having a more favorable context of reception may not prove especially beneficial to immigrants from low economic starting points.

Human capital characteristics and context of reception are likely to interact with one another, but only recently has segmented assimilation research attempted to tease out how experiences of incorporation differ by economic starting points. The studies that do so use interactions—either mathematically or by studying different levels of starting point characteristics—to examine outcomes. Some of these studies examine group-level starting points rather than individual-level ones (Xie and Greenman 2005; Martinez, Lee, and Nielsen 2004; Wildsmith 2004). Others include only descriptive analyses by starting point (Zhou and Xiong 2005; Feliciano and Rumbaut 2004; Hao and Pong 2008). Fernandez-Kelly's (2008), Portes's (Portes and Fernandez-Kelly 2008), and Konczal and Haller's (2008) recent qualitative works examine academic achievement but focus solely on disadvantaged children of immigrants. Valdez's (2006) examination of earnings among individuals of Mexican origin in the Southwest is the only quantitative study that analyzes an indicator of assimilation by starting point (skill level, in this case) at the individual level—although she does not examine change in earnings over time at the individual level.

In their theoretical formulations, segmented assimilationists focus more on economic than cultural starting points. Their discussions of cultural starting points are largely limited to considerations of communal contexts of reception and focus more on how cultural attachments influence economic incorporation than cultural change (or lack thereof). They do not consider how the factors associated with cultural change may differ depending on their cultural starting points.

The Intergenerational Nature of Assimilation

Most researchers agree that assimilation is a multigenerational process (Warner and Srole 1945; Gordon 1964; Lieberson 1980; Alba and Nee 1997, 2003; Alba 1999; Brubaker 2001). Segmented assimilation theorists and researchers, however, tend to focus their theoretical and empirical work solely on the second generation, or, more specifically, on children of immigrants. While this generation's experiences are a vital part of the incorporation process, distinct from that of their parents, assimilation is about change, and greater changes can occur over generations than during an individual's life. To understand assimilation more completely at the individual level, segmented assimilation theory needs to include a focus on how change occurs from one generation, parents, to the next, their own children (Zhou et al. 2008).

Along with segmented assimilation's lack of theoretical focus on intergenerational mobility, there has been a dearth of true intergenerational empirical analysis in the assimilation literature. Most researchers who discuss assimilation across the generations do not focus on genuine intergenerational change; instead, they infer intergenerational change by comparing different generations-since-immigration of approximately the same ages at the same point in time (see, for example, Portes and Rumbaut 2001a; Harris 1999; Kao and Tienda 1995). This method of investigation does not appropriately consider intergenerational change from one generation to its descendant generation. Examining assimilation in this way assumes that the process of intergenerational change will be the same for immigrants today as it was in the past. Perlmann (2001: 2) notes that "...because historical development matters, we cannot say that the third-and-later generation of today is like the third generation that will emerge as the children of today's second generation."

With their remarkable data source, Telles and Ortiz (2008) examine true intergenerational change (and lack thereof) from Mexican-origin parents to their own children (and grandchildren) across a variety of possible assimilation indicators. However, they limit this examination to descriptive analyses. For their multivariate analyses, Telles and Ortiz infer intergenerational change by comparing a cohort of individuals across generations-since-immigration.

Perlmann (2001) and Smith (2003, 2006) use methods to overcome this bias. They analyze intergenerational assimilation more accurately at the group level, comparing different generations of immigrants over time. They compare a cohort of first generation immigrants to their hypothetical children, who are about 25 years younger than the parent cohort, and, in the case of Smith (2003, 2006), to their (hypothetical) grandchildren 25 year later still, to determine trends in various economic indicators across the generations. Using these methods, Perlmann and Smith are able to examine, rather than infer, intergenerational assimilation across generations, and their research reveals outcomes different from other forms of generational comparison. For example, Smith (2003) reveals much more positive intergenerational economic mobility outcomes among Latino men when comparing their economic characteristics across generations rather than inferring generational change.

However, even Perlmann and Smith's methods do not tell the full story of assimilation. They only permit researchers to consider assimilation as a group-level phenomenon. While some (Brubaker 2001) argue that assimilation occurs intergenerationally at the population-level, others (Alba and Nee 2003) argue that it is primarily an individual process, although it involves both individual and group components. Most of the previous research into segmented assimilation has focused on intragenerational assimilation at the individual level; however, *inter*generational assimilation studies, using the aforementioned methods, have been unable to tap into individual-level experiences of assimilation.

A Gendered View of Mobility and Assimilation

Gender is an integral factor in social processes. Vast numbers of studies show how gender is related to educational outcomes among the U.S. population at large, with some negative repercussions for women (e.g., Gilligan 1982; American Association of University Women 1992) and other, more positive outcomes for them (e.g., Mickelson 1989; Bae et al. 2000). Even more than education, gender is highly associated with occupational outcomes (Padavic and Reskin 2002), with men and women generally holding different kinds of jobs that are valued differently and experiencing different levels of attachment to the labor force. There is also evidence that gender differences exist in cultural characteristics, such as language ability and use, among first and second generation immigrants (Stevens 1986, 1992; Noh 2008). As these and other studies suggest, from birth (or even earlier) to death, gender shapes individuals' life experiences. Yet, somehow, gender has been mostly excluded from discussions of assimilation.

Portes and colleagues rarely have mentioned gender in their segmented assimilation writings, and, when they have discussed gender, it has been mostly cursory and with unsophisticated views of "gender roles." For example, in their first mention of how gender is associated with assimilation outcomes in their influential book, *Legacies: The Story of the Immigration Second Generation*, Portes and Rumbaut present a figure illustrating that gender, along with parental human capital, modes of incorporation, and family composition, affects first and second generation socioeconomic and cultural outcomes (68). The only explanation provided for these associations is "the different roles that boys and girls occupy during adolescence and the different ways in which they are socialized. As a general rule, females tend to be more under the influence of their parents because of the less autonomous and more protective character of their upbringing" (Portes and Rumbaut 2001a: 64).

This gender-roles framework considers gender as a characteristic of individuals rather than a characteristic of society. In their writings, Portes and colleagues have a more sophisticated understanding of race, which they consider a social rather than a personal attribute, but this sophisticated understanding does not extend to gender. They do not acknowledge that gender is a system of stratification—based on physical differences between individuals but played out at the individual, group, and societal level (Kessler et al. 1985). Gender and gendered behavior, then, result from social structures while socialization is really just "a means of *maintaining* a gender stratification system" (Ferree and Hall 1996: 935). In considering how gender is tied up with experiences of incorporation, we must consider the social structures that uphold gender difference and dominance.

Young men and young women are likely to have very different experiences of assimilation and mobility. There is certainly evidence in the migration literature that the experiences of migration and settlement differ significantly for men and women (Donato 2010; Donato et al. 2006; Cerrutti and Massey 2001; Pessar 1999a, 1999b; Valenzuela 1999; Hondagneu-Sotelo 1994.) Evidence focusing on the U.S.

adolescent and young adult non-immigrant population also suggests that economic expectations and attainment experiences differ by gender (see, for example, Rosen and Aneshensel 1978; Haggstrom, Kanouse and Morrison 1986; Marini 1984; Randour, Strasburg, and Lipman-Blumen 1982; Mickelson 1989; Jacobs 1996; Anker 1998; Blau, Ferber, and Winkler 1998; Blau, Simpson, and Anderson 1998; Schneider and Stevenson 2000). In addition, research on children of immigrants reveals different outcomes for males and females (Kao and Tienda 1995; Fuligni 1997; Portes and Rumbaut 2001a; Zhou and Bankston 2001; Fuligni and Witkow 2004; Rumbaut 2005).

Most studies, however, include gender only as a covariate to be controlled. This method reveals that a difference exists between males and females but not how the factors predicting a particular outcome are differently associated for males and females. Assimilation researchers have rarely examined assimilation experiences separately for males and females, with some exceptions (Lutz and Crist 2008; Valdez 2006; Feliciano and Rumbaut 2005; Waldinger and Feliciano 2004). Examining gender in this way allows for variation within males' and females' experiences and thus offers a more accurate picture than merely having a single "gender" variable.

Lack of Non-Immigrant Comparisons

Although not all questions of assimilation are applicable to non-immigrants, matters of economic mobility pertain to both immigrants and non-immigrants alike; individuals of every ethnic origin and every generational status experience downward, horizontal, and upward mobility across generations and over their own lifetimes. Moreover, the factors that segmented assimilation theorists predict shape assimilation experiences for children of immigrants—modes of incorporation, downward leveling factors, and protective factors—have counterparts among the third and later generations as well. "Modes of incorporation," specifically, human capital, governmental policies, societal beliefs and stereotypes, and community characteristics, shape third and later generation individuals' experiences of mobility. Children of non-immigrant parents, similarly, have to deal with the downward-leveling factors of racial discrimination, the hourglass economy and growing inequality, and inner-city subcultures.

Like children of immigrants, third and later generation individuals can benefit from the protections of their families' social capital. A second protective factor, parent-child acculturation, is less pertinent to this population; however, at the root parent-child acculturation issue, suggest Portes and colleagues, is the quality of the relationship between parent and child: Are parent and child able to communicate? Do they communicate? Who holds the authority? These kinds of issues of relationship quality most certainly apply to third and later generation youths and their parents. But non-immigrant comparisons have been lacking to some extent from the segmented assimilation literature, in part. This lack of non-immigrant comparison is, in part, due to the relative recency of the "new" immigrants and the young ages of their children, although the Mexican-origin population is the exception (Telles and Ortiz 2008).

Other assimilation research does incorporate later generation comparisons. For example, in their recent investigation of assimilation, Kasinitz et al. (2008) analyzed incorporation experiences from their own data on children of immigrants (Dominicans, South Americans, Chinese, West Indians, and Russian Jews), making use of native-born comparison groups (African Americans, native whites, and Puerto Ricans) in New York City. But this and similar research provide only a partial understanding of economic mobility experiences. In multivariate analyses, including the work of Kasinitz et al., studies comparing individuals across a variety of generational statuses tend to include generational status (or some combination of race-ethnicity-and generation) as a covariate (or set of covariates) to be controlled. Through this method, researchers either infer generational change or compare a variety of racial-ethnic-generational-status groups to some reference group (usually third and later generation whites). While these are useful comparisons, they do not allow for the possibility that factors associated with economic mobility vary by generational status; that is, these models assume that parental human capital, parent-child relationships, and other predictors have the same relationships with economic mobility measures regardless of generational status.

A number of theorists argue that experiences of incorporation (and mobility) differ by generational status. Rumbaut (2004), for example, reveals significant (and at time, non-linear) differences in educational and occupational status by immigrant generations.[21] Kao and Tienda (1995) argue that the most significart divide exists between those with and without immigrant parents. Their immigrant optimism hypothesis suggests that the experiences of children of immigrants and other children are qualitatively different because immigrant parents differ from non-immigrant parents. Kao and Tienda (1995) argue that immigrant parents have higher levels of motivation and higher expectations for success. Moreover, because their frames of reference are their countries of origin, where they often may have faced more difficult circumstances than in the United States, they are inspired and able to overcome problems here (Ogbu 1991). These highly motivated immigrant parents provide encouragement and support, found to a lesser degree among non-immigrant parents, that spurs their own children's economic achievement. Even so, researchers examining this hypothesis have failed to examine fully how experiences of mobility and the factors associated with them differ by parental immigration status (see, for example, Kao and Tienda 1995; Hirschman 2001). The lack of non-immigrants in segmented assimilation research has skewed its conclusions. Kasinitz, Mollenkopf, and Waters (2002) observe that because segmented assimilation research fails to incorporate third and later generation whites, blacks, and Latinos, it fails to recognize the diversity of experiences within these groups, specifically, that minority group members are often quite successful and that whites, in addition to minorities, take part in oppositional subcultures.

Mobility and Assimilation from a Life Course Perspective

Although Crul and Schneider (2010: 1263) recently argue that "[l]ooking at life courses up and into adult life rather than only a particular part of that trajectory may help to soften the rigidity of certain [assimilation] concepts (and their critique)," previous theoretical statements on assimilation—classical, segmented, or otherwise—have rarely taken into account the possibility that experiences of assimilation are likely to differ over the life course. The vast life course and developmental literature, however, reveals that individuals have different abilities, resources, needs, and desires at different stages in their lives. Individuals' lives are socially structured over time. As individuals progress through the life course, their experiences change and those factors that influence these experiences also change; therefore, mobility and assimilation are likely to be influenced by different factors at different stages in an individual's life. Ignoring these changes risks assuming that findings in one life course stage will necessarily hold across the life course.

In some assimilation work, there is an *acknowledgement* that developmental stage is likely to influence assimilation outcomes. For example, many researchers (e.g., Rumbaut 1997b; Portes and Rumbaut 2001a) actually consider the experiences of immigrants who come to the United States at younger ages to be different enough from those of late arrivals that they classify these immigrants into different generational categories. Rumbaut (1997b), for example, goes so far as to separate those born outside the United States to foreign-born parents into the first generation (adult arrivals), the 1.25 generation (arrivals between 13 and 17 years of age), the 1.5 generation (arrivals between 6 and 12), and the 1.75 generation (arrivals between 0 and 5). Rumbaut and others suggest that those who spend more time in the United States are not only different from each other because of greater levels of exposure to American society but also because experiences after arrival at distinct developmental stages have different effects on individuals. This idea, however, has not been translated into theoretical statements relating to individual immigrant incorporation over the life course.

The one exception is Rumbaut's (1997a) discussion of differences in language acquisition propensities across the life course, although he does not examine this matter empirically. Rumbaut cites literature that shows that individuals more rapidly acquire language skills at younger ages (Lenneberg 1967; Laponce 1987; Bialystok and Hakuta 1994), although recently this statement has been subject to debate (see Bialystok 1997; Singleton and Ryan 2004). One's ability to assimilate linguistically, then, may be associated with one's development or position in the life course. Rumbaut and others have failed to consider other indicators of assimilation or mobility from a developmental or life course approach.

Assimilation research has examined many factors that are intimately tied to the life course, including health, education, earnings, and marriage (see, for example, Harris 1999; Arias 2001; Hirschman 2001; Feliciano and Rumbaut 2005; Portes, Fernández-Kelly, and Haller 2005; Rumbaut 2005). However, they have not examined if or how these characteristics and the factors associated with them differ over time. Even in the rare instances in which researchers have examined change over time (Feliciano and Rumbaut 2005), they have not provided comparisons across different life course stages.

A life course approach adds insight to assimilation frameworks in a number of ways. First, additional time in the United States means greater exposure to U.S. institutions, norms, and values. As children of immigrants age, their experience with American society and its institutions accumulates, perhaps influencing their cultural and economic characteristics. Second, for immigrants and non-immigrants, life course stage is related to cognitive development, which may, in turn, influence assimilation and mobility outcomes. For example, cognitive skills increase over adolescence, particularly the ability to think abstractly (Keating and Clark 1980; Martorano 1977; Petersen 1983). Cognitive skills certainly help predict educational outcomes (see, for example, Cameron and Heckman 2001). Similarly, many researchers consider adolescence—and emerging adulthood—to be an important stage in life for the development of an identity (Erikson 1968; Rumbaut 1994; Arnett 2000). All of these indicators of assimilation and mobility, then, may be influenced by factors associated with life course.

Finally, individuals' lives are socially structured over the life course. For example, in the United States, most children start out living with parent(s) or adult guardian(s). These living arrangements generally continue through high school (see Arnett 2000). After high school, there is greater variability, although most youths move away from home, either for college or to live and work independently. Social arrangements such as these may have an impact on youths' assimilation and mobility experiences. Parents' behaviors and characteristics are likely to have more of an impact on youths' lives while they are living together at younger ages than when youths are living on their own. Post-high school living arrangements generally allow youths greater independence and autonomy. While the influence of parental characteristics on assimilation and mobility paths may diminish over time, it is possible that peer influences remain strong or gain in strength. By failing to consider the life course, segmented assimilation theory overlooks important age, cognitive, and structural influences on immigrant incorporation. Moreover, it may reify outcomes that are really short term occurrences rather than longer term patterns.

Addressing the Issues of Segmented Assimilation

I remedy these problems in this book by analyzing both intergenerational and intragenerational *paths* of mobility and assimilation, taking into account starting points, gender, the life course, and non-immigrant comparisons. I focus solely on paths of assimilation, analyzing segments of assimilation elsewhere (Faulkner and Jakubowski 2007). I define a path as the direction of change from one point in time, a designated "starting point," to another point in time, a designated "ending point." I identify paths of economic mobility, specifically, educational and occupational mobility, and cultural assimilation, specifically, linguistic assimilation and identificational assimilation (Milton Gordon's [1964] term for assimilation in terms of ethnic self-identity).

The paths I examine differ for economic mobility and cultural assimilation. The segmented assimilation framework suggests that there are three possible directions of economic mobility: upward, downward, and horizontal (no mobility). With respect to acculturation, segmented assimilation describes three possible types: (1) middle class, (2) underclass, and (3) partial or selective. The first two reference endpoints rather than paths; however, they can also be thought of being in the direction of the endpoints. The first type signifies a classical path form of acculturation; the second indicates acculturation in the direction of the underclass (which may or may not differ from classical acculturation, depending on the indicator). The third involves some form of classical acculturation along with cultural maintenance, or lack of cultural change (horizontal acculturation), and/or reemergence of an immigrant's cultural traits (acculturation contrary to classical assimilation's predictions). Individuals experiencing this third pattern follow different trajectories of acculturation for different cultural indicators.

I do not examine acculturation into the underclass in this book. Portes and colleagues suggest that underclass acculturation involves a rejection of mainstream cultural attitudes and norms, particularly those relating to socioeconomic advancement; however, the underclass literature reveals that characteristics of the underclass, including cultural traits, are tied explicitly to economic position. Moreover, as Waldinger and Feliciano (2004) note, individuals can and do have characteristics associated with an oppositional subculture without being part of the "underclass." Even if there were definitive indicators of underclass or oppositional culture, the forms of cultural assimilation that I examine, language use and ethnic identification, do not include any obvious "underclass" or oppositional pathway.[22] Accordingly, I consider the following remaining paths of acculturation: (1) classical, (2) horizontal or stable, and (3) anti-classical, in opposition to the mainstream but not necessarily in the direction of the underclass.

Unlike much previous segmented assimilation research, I analyze true intergenerational assimilation. Rather than inferring generational change, I compare parent characteristics to their own children's characteristics to demarcate various paths of assimilation across generations, in both descriptive and multivariate analyses. In my intragenerational analysis, I examine change, or lack thereof, in children of immigrants and other youths' characteristics over time from a life course perspective. I compare and contrast a shorter time period, adolescence, from about eighth grade to twelfth grade, with a longer, transitional period from adolescence to emerging adulthood, from about eighth grade to individuals' mid-twenties. I select these two time periods for a number of reasons. First, they are associated with important developmental and social stages in youths' lives. Second, they are comparable in the data sets that I use. Third, analyzing these specific time periods allows me to compare paths of mobility and assimilation over time among the same individuals—defined by their starting points. Finally, these two time periods allow me to understand assimilation from both a short-term and longer-term perspective.

My analyses also take into account starting point, gender, and parental immigration status. I operationalize starting point as one's level of a particular characteristic of interest at the time of the first survey. For the intergenerational analysis, I define the starting points as parental economic and cultural characteristics. For the intragenerational analysis, I define the starting point at the earliest point in time available in the data: eighth grade. I use this starting point information to define the paths of mobility and assimilation during adolescence and the transition to emerging adulthood. For both the inter- and intragenerational analyses, I examine the factors associated with the paths of assimilation separately by their various economic and cultural starting points. I also examine these paths separately by gender whenever possible to examine how girls' and boys' experiences of mobility and assimilation compare, although data limitations do not permit me to consider gender differences fully for every mobility and assimilation indicator. Finally, I compare experiences of children of immigrants to children of non-immigrants by examining paths of economic mobility in two data sets—one focused on children of immigrants exclusively (Children of Immigrants Longitudinal Study) and the other (National Educational Longitudinal Study) a nationally representative data set, from which I select third and later generation youths for analysis.[23]

Expected Outcomes

With this research, I attempt to answer the question, how do paths of inter- and intragenerational mobility and assimilation and the factors associated with them differ by starting point, gender, parental immigration status, and, where appropriate, life course stage? I expect to find that children of immigrants and other youths experience all possible paths of mobility and assimilation—both inter- and intragenerationally—though some paths will be more common than others. Intergenerationally, I expect to find that few youths experience downward educational mobility; because the educational levels of the U.S. population have risen over the years (Planty et al. 2008), most youths will maintain or exceed their parents' educational status. It is less clear that this pattern will hold for occupational mobility. I measure youths' occupational attainment in their mid-twenties. They are not likely to have reached their highest occupational status at this point, in contrast with their parents, who are older at the time I measure their occupational status. Thus, there will be greater variation in intergenerational occupational mobility paths than intergenerational educational mobility paths.

In terms of intergenerational cultural assimilation, again, I expect to find that children of immigrants experience all possible paths of assimilation. I expect more mixed results for intergenerational identificational assimilation than linguistic assimilation. Previous research on English language ability and use has revealed a strong pattern of increased English skills and use over time and across generations (Portes and Schauffler 1994; Portes and Rumbaut 2001a; Alba et al. 2002; Portes and Hao 2002). Portes and Rumbaut's (2001a) research on identificational assimilation suggests greater variability in paths of this form of cultural assimilation, with many more youths experiencing anti-classical identificational assimilation than anti-classical linguistic assimilation.

Turning to intragenerational assimilation, I expect to find substantial differences in the distribution of educational mobility paths by life course stage. During adolescence, I examine shifts in educational expectations alone; in the transition to the emerging adulthood period, I examine the extent to which youths attain their educational expectations. Of course, it is far easier to maintain or raise one's expectations than to meet or surpass them in terms of attainment.

As with intergenerational linguistic assimilation, I expect to find the distribution of the paths of assimilation to be heavily classical. Again, previous research suggests that it is difficult for youths to maintain their non-English languages and that English use rapidly increases over time (Portes and Schauffler 1994; Portes and Rumbaut 2001a; Portes and Hao 2002). I expect much more anti-classical identificational assimilation.

I also expect that the intergenerational and intragenerational paths of mobility and assimilation and the factors associated with them will vary by starting point, gender, parental immigration status, and life course stage, where applicable. Below, I will discuss more specific expectations about associations between the input factors and paths of mobility and assimilation for each of the inter- and intragenerational indicators in the next two chapters. Here, I will provide some general expectations about differences in the paths themselves. First, and most obviously, the paths of mobility and assimilation that youths can follow are limited by their starting points.

Second, I expect to find associations between the various paths and gender. Since, as described above, females generally have more educational success than males, I expect to find that females are more likely to experience upward educational mobility (or horizontal mobility from high starting points) than males. Conversely, females have not had as much occupational success as males; therefore, I expect that young men will more often experience positive forms of occupational mobility than young women. Some researchers suggest that females are more tied to their homes and ethnic identities and often function as "keepers of the culture" for their families (Billson 1995; Waters 1996; Das Gupta 1997; Valenzuela 1999; Dion and Dion 2001; Espiritu 1999; Ginorio and Huston 2001; Williams, Alvarez, and Hauch 2002; Suárez-Orozco and Qin 2006); therefore, young women may be less likely to experience classical acculturation than young men. Third, I expect, then, to find that, for both inter- and intragenerational economic mobility, children of immigrants will more often experience upward mobility or horizontal mobility from high starting points than children of non-immigrants, controlling for their starting points, because of their immigrant parents' optimism (Kao and Tienda 1995).

Finally, I expect that patterns of intragenerational mobility will differ by life course stage. As I noted above, this is very likely to be the case for educational mobility because I compare changes in educational expectations in adolescence to attainment (or failure to attain) expectations by emerging adulthood. I expect to find differences in acculturation across the time periods. First, exposure to American society and its values and norms increases with time spent in the United States; therefore, youths likely will experience classical assimilation—particularly linguistic assimilation—over the longer transition-to-emerging-adulthood period than the shorter adolescent one. Second, since language acquisition appears to be easier at younger ages, youths may be better able to maintain or improve their non-English language skills during adolescence than over the emerging adulthood period. There has been far less research on identificational assimilation than linguistic assimilation. However, Erikson and others (Erikson 1968; Rumbaut 1994; Arnett 2000) suggest that adolescence and emerging adulthood are important times for identity development. Their work suggests that youths are likely to change their identity over these time periods; however, it is not clear how they are likely to change them and how these changes may differ across the two time periods I examine.

In the next chapter, I turn to my examination of intergenerational assimilation. I first provide additional information on the theoretical framework for the chapter. Then, I present my plan for analysis, detailing the paths of mobility and assimilation that I examine, as well as how these paths differ by starting point, gender, and generational status. I discuss my data and methods and then provide descriptive and multivariate results of my analysis and a brief discussion of them. In chapter three, I discuss intragenerational assimilation. Again, I first give additional theoretical framing for my analysis. I also detail how the paths of mobility and assimilation that I study are likely to differ by starting point, life course stage, gender, and immigrant generational status. Following my data and methods section, I report the descriptive and multivariate results of this analysis and provide a discussion of them. In the final chapter, I discuss how this book adds to the assimilation literature, and I provide suggestions for possible future data collection and research.

NOTES

[1] I use the term "mobility" instead of subsuming economic mobility in the term "assimilation." Economic mobility is not the equivalent of economic

assimilation. Economic mobility refers to (upward, downward, or no) change in economic status while economic assimilation's meaning is more disputed. For example, economic assimilation may suggest regression to the mean. Furthermore, as Portes, Rumbaut, and Zhou point out, economic advancement in some cases, for example among some Cubans' in Miami (Portes and Zhou 1993), occurs outside of mainstream economic structures. It is not clear that economic "assimilation" has really occurred in such cases. Finally, the term "mobility" can be applied to both immigrants and non-immigrants alike.

[2] I use the term "starting point" to refer to a baseline measure of individuals' characteristics, for example, parent's level of education or occupational status. It is from this point that one examines a trajectory of change. Other researchers have used the term starting point similarly, including Perlmann and Waldinger (1997), Rumbaut (1997a, 1997b), Glick and White (2003), and Bean, Brown, and Rumbaut (2006).

[3] "Children of immigrants" refers to second generation immigrants (those born in the United States to at least one foreign-born parent) and children born outside of the U.S. to at least one foreign-born parent who migrated at an early age, generally before age 12, also known as the 1.5 generation.

[4] I am unable to perform other analyses (the cultural analyses) using both data sets because the nationally representative data lacks appropriate cultural indicators.

[5] Gordon, however, predicted that the most likely outcome of assimilation would be acculturation to Anglo Saxon forms but structural pluralism.

[6] Other researchers (Perlmann and Waldinger 1997; Alba and Nee 2003) disagree with this view. They argue that it does not take into account the changing construction of race and the fact that many previous European groups were considered non-white upon their arrival.

[7] Other researchers suggest that previous immigrants faced a much greater challenge to economic advancement, the Great Depression, and yet were still able to succeed economically over generations (Alba and Nee 1997, 2003). Furthermore, many researchers (Alba and Nee 2003; Perlmann and Waldinger 1997), including Portes and his colleagues (Portes and Zhou 1993, Zhou 1997a) suggest that the middle of the job ladder is not (yet) as hollowed out as the "hourglass economy" idea suggests.

[8] Alba and Nee also proposed a new theory of assimilation, a revision of the classical formulation. They argue that assimilation is still the foremost model of immigrant incorporation and define it as "...the decline of an ethnic distinction and its corollary cultural and social differences" (2003: 11).

[9] While Portes and colleagues focus on these characteristics within an immigrant framework, they can be applied, in many cases, to non-immigrants as well.

[10] These communal resources, or lack thereof, are also part of immigrants' social capital, a protective factor for immigrant incorporation and another factor that Portes and colleagues argue influences assimilation, which I discuss further below.

[11] Segmented assimilation researchers do not include the hourglass economy as a variable. It is a factor that influences assimilation outcomes for all immigrants, but it is additionally influenced by parental resources.

[12] Portes and Rumbaut (2001a) actually focus more on the negative consequences of acculturation when parents and children integrate into American culture at different rates; however, they also talk about the positive consequences of mutual acculturation—and shared lack of, or partial, acculturation. I focus on the positive effects of acculturation here.

[13] Portes and Rumbaut (2001a) include family structure as both a mode of incorporation and a protective factor or measure of social capital.

[14] Some of these authors, Astone and McLanahan, in particular, suggest that family structure alone cannot fully capture the familial form of social capital. The strength of parent-child ties better measures this concept.

[15] In this book, I consider parental and family economic resources separately from less-economically-based social ties between youths and their families and individuals in their community—including relatives, friends, peers, and others.

[16] It does seem, however, that a minimum standard of well-being is necessary for social capital to have a marked positive influence on members of a social network.

[17] Although segmented assimilationists rarely find evidence contrary to their predictions, Portes, Fernández-Kelly, and Haller (2005) find that, after controlling for a variety of factors, Haitian and West Indian children of immigrants in Miami actually performed better than average academically. Out of the six characteristics the authors examined, educational attainment was the only one for which they found evidence that disputed segmented assimilation theory's claims. Other researchers have recently reported little support for the pattern of downward assimilation into the underclass (Boyd 2002; Hirschman 2001; Farley and Alba 2002; Kasinitz, Mollenkopf and Waters 2002; Smith 2003; Waldinger and Feliciano 2004; Waldinger and Reichl 2007; Kasinitz et al. 2008).

[18] Other researchers, however, have found that this association between bilingualism and educational outcomes does not hold over the long term (Mouw and Xie 1999).

[19] The descriptions of the segments of American society clearly conflate race, ethnicity, and nation with class. For example, the only path identified in this theory that includes native-born minorities assumes that they are all a particularly dysfunctional version of the poor, the "underclass." Researchers and the media have most often used the term to refer to a group of extremely poor, inner-city, socially "maladjusted" African Americans with little to no attachment to the labor force (Rolison 1991; Katz 1993). However, this theory and the researchers working within it also describe U.S.-born Puerto Rican and Mexican "underclasses" (see, for example, Portes, Fernández-Kelly, and Haller 2005). Interestingly, segmented assimilationist theorists do not discuss the possibility of white, Cuban, or Asian versions of the "underclass." In fact, in this conflation of race and class, segmented assimilation theory assumes that all whites are middle class. Segmented assimilation theory overlooks very poor whites (underclass or otherwise) as well as the working class and the working poor (regardless of race-ethnicity). Asians and Cubans are generally associated with the pseudo-segment ("middle class" with cultural maintenance) (see Portes and Rumbaut 2001a, 2001b).

[20] There are a number of problems with these conceptualizations of oppositional subcultures. First, oppositional subcultures are not limited to (American) minorities (see Willis 1977). Second, there is evidence that the characteristics (such as violence, negative attitudes towards authority, etc.) thought to comprise minority "adversarial subcultures" are far from universal among inner city, poor minorities (see Anderson 1999; Newman 1999). The association between minority status and an adversarial subculture in this theory disregards the diversity of minority experiences and the diversity of the population in poverty.

[21] Rumbaut (2004), in fact, breaks down the foreign-born first generation by age at arrival into four distinct generations (1.0, 1.25, 1.5, and 1.75). He also distinguishes the "pure" second generation (U.S.-born individuals with foreign-born parents) and the 2.5 generation (U.S.-born individuals with one U.S.-born parent and one foreign-born parent).

[22] Portes and Rumbaut (2001a) suggest that acquisition of a racial/pan-ethnic identity is evidence of underclass acculturation, though, as I explain below, I disagree.

[23] Lack of appropriate cultural information for non-immigrants prevents me from using non-immigrant comparisons for cultural shifts over time.

CHAPTER 2

Intergenerational Paths of Assimilation

Many researchers argue that the process of assimilation is better understood as one that occurs over generations rather than during the lifetime of an individual. Segmented assimilation theory focuses on individual-level change (or lack thereof) but has largely failed to examine the paths of change from parents to their own children. In this chapter, I employ the segmented assimilation framework to examine mobility and assimilation intergenerationally, from parents to their own children. I focus specifically on paths of change from one generation to the next for economic characteristics (education and occupational status) and cultural characteristics (English language use and ethnic identification). I examine how the paths and the factors associated with them differ depending on parents' initial education, occupational status, level of English use, and ethnic identity. I also analyze paths separately by gender, where possible, and, in the case of economic mobility, I compare children of immigrants' experience to that of youths with non-immigration parents.

Economic Indicators of Mobility

I examine two indicators of economic mobility: educational attainment and occupational status. Education "characterize[s] the placement of persons, families, households...with respect to the capacity to create or consume goods that are valued in our society" (Hauser and Warren 1997: 178). It has important effects on individuals' lives through its socialization, allocation, cognitive, and class effects (Kingston et al.

2003). For this sample, educational attainment is a valid measure of economic success because, in the waves of data that I use, youths are, on average, in their mid-twenties and, therefore, are likely to have reached, or be well on their way to, their ultimate educational level. Intergenerational educational mobility, then, reveals the extent to which later generations' economic standing, in this respect, falls behind, remains the same as, or surpasses their parents' economic standing.

Occupational status, like education, is related to various indicators of well-being (Adler and Newman 2002; Marmot et al. 1997; Williams and Collins 1995; Dahl 1994);[1] however, it is more constrained by the opportunity structure than educational attainment (Mare 1997). Occupations are intimately tied to social networks and ways of living. Because of the young age of my samples, occupational status at the time of the surveys is not likely to represent these young adults' ultimate occupational standings; however, this comparison provides an early indication of youths' success compared with their parents.

I categorize paths of mobility according to Portes and colleagues' descriptions. Downward mobility occurs when parents have higher economic status than their children. When parents and their children share the same status, youths experience a horizontal or stable path of mobility. Upward mobility occurs when youths surpass their parents' economic status.

The paths of intergenerational economic mobility that youths can take depend upon parents' initial educational and occupational characteristics. Those starting at the middle rungs of the ladder can experience all three forms of mobility, but those at the top and bottom are limited to two possible directions of mobility—horizontal or downward for those starting from the top and horizontal and upward for those starting at the bottom. Furthermore, the meaning of these forms of mobility differs depending on parents' initial economic characteristics. For example, downward mobility from a high point is likely to have fewer negative consequences on an individual's life than downward mobility from a lower point. Because mobility and it meaning differ so much depending on parents' initial educational and occupational levels, I examine mobility experiences separately for those at the bottom, middle, and top of the educational and occupational scales. Regardless of starting point, I expect that positive forms of educational mobility will be more common than positive forms of occupational mobility because of the young age of my sample (see Table 2.1 for hypotheses).

Table 2.1. Intergenerational Mobility and Assimilation Hypotheses

1. Children of immigrants and 3rd and later generation youths will experience all possible forms of mobility and assimilation.

2. More negative forms occupational mobility will be more common than downward or more negative educational mobility across the various starting points.

3. Classical linguistic assimilation will be more common than classical forms of identificational assimilation. Anti-classical linguistic assimilation will be less common than anti-classical identificational assimilation.

4. The distribution of paths of mobility and assimilation and the factors associated with them will differ by starting point, gender, and parental immigration status.

   a. Starting point:
      i.   By definition, the possible paths of mobility and assimilation differ from each starting point.
      ii. Upward mobility is more likely from lower starting points. Downward mobility is more likely from higher starting points.
      iii. Classical mobility is more likely from less
   b. Gender:
      i.   Females will be more likely to experience positive forms of educational mobility than males.
      ii. Males will be more likely to experience positive forms of occupational mobility than males.
      iii. Females will be less classical in terms of cultural assimilation than males, especially linguistic assimilation.
      iv. Females will be more likely to hold on to their parents' identities than males.
   c. Parental immigration status: Children of immigrants will be more likely to experience positive forms of economic mobility than third and later generation youths.

The distribution of these educational and occupational mobility pathways and the factors associated with them are also likely to differ by gender. Although there has been little research examining educational mobility by gender, the education literature suggests that young men's and young women's attainment experiences differ substantially. For example, while disparities in college attendance and completion are much larger between non-white males and females than white males and females (Kimmel 2004), young women, in general, have surpassed young men in terms of educational attainment in recent years (Morgan 2005; Planty et al. 2008). Consequently, young women may be less likely to experience negative forms of educational mobility and more likely to experience positive forms of mobility than young men. Furthermore, research indicates that the factors explaining educational attainment differ by gender as well. For example, Stromquist (1989) found that parental education and economic resources were stronger predictors of educational outcomes for girls than for boys. But Kasinitz et al. (2008), in their examination of children of immigrants and native-born comparison groups in New York City, found that parental educational attainment and family structure were stronger predictors of educational attainment for young men than young women. Different factors also help explain school leaving among young men and women (Jacobs 1996).

More research has focused on differences between men's and women's occupational mobility. Young men and young women have very different experiences in the labor market, and these differences are likely to have an impact on their occupational status. There is much evidence of gender segregation in occupations (Reskin 1988, 1993; Padavic and Reskin 2002; Beller and Han 1984). Specifically, women are overrepresented in lower status occupations than men. In tandem with this occupational gender segregation, on average, women earn less than men, although this wage gap has been narrowing over time (Marini 1989; England 1992, U.S. Bureau of the Census 1995). These two factors suggest that young women may be less likely to experience positive forms of intergenerational occupational mobility than young men.

As with educational attainment, there is evidence that the factors associated with occupational status differ for men and women. Hauser and his colleagues, for example, (Sewell, Hauser, and Wolf 1980; Hauser et al. 2000) found different effects for educational attainment and parental occupational status on men's and women's occupational attainment. There are also gender differences in attachment to the labor force, with women exhibiting higher rates of part-time work than men, that may influence patterns of intergenerational occupational mobility and the factors associated with it. This previous research suggests that because the process of attainment of occupational status differs for men and women, it is best to examine intergenerational occupational mobility by gender when possible.

It is also possible that economic mobility will differ by parental immigration status and ethnic origin. According to segmented assimilation theory, immigrants who have strong ethnic communities and remain tied to these communities are protected from negative outside influences and will outperform non-immigrants in terms of economic outcomes and mobility. Segmented assimilation theory suggests more negative economic outcomes are likely for immigrants for whom a large, downtrodden co-ethnic community already exists in the United States. Youths who see their parents and other co-ethnics stuck in low-end jobs may view no possible means of escaping these occupational futures. Following Ogbu's (1978) logic, these youths are likely to adopt an "oppositional outlook," rejecting traditional, mainstream norms of success, such as educational achievement, which, in turn, leads to failure in the labor market. This experience, however, is not limited to immigrants. Instead, it applies to those whom Ogbu (1978) classifies as "involuntary immigrants" and "castelike minorities," including Mexicans, Puerto Ricans, and blacks. Therefore, some immigrants and some native minorities may be less likely to experience more positive forms of economic mobility.

While segmented assimilation theory does not have one clear expectation for children of immigrants compared to non-immigrants, the immigrant optimism hypothesis (Kao and Tienda 1995) predicts more positive economic outcomes for children of immigrants compared with other youths. This hypothesis is grounded in the idea that immigrants to the United States are positively selected to integrate into American society (Chiswick 1979, Borjas 1990, Ogbu 1991). Immigrant parents generally have high expectations for themselves and their children and tend to be more optimistic about their children's chances for success than non-immigrant parents (Kao and Tienda 1995). These parents provide emotional and other kinds of supports, then, that help their children do better than children of non-immigrants in areas such as education. In other words, "differences between immigrant and native *parents* are the essential ingredients to explaining generational differences in performance among youth" (Kao and Tienda 1995: 5). In particular, Kao and Tienda (1995), along with

Caplan, Choy, and Whitmore (1991), argue that cultural factors promoting educational success are particularly important for explaining children of immigrants' outperformance of other youths. The immigrant optimism hypothesis suggests, then, that children of immigrants, in general, will be more likely to experience upward economic mobility (or horizontal mobility when starting out from a high rung on the economic ladder) than the general population. It also suggests that cultural factors and parental practices will be particularly important for explaining children of immigrants' success.

   In addition to the immigrant optimism hypothesis, there are further reasons to expect differences in occupational mobility between children of immigrants and other youths, even after controlling for parents' initial occupational status. Immigrant parents, regardless of educational background, are likely to have lower status occupations than the non-immigrant population because of problems transferring credentials and work experience from abroad into equivalent jobs in the United States. Additionally, lack of acculturation—particularly in terms of English language ability—is likely to create obstacles for or, at least, delay immigrants' ability to achieve the same occupational positions that they held in their home countries. Immigrant parents, then, are likely to start out in lower status occupations in the United States given their level of skills compared with educationally equivalent non-immigrant parents, on average. For children of immigrants whose parents have relatively high levels of education for their occupational status, starting out from a lower economic position may give them greater resources for upward occupational mobility than children of non-immigrant parents from the same starting point.

Cultural Indicators of Assimilation

The cultural indicators that I examine are linguistic assimilation, specifically, changes in English language use across generations, and identificational assimilation, i.e., intergenerational changes in ethnic identification. There are a number of differences between the analysis of economic and cultural indicators of assimilation. First, I am not able to include later generation individuals from the NELS data in my analysis of acculturation; therefore, I cannot examine generational status differences in these paths. The data either lack the appropriate information, in the case of ethnic identity, or the indicators are not applicable to most sample members, in the case of English use.

Second, as I discussed in the introductory chapter, the paths of cultural assimilation that I examine differ from those of economic mobility. Cultural assimilation cannot be upward or downward; instead, I use a different metric. I define three possible paths of acculturation for this analysis in terms of their similarities to or differences from predictions of classical assimilation theory: (1) classical, (2) horizontal or stable, and (3) anti-classical. Classical forms of cultural assimilation include the acquisition of more mainstream American cultural characteristics or the loss of traits from other cultural backgrounds. Anti-classical forms of assimilation follow the opposite patterns: loss of more mainstream American or acquisition of other cultural traits. As was the case for educational mobility, parents' initial levels of the indicators matter when considering direction of linguistic and identificational acculturation.

Language is an important, and easily identifiable, indicator of cultural attachment. I focus on differences (or the lack thereof) in English use among parents and their own children. For many immigrants and their descendants, English use is an indicator of distance or separation from their cultures of origin and association with (possibly) more mainstream U.S. society (Stevens 1992).[2] The frequency and consistency with which immigrants and the children of immigrants use English reveals the degree of their involvement and embeddedness within an English-speaking social sphere. Of course, this English-speaking social sphere may be of any ethnic background; nevertheless, English language networks are likely to include the native-born and/or co-ethnics with greater U.S. experience and are less likely to involve recent immigrants. Even in cases in which English language networks include many recent immigrants, greater levels of English use indicate weakened ties to one's native language and, thus, they have greater possible exposure to more "American" norms and values.

Youths who use English less than their parents experience anti-classical assimilation, a path that previous research suggests will be uncommon (Portes and Rumbaut 2001a). Those who use English the same amount as their parents follow a stable path. Youths who use English more than their parents follow the classical path of assimilation; they exhibit greater attachment to and involvement in American mainstream culture.

As with all forms of assimilation, the initial level of the characteristic is important for determining the possible assimilation paths and their meanings. In the case of intergenerational English use assimilation, youths whose parents use a non-English language exclusively can experience only classical or stable forms of assimilation. Children of English-only parents can experience anti-classical or stable assimilation. Only those youths whose parents use some English can experience all three forms of assimilation. The meaning of stable assimilation, then, differs depending on parents' level of English language use. The meaning of classical linguistic assimilation differs also depending on whether parents start at a very low or intermediate level of English use. Youths who experience classical linguistic assimilation from a higher parental level of use are likely to have greater involvement in mainstream American culture than youths whose parents use a language other than English only. Similarly, anti-classical assimilation has different meanings for children of immigrants' lives depending on whether their parents use English only or English along with some other language initially.

Previous research suggests that young men and women are likely to have different experiences of this form of linguistic assimilation. Men and women, in many instances, tend to participate in different social circles and use their time differently (Sayer 2005; Gager, Cooney, and Call 1999; Mauldin and Meeks 1990), which may influence their levels of English use (Stevens 1986; Arriagada 2005). Specifically, segmented assimilation theorists and others suggest that girls and women may be more restricted to the home than boys and men, strengthening their native language ability, increasing its use, and limiting their exposure to English (Arriagada 2005; Portes and Hao 2002; Urciuoli 1991; Stevens 1986). Researchers have found that women, particularly Latinas, are more attached to their languages of origin than men in terms of both ability and use (Arriagada 2005; Lutz 2006; Portes and Hao 2002; Portes and Schauffler 1994; Stevens 1986; Veltman 1981). As a result of this research, I expect that young women will be less likely to experience classical linguistic assimilation than young men. It is unclear, however, how factors associated with linguistic assimilation will differ by gender, as there has been little previous research. The lone available study by Akresh (2007) found very few gender differences, with the exception of different relationships between time spent in the United States and English use for men and women.

The other form of acculturation I examine is intergenerational identificational assimilation. Ethnic self-identification interests assimilation researchers because it represents an individual's emotional connection to his or her ethnic group (Ontai-Grzebik and Raffaelli 2004; Phinney 1992; and Tajfel 1981). But ethnic identification is not so straightforward. It is not static but situational and contextual (Cerulo 1997; Conzen et al. 1992; Glenn 1992, 2000; Hondagneu-Sotelo 2003; Messerschmidt 1993; Waters 2004). Ethnic self-identification is a symbolic experience, constructed through social interactions with others (Gans 1979; Glenn 2000; Omi and Winant 1994; Portes and Rumbaut 2001a; Waters 1990, 1999). It reveals something about how individuals believe they fit into the larger social world (at a particular point in time and situation) and reflects, in many cases, constraints that the social world places upon them. Ethnic identities show who or what an individual is like but also from whom or what an individual differs (Portes and Rumbaut 2001a). Both immigrant parents and children of immigrants must negotiate between identities based on their (parents') places of origin and their (new) home country.

In order to perform this examination of ethnic identification within the segmented assimilation framework and make it comparable to previous studies of ethnic identity, I make use of Portes and Rumbaut's (2001a) system of ethnic identity classification. Though there are many possible ethnic identities to which individuals ascribe, Portes and Rumbaut (2001a) collapse these identities into four categories: (1) national origin identities, such as Vietnamese or Cuban; (2) hyphenated-American identities, such as Mexican-American; (3) racial or pan-ethnic identities, such as black or Asian[3]; and (4) plain "American" identities. The first two forms of identities are explicitly linked to an individual's place of origin. Hyphenated identities project a dual identity; they reveal a thinning of the national origin identity (Portes and Rumbaut 2001a). In contrast, racial/pan-ethnic and plain American identities are, according to Portes and Rumbaut, "made in the USA." While the other identities refer to specific national ties, the racial or pan-ethnic identity "reflects a denationalized identification with racial-ethnic minorities in the United States and self-conscious differences in relation to the white Anglo population" (154). Such identities simultaneously reveal a sense of membership in American society and separation from it—a sense of "otherness" while still being a part of American society.

Portes and Rumbaut (2001a) define identity shifts by three paths of identificational assimilation. The first is a linear path, associated with classical assimilation and acquisition of a more "American" identity over time. The second is a racialized path, whereby one adopts a made-in-America identity that is associated with minority group status. Portes and Rumbaut (2001a) suggest that the racialized path is associated with the downward pattern of assimilation into the underclass. I disagree and consider this path a variant on classical assimilation in most cases because there are few other identity options for native-born racial minorities (Waters 1990).[4] Furthermore, it is indefensible to associate the identity of a minority group as a whole with the underclass. While a large proportion of the underclass may be racial-ethnic minorities, most minorities are not underclass members however one defines the underclass (Wilson 1987; Jencks 1992). The third and final path that Portes and Rumbaut (2001a) identify is a resurgent or anti-classical path, associated with acquisition of a more national origin (less American) identity over time. To these three paths, I add a fourth path of stability over time.

Table 2.2. Possible Paths of Intergenerational Identificational Assimilation

Parent Identity	Youth Identity			
	American	Hyphenated	National origin	Racial/pan-ethnic
American	Stable	Resurgent	Resurgent	Racialized
Hyphenated	Linear	Stable	Resurgent	Racialized
National origin	Linear	Linear	Stable	Racialized
Racial/pan-ethnic	Linear	Resurgent	Resurgent	Stable

The paths of intergenerational identificational assimilation depend on parents' initial ethnic identities. Table 2.2 shows the possible identificational assimilation paths open to youths whose parents initially hold each of the four ethnic identities. As the table reveals, not all paths are open to all youths. Furthermore, the meanings of these paths are likely to vary depending on the starting point. For example, linear assimilation can include acquisition of a hyphenated identity for those whose parents initially hold national origin identities. For those whose parents have hyphenated identities originally, it requires the acquisition of a plain American identity. These paths may be influenced by different factors and are likely to have different meanings in individuals' lives. For these reasons, I have chosen to analyze the paths of identificational assimilation by initial ethnic identity.

Paths of intergenerational identificational assimilation may also differ by gender. According to Phinney's (1990) review of articles on ethnic identification, research on gender suggests that women are more involved in maintaining ethnic connections and traditions than men, although there is variation by cultural group. Some research suggests that female immigrants and children of immigrants are more tied to their homes and families than males (Bankston 1995; Gibson 1988; Lopez 2002; Warikoo 2005); therefore, they may be less likely to experience more classical forms of assimilation and more likely to hold on to their parents' more national origin identities. More intimate relationships with their parents, in general, may be associated with higher odds of maintaining parental identities among young women— no matter what their parents' initial identities. While there have been no multinomial analyses of intergenerational identificational assimilation, analyses of intragenerational identificational assimilation reveal that young women have more stable ethnic identities than young men (Golash-Boza 2006; Portes and Rumbaut 2001a). While I am able to examine these predictions of gender differences in identificational assimilation at a bivariate level in this analysis, data restrictions prevent me from predicting paths of intergenerational identificational assimilation separately for boys and girls.

In order to deal with the problems of segmented assimilation theory and incorporate more fully these key elements into our understanding of assimilation, I examine pathways of assimilation intergenerationally from parents to children in terms of education, occupation, English language use, and ethnic identity. I perform these analyses separately by parents' initial characteristics for each of these and analyze paths of intergenerational assimilation separately for young men and young women. I am thus able to examine how assimilation varies by immigrant starting points and gender and allow for variation of experience within each category. Finally, I compare economic mobility experiences of children of immigrants and the general U.S. population. With this method, I am able to assess the extent to which certain patterns of mobility outcomes apply primarily to children of immigrants and which patterns are more widespread.

Data

I use two data sets for this analysis: the Children of Immigrants Longitudinal Study (CILS) and the National Education Longitudinal Study of 1988 (NELS:88). Portes and Rumbaut directed the collection of CILS, a longitudinal study focusing on the incorporation experiences of children of immigrants in the Miami and San Diego metropolitan areas, two areas heavily affected by recent immigration. For the first wave of data collection in 1992, they surveyed a sample of eighth and ninth graders of foreign parentage from 49 public and private schools in the two areas (Portes and Rumbaut 2001a). They selected youths with at least one foreign-born parent who were born in the United States or were born abroad but had lived in the United States for at least five years. Although respondents represented 77 different nationalities, Cubans, Haitians, Nicaraguans, and West Indians, dominate the Miami sample while Mexicans, Filipinos, and Southeast Asians made up the bulk of the San Diego sample (Portes and Rumbaut 2001a). The original sample was evenly split by grade, gender, and place of birth (U.S. vs. foreign-born), but nationality and place of birth were closely linked for some groups. For example, most Southeast Asians were foreign-born. There were more Miami (54 percent) than San Diego respondents (46 percent).

Portes and Rumbaut followed up with the 5,262 original survey participants three to four years later (1995-1996), regardless of school enrollment or region of residence (Portes and Rumbaut 2001a). Most youths were high school seniors at the time of the first follow-up. The response rate for this survey was approximately 82 percent. Portes and Rumbaut's (2001a) analysis of sample attrition revealed that, for the most part, the follow-up sample was very similar compositionally to the original sample. There was a slight overrepresentation of higher status and more stable families.

At the same time as the follow-up survey for youth respondents, Portes and Rumbaut organized a data collection for a subsample of parents.   This subsample targeted half of the initial respondents' parents. Approximately 92 percent of this subsample participated. The parent sample was drawn randomly; however, Portes and Rumbaut (2001a) used probabilities so that smaller nationalities would be represented among the parent subsample. The survey was translated into eight different languages so that the largest number of immigrant parents could participate (Portes and Rumbaut 2001a).

The youth respondents were followed-up for a second and final time from 2001 to 2003, when they averaged 24 years of age (Portes and Rumbaut 2005). In this final wave of data collection, 84 percent of the first follow-up, or 69 percent of the original sample, were interviewed. There was a higher percentage of original San Diego respondents than Miami respondents in this final wave. It was more difficult for the survey team to reach the youths in the final wave because there was a longer interim between surveys and most youths were no longer in school. Although the sample composition in terms of age, gender, and nationality was similar to the previous two waves, there was more sample selectivity based on family structure, family socioeconomic status, and youths' grades. Portes and his colleagues (Portes, Fernández-Kelly, and Haller 2005; Rumbaut 2005), however, found that results did not differ greatly whether or not one adjusted for selection bias. I discuss methods for dealing with selection bias below.

The CILS data set includes a unique and diverse sample and provides a wide variety of indicators of assimilation and explanatory variables unavailable in most other data sets; however, there are a number of problems with this data for my intergenerational analysis. First, as noted above, parent surveys are only available from a subsample of respondents. Although youths provided some information on their parents' characteristics, they did not provide information on parent language ability or use. Moreover, youth reports of some parental characteristics have validity problems. I compared youth reports from the second wave of data collection of occupation and ethnic identity to parent reports, which came from the same time period, and found quite sizeable differences between parent and youth reports. I decided to make use of the parent survey to construct the paths of intergenerational mobility and assimilation because of their greater accuracy, although it cut my sample size in about half.

A second problem with the CILS data is its lack of national representativeness. San Diego and Miami, especially, are unique immigrant destinations. For example, the Cuban enclave in Miami provides ethnic solidarity and job opportunities for its members that are not available in other parts of the country. Patterns of mobility and assimilation found in these two areas very well may not be applicable to other parts of the country.

Finally, these data do not include information on the U.S.-born population of U.S. parentage. Because of the lack of a comparison group, it is not possible to determine if the paths of economic mobility that I find are limited to this group or are more widespread among youths in the United States or even in San Diego and Miami. For this reason, I have chosen to supplement the CILS data with a nationally representative data set, NELS:88.

The National Center for Education Statistics (NCES) within the U.S. Department of Education collected the NELS data, beginning in 1988. The baseline sample of NELS was based on a stratified probability design, resulting in a sample of 1,057 schools. From these schools, NCES researchers selected a random sample of eighth graders, resulting in 24,599 participants in the student survey (Ingels et al. 1994). At the same time, NCES also administered questionnaires to a parent or guardian of each of the youth survey participants. Of the youths who participated in NELS:88, approximately 92 percent of them also had completed parent surveys.

NCES then followed these students several times, including a 1992 follow-up of youths, when most were in twelfth grade, and their parents and a 2000 follow-up when respondents were in their mid-twenties. In the1988 base-year survey, approximately 93 percent of respondents who were selected for inclusion in the NELS student survey participated (Curtin et al. 2002). The follow-ups included subsamples of the base-year sample, with fewer respondents in the sampling frame every year. Of those who were contacted for interview in 2000, approximately 90 percent, or 14,915 cases, completed the interview. The NELS data, appropriately weighted, provide a nationally representative sample of all youths who were in eighth grade in the United States in 1988.

NELS contains excellent information on educational achievement and attainment, key indicators of economic mobility; however, NELS was not geared towards the study of immigrant assimilation. In fact, students who could not participate meaningfully in the survey—including those with limited English skills—were ineligible for NELS in the first wave, excluding most recent immigrants.[5] For this reason, the sizes of the various immigrant groups included in the data are small. Furthermore, NELS also lacks questions directed at measuring assimilation—particularly in non-economic ways. The NELS data, however, serve as a useful comparison of economic mobility among third and later generation youths.

Several waves of the NELS data are approximately equivalent to the waves of CILS data, although the NELS cohort came from a slightly earlier time period. The NELS 1988 base-year survey includes a sample of eighth graders similar to the sample of eighth and ninth graders from the first wave of CILS. The NELS second follow-up in 1992 includes youths in twelfth grade and their parents, like the CILS wave two data and parent subsample data. Finally, the NELS fourth follow-up in 2000 includes youths in their mid-twenties, like the CILS wave three data, although the NELS participants were a bit older than the equivalent CILS participants.

For the intergenerational analysis, I make use of CILS parent and youth surveys from the time when youths were typically in twelfth grade (1995-1996) and the final youth interview (2001-2003) when respondents were in their mid-twenties. I limit my NELS sample to only third and later generation youths (defined as youths born in the United States to two U.S.-born parents) who identify as non-Hispanic white, non-Hispanic black, and of Mexican origin on questions of racial and ethnic identity. There are not enough third and later generation other Latinos, Asians, or American Indians to include in my analysis. For the NELS intergenerational analysis, I use information from parent and youth surveys, when youths were generally in twelfth grade (1992), along with youth surveys from the last wave of data collection in 2000 when youths were in their mid-twenties. I use the survey information from when youths were typically in twelfth grade because it is the only wave in which parent surveys are available for CILS. When defining paths of mobility and assimilation, I compare parent information from that wave to youth information in their mid-twenties so I can be confident that the youths' outcomes came after their parents' outcomes—rather than coincident with them. I also use this time point so that youth educational and occupational statuses are more comparable to their parents' economic statuses.

Dependent Variables

Indicators of Economic Mobility

For both the CILS and NELS data, to create indicators of economic mobility, I compare parent educational and occupational attainment, from the time youths were in about twelfth grade, to youth levels of educational and occupational attainment, from the time youths were in their mid-twenties. For the CILS data, to make the parent and youth educational categories equivalent for comparison, I collapse parent response options into the following four educational outcomes: (1) less

Table 2.3. Post-Imputation Percentage of Indicators Used to Create Intergenerational Mobility and Assimilation Dependent Variables

	CILS: CHILDREN OF IMMIGRANTS		NELS: 3RD AND LATER GENERATION	
Educational status	Parents	Youths	Parents	Youths
Less than high school	23	3	7	4
High school degree	15	12	21	16
Some college	31	37	42	44
College degree or more	31	48	30	36

	CILS			
Occupational status	Parents	Youths		
Lowest parent SEI quartile	25	22		
2nd parent SEI quartile	25	22		
3rd parent SEI quartile	25	33		
Highest parent SEI quartile	25	23		

	NELS	
Occupational status	Parents	Youths
Not working, laborers, operators, service workers	19	20
Clerical, craftspersons, farmers, military, protective service, and sales	27	39
Professional, technical, and managerial occupations and proprietorships	54	41

	CILS	
English use	Parents	Youths
English mostly user	15	83
Not English mostly user	85	17

	CILS	
Ethnic identity	Parents	Youths
National origin	54	28
Hyphenated	14	40
Racial/pan-ethnic	29	29
American	3	3

than high school, (2) high school degree only, (3) some college, and (4) college degree or more. I compare the two parents' levels of education and select the parent with the higher level of education for comparison with the youth (see Table 2.3 for distribution[6]). I categorize youth education similarly, using several questions from the survey. Because of the young age of the sample, I treat those youths who were currently enrolled in a four-year degree program to be equivalent to college graduates.

Table 2.4. Post-Imputaton Distribution of Intergenerational Educational Mobility Paths from Parents to their Young Adult Children by Parent Education and Gender

	CILS: 3RD AND LATER GENERATION			NELS: CHILDREN OF IMMIGRANTS		
Low Parental Educational Status						
	Males	Females	Total	Males	Females	Total
Stable	50	51	101	14	11	25
Up	148	263	411	161	221	382
Total	198	314	512	175	232	407
% Up	74.7	83.8	80.3	92.0	95.3	93.9
Intermediate Parental Educational Status						
	Males	Females	Total	Males	Females	Total
Down	369	321	690	54	42	96
Stable	1047	1083	2130	126	105	231
Up	821	1143	1964	208	259	467
Total	2237	2547	4784	388	406	794
% Up	36.7	44.9	41.1	53.6	63.8	58.8
% Down	16.5	12.6	14.4	13.9	10.3	12.1
High Parental Status						
	Males	Females	Total	Males	Females	Total
Down	733	776	1509	103	92	195
Stable	405	335	740	166	188	354
Total	1138	1111	2249	269	280	549
% Down	35.6	30.2	32.9	38.3	32.9	35.5

To create educational attainment measures with the NELS data, I use a variable that the NCES staff constructed to code parents' highest education. These parent educational categories are: (1) less than high school degree, (2) hig school degree or equivalent, (3) some post-secondary education, and (4) a college degree or higher. I classify youths' educational attainment into the same four categories, using variables on post-secondary educational completion, ever attendance of post-secondary education, and high school degree information. For both the CILS and NELS data, I compare the parent's and child's information to determine if youths experience (1) downward, (2) horizontal, or (3) upward intergenerational educational mobility. See Table 2.4 for the distribution of intergenerational educational mobility paths by parent education and gender for both the CILS and NELS data.

Table 2.5. Post-Imputation Distribution of Intergenerational Occupational Mobility Paths from Parents to Their Young Adult Children by Parent Occupational Status and Gender

	NELS: 3RD AND LATER GENERATION			CILS: CHILDREN OF IMMIGRANTS		
Low parental occupational status						
	Males	Females	Total	Males	Females	Total
Stable	138	230	368	41	55	96
Up	491	567	1058	165	179	344
Total	629	797	1426	206	234	440
% Up	78.1	71.1	74.2	80.1	76.5	78.2
Intermediate parental occupational status						
	Males	Females	Total	Males	Females	Total
Down	174	267	441	121	153	274
Stable	421	404	825	120	137	257
Up	369	398	767	166	177	343
Total	964	1069	2033	407	467	874
% Up	38.3	37.2	37.7	40.8	37.9	39.2
% Down	18.0	25.0	21.7	29.7	32.8	31.4
High parental occupational status						
	Males	Females	Total	Males	Females	Total
Down	1053	1076	2129	156	156	312
Stable	927	1030	1957	63	61	124
Total	1980	2106	4086	219	217	436
% Down	53.2	51.1	52.1	71.2	71.9	71.6

To create the occupational mobility measures for CILS, I compare the SEI score of the parent with the higher occupational status, from parent survey reports, to the SEI score of the youth's occupation. Occupational information in CILS is based on Census occupational classifications from the 1980s (Haller 2006) plus several additional occupational titles that did not fit into the Census scheme. I apply Hauser and Warren's (1997) 1990 SEI scores to the CILS occupational categories. I recode some of the occupations included in the CILS data, although the differences between the 1980 and 1990 Census occupational titles are minor.

I next categorize parent SEI scores into quartiles and divide youths' SEI scores into these same categories. These quartiles generally signify major differences in occupational situation. Furthermore, they allow enough cases for analysis of occupational mobility at the bottom, middle, and top of the occupational status distribution. I compare parent and youth occupational status quartile to determine if youths experience (1) downward, (2) horizontal, or (3) upward intergenerational occupational mobility.

In the NELS data, the parent survey asks respondents to select one of the following categories that best describes their occupations: (1) clerical, (2) craftsperson, (3) homemaker; (4) farmer or farm manager; (5) laborer, (6) manager or administrator, (7) military; (8) operative, (9) professional, (10) other professionals, (11) proprietor or owner, (12) protective service, (13) sales, (14) school teacher, (15) service, and (16) technical. I reduce these occupations into three ranked occupational categories based on earnings and SEI score information from Hauser and Warren (1997) and Buckley (2002). The lowest category includes those not working for pay and the low-skilled: laborers, operators, and service workers. The highest status occupational category encompasses professional, technical, and managerial occupations and proprietorships. The intermediate category includes the remaining occupations. While these categories are imperfect and overlap is possible in a few cases, they typically reflect sizable and meaningful differences in occupational experiences and income. For youths, there are 40 different occupations that I classify similarly into the three categories. As with CILS, I compare the higher occupational status parent to his/her child to determine if the youth experiences (1) downward, (2) stable, or (3) upward intergenerational occupational mobility. Table 2.5 presents the distribution of occupational mobility paths by data set, gender, and starting point.

Indicators of Cultural Assimilation

I next turn to paths of cultural assimilation, applicable only to CILS respondents due to NELS data limitations. To examine intergenerational linguistic assimilation, I define equivalent measures of parent and child English language use; however, the CILS parent and youth surveys do not contain exactly the same English use items. I compare parents' use of English with their children, when most were in twelfth grade, to youths' use of English with their friends when they were in their mid-twenties.[7]

Table 2.6. Post-Imputation Distribution of Intergenerational Linguistic (English Use) Assimilation Paths from Parents to Their Young Adult Children by Parent English Use and Gender for CILS Data

Non-English Mostly Parents			
	Males	Females	Total
Stable	227	239	466
Classical	480	545	1025
Total	707	784	1491
% Classical	67.9	69.5	68.7
English Mostly Parents			
	Males	Females	Total
Anti-classical	5	5	10
Stable	120	129	249
Total	125	134	259
% Anti-classical	4.0	3.7	3.9

Parent English use information comes from an item that asks: "In what language do you mostly speak to your child?" Response options in the questionnaire included English, "other," and "mixed." I code those parents who respond "English" as English mostly users and all other parents as non-English mostly users (see Table 2.3 for distribution). The youth language use item asks respondents the language(s) they speak with their closest friends. Response options include (1) English only, (2) English mostly, (3) English and non-English about the same, (4) mostly non-English language, and (5) non-English language only. I code all those who report using English only or mostly with their friends as English-mostly users. I code all other respondents with non-missing information as other language users.

I then compare parents' and youths' English use. If the parent reports using English more than his/her child, I consider the direction of assimilation to be anti-classical. If the parents and youths report the same level of English use, I classify assimilation as stable. If the parent reports using less English than his/her child, I consider the direction of assimilation to be classical. I provide the distribution of the directions of assimilation by starting point and gender in Table 2.6.

To measure identificational assimilation, I use responses to open-ended items from the parent and youth surveys that ask respondents, "How do you identify, that is, what do you call yourself?" Following the question is a list of example responses, such as American, Asian, Hispanic, African-American, Black, Chinese, Chinese-American, Haitian, Haitian-American, etc (Portes and Rumbaut 2001a). For both youths and their parents, these questions on ethnic identification come relatively late in the survey, after respondents had completed questions on immigration status, place of origin, and language ability. It is likely, therefore, that matters of ethnic identification—and particularly their connections to their countries of origin—had been primed as a result of the survey context.

I code parent and youth ethnic identification responses into Portes and Rumbaut's (2001a) four identification categories: plain American, national origin, hyphenated American, and racial or pan-ethnic. See Table 3 for the distributions. I then compare parent and youth ethnic identities to determine the direction of assimilation. As noted above, there are four possible paths of identificational assimilation: (1) linear, associated with classical assimilation; (2) stable or horizontal, or no change over time; (3) resurgent, in the opposite direction expected by classical assimilation; and (4) racialized, whereby one adopts a made-in-America identity but one that is associated with minority group status. Of course, these paths depend on the starting points, parents' ethnic self-identification, and the ending points, youths' ethnic self-identification, of assimilation (see Table 2.2, above). Only when parents have hyphenated identities can youths experience all four paths of assimilation. See Table 2.7 for the distribution of paths of identificational assimilation by gender and starting point.

Table 2.7. Post-Imputation Distribution of Intergenerational Identificational Assimilation Paths from Parents to Their Young Adult Children by Parent Ethnic Identity and Gender for CILS Data

Parents with American Identities			
	MALES	FEMALES	TOTAL
Resurgent	6	14	20
Stable	3	5	8
Racialized	7	16	23
Total	16	35	51
% Resurgent	37.5	40.0	39.2
% Racialized	43.8	45.7	45.1
Parents with Hyphenated American Identities			
Resurgent	35	32	67
Stable	63	63	126
Linear	6	4	10
Racialized	20	31	51
Total	124	130	254
% Resurgent	28.2	25.8	27.0
% Linear	4.8	3.2	4.0
% Racialized	16.1	25.0	20.6
Parents with Racial or Pan-Ethnic Identities			
Resurgent	157	153	310
Stable	85	97	182
Linear	7	5	12
Total	249	255	504
% Resurgent	63.1	61.4	62.2
% Linear	2.8	2.0	2.4
Parents with National Origin Identities			
Stable	136	147	283
Linear	198	213	411
Racialized	109	138	247
Total	443	498	941
% Linear	44.7	48.1	46.4
% Racialized	24.6	31.2	27.9

CILS Independent Variables

I create three groups of independent variables from the CILS data: demographic characteristics, downward leveling factors, and protective factors. These variables primarily come from the youth and parent surveys when youths are typically in twelfth grade. The demographic factors include gender, year of birth, ethnic origin, family structure, family size, parent education, parent occupational status, and income.[8] Gender, of course, distinguishes females from males (the reference group). Because of the lack of variation in year of birth, I collapse responses into two categories: youths born in 1978 or 1979 and those born from 1975 to 1977 (the reference category).

To determine youths' ethnic origin, I followed Portes and Rumbaut's (2001a) method of using information on parents' place of birth. When this information conflicts, I use youth's place of birth and language information to assign ethnic origin. I collapse groups into the following categories to maintain suitable cell sizes: Cuban (16 percent of the sample), Mexican (13 percent), Nicaraguan (9 percent), West Indian (8 percent), Filipino (17 percent), Southeast Asian (18 percent), and "other" immigrant groups (18 percent). Other Latinos and Asians as well as individuals of European, Canadian, and African origin make up this "other" group. Although Rumbaut (2004) argues persuasively that examining children of immigrants by generational status is important for a full understanding of their experiences, I do not divide these groups by generational status because the relatively small number of cases, divided by starting point and gender, do not allow for it. In addition, ethnic origin and generation are quite strongly linked. Most Cubans and Mexicans in the sample are second generation. The vast majority of Nicaraguans and Southeast Asians in the sample are first generation. West Indians, Filipinos, and individuals of "other" ethnic origin are more evenly split.

To measure family structure, I create a dummy variable indicating that the youth live with both biological parents in twelfth grade. Other living situation is the reference group. Research suggests that the more thinly spread family resources are over additional siblings/dependents, the poorer youths' educational performance (Blake 1989; Steelman and Powell 1991; Downey 1995); therefore, I include an indicator of family size from the parent survey.

Information on parents' education, occupational status, and income comes from the parent survey. The exact parental education, occupational status, and income explanatory variables I use differ across the analyses, due to their associations with the starting point I examine. For education and occupation, I use some combination of the status variables described above. For the income measure, I divide family income from all sources into four quartiles. Again, I use some combination of the four quartiles in each set of analyses.

I also created several sets of downward leveling factors. The first set deals with negative influences stemming from peers and friends. I include a dummy variable indicating that the youth has at least one dropout friend. The reference category indicates no dropout friends. I also create two scales indicating parent opinions of negative friend influences. For the first scale, parents' views of negative peer influences, I sum two survey items that ask parents how worried they are about negative influences on their children from (1) other students in school and (2) from their children's own close friends.[9] I created a second scale by summing up responses to the items inquiring how different (1) parents' and their children's friends' views and ideas are and (2) parents' and their children's friends' messages about becoming a successful person are.[10] Response options in both cases range from (0) not at all for both to (6) very for both.

I also create a scale to represent youths' negative experiences at school from items that ask respondents how often during the current school year (1) they had something stolen from them at school, (2) someone offered to sell them drugs, (3) someone threatened to hurt them, and (4) they got into a physical fight at school. The response options range from (0) never for all to (9) more than twice for all.[11]

A second set of downward leveling factors relates to respondents' neighborhoods. For one scale, parents report how much of a problem in their neighborhoods are (1) different racial or cultural groups who do not get along with each other, (2) little respect for rules, laws, and authority, and (3) assaults or muggings. For the second scale, they report how much of a problem (1) gangs and (2) drugs are in their neighborhoods. Response options for both sets of items (before adding the responses) are (1) not a problem, (2) somewhat of a problem, and (3) a big problem.[12]

The final set of downward leveling factors represents race problems. The first variable is a dummy indicating whether the youth feels that he/she has ever been discriminated against or not (the reference group).[13] The second variable represents youths' views of racial problems in the United States. To create this variable, I sum responses to survey items inquiring about the degree to which respondents agree that (1) there is racial discrimination in the United States and (2) there is much conflict between races in the United States.[14] Response options range from (0) disagree a lot for both and (6) agree a lot for both.

I also include five sets of protective factors. The first set of variables indicates (hypothetically) protective friend influences. These variables are counts of the respondents' friends with (1) college plans and (2) foreign-born parents. Response options are (1) none, (2) some, and (3) many or most. Because the results are skewed for both variables, I collapse categories, creating a dummy variable to indicate that many or most friends had college plans or foreign-born parents. The reference group indicates that some or fewer friends had college plans or foreign-born parents.

The second set of protective factors deals with the parent-child relationship. Although segmented assimilation theory explicitly discusses parent-child acculturation, it suggests that the parent-child relationship generally is important for understanding mobility and assimilation. It indicates that youths will have greater success when parents and children have better relationships and relationships in which parents maintain authority and responsibility over their children. Such qualities are applicable to relationships between youths and immigrant and non-immigrant parents alike.

I create an additive scale measuring the quality of the parent-youth relationship from three survey items in which respondents rate the truthfulness, from (0) very true for all to (9) very untrue for all, of the following statements: (1) "My parents don't like me very much"; (2) "My parents and I often argue because we don't share the same goals"; and (3) "My parents are usually not very interested in what I say."[15] Because these statements are all negative, the less true respondents rate them, the higher the score and the better the quality of the parent relationship. I also create an additive scale representing family closeness from three survey items that inquire of the youth respondents how often each of the following is true: (1) family members like to spend time together, (2) family members feel close, and (3) family togetherness is important. Responses ranged from (0) never for all to (12) always for all.[16]

In addition, I create a dummy variable indicating that parents talk regularly with their children about their experiences in school and their educational plans. The reference category is that they do not talk regularly about these things. I also create a count of the number of the following activities that the parent reports that he/she or his/her partner participate in at school: (1) belonging to the parent-teacher organization, (2) attending PTO meetings, and (3) acting as a volunteer in the school.[17] Finally, I include a count of family rules related to watching television, specifically, rules about (1) what programs one's child may watch, (2) how early or late he/she may watch television, and (3) how many hours he/she may watch.[18]

The third set of protective factors involves forms of social capital and the youth and his/her family's wider social network. The first variable is a neighborhood social capital scale based on parents' summed responses to the following three items: (1) "There are a lot of adults around that my children can look up to"; (2) "My neighbors have similar views about how to raise children"; and (3) "I can count on people in the neighborhood to let me know about opportunities for my kids." The response options for each range from (0) strongly disagree for all to (12) strongly agree for all.[19]

In addition, I create an additive scale measuring neighbor intervention from survey items that ask parents if people in their neighborhood would intervene if (1) someone were trying to sell drugs to one of the respondent's children in plain sight and (2) the respondent's kids were getting into trouble. Response options range from (0) very unlikely for both to (6) very likely for both.[20] Additionally, I create a dummy variable indicating that the family has not moved in the last three years. The reference category includes those who have moved in the last three years.

The fourth set of protective factors measures attachment to one's culture of origin. For one measure, I assign a score of one for parents who report feeling a lot of pride in their countries of origin and wanting to share it with their children. The reference group includes those parents who do not report a lot of pride. Another dummy variable distinguishes parents who report socializing mainly with other persons from their own country of birth from those who do not (the reference group).

I create two dummy variables from youth survey items asking how much youths and their parents prefer American ways. Youths, then, provide their views of their parents' preferences for American ways. The first dummy variable represents those cases in which neither the youth nor his/her parents prefer American ways most of the time. The second dummy variable indicates that either the youth or the parent prefers American ways most of the time.[21] The reference category represents those cases in which both the youth and his/her parents prefer American ways most of the time.

I also create a scale measuring relatives' importance from the following three youth survey items: (1) "If someone has the chance to help a person get a job, it is always better to choose a relative than a friend"; (2) "When someone has a serious problem, only relatives can help"; and (3) "When looking for a job a person should find a job near his/her parents even if it means losing a better job somewhere else." The scale ranges from (0) disagrees a lot for all to (9) agrees a lot for all.[22]

The final ethnic protectiveness variables I include in the analysis are measures of non-English language ability and frequency of non-English language use at home. The non-English language ability scale ranges from respondent understands, speaks, reads, and writes a non-English language (0) very little to (12) very well. The response options for the non-English language use in the household item range from (0) never to (4) always.[23]

NELS Independent Variables

I create similar measures for my NELS analysis primarily from youth and parent surveys when youths were in twelfth grade. Again, gender and year of birth are dummy variables. For year of birth, a value of one indicates the respondent was born in 1974 or 1975. The reference group includes those born in 1972 or 1973.

A series of dummy variables indicate racial-ethnic origin. Race-ethnicity information comes from the youth eighth grade survey items on race and Hispanicity, although, when it is missing, I use information from later survey waves. Due to cell size issues, I am able to retain only the following third and later generation categories for analysis: (1) whites (the omitted group), (2) blacks, and (3) Mexicans.

I also include indicators of family structure and size when youths were in twelfth grade. I create a dummy variable representing that the youth lives with two biological parents. The reference group comprises all other families. Additionally, I include a count of the number of dependents that parents report.

As is the case with CILS, controls for parents' educational and occupational status depend on the model I am examining. For parental educational status, they involve some combination of the following dummy variables (with appropriate reference groups): less than a high school degree, a high school degree only, some college, and a four-year college degree. For parental occupational status, I use some combination of dummies (with appropriate reference group) indicating that it falls in the first, second, third, or fourth quartile. Finally, dummy variables indicate parental income quartile, from a parent-survey variable. As with the educational and occupational information, I include some combination of these dummy variables in the analyses. These variables differ across models because of different associations between them and the parental educational and occupational starting points.

The first set of downward leveling factors in NELS are related to youths' current schools (in twelfth grade, primarily) or their most recent schools if they had dropped out. First, I create a dummy variable to indicate that the youth's school is in an urban area. Non-urban schools are the reference group. Another variable is a scale representing the extent to which there are (1) racial and (2) gang problems at school. Responses for this scale range from (0) strongly disagree to both to (6) strongly agree to both.[24] Another item asks respondents how much they agree with this statement: "I don't feel safe at this school." Reverse-coded responses range from (1) strongly disagree to (4) strongly agree.

I also create a scale to represent problems at youths' schools. Respondents are asked how much they agree that the following issues are problems for the school: (1) drug use on school grounds, (2) the sale or use of drugs on the way to and from school, (3) theft, (4) violence, and (5) lack of discipline. Summing the scores to these items, response options range from (0) strongly disagree to (15) strongly agree.[25] I also include a scale representing negative peer influences. Respondents are asked how important it is to their close friends to (1) go to parties, (2) have sex, and (3) drink alcohol. The summed responses range from (0) not important for any to (6) very important for all.[26]

The last downward leveling factor I include is a count of dropout friends. Respondents report the number of their friends who have dropped out of high school: (1) none to (5) all of them. I use this variable as is for the models of educational mobility among youths whose parents have less than a high school degree. In all other models,

I use a dummy variable indicating that the youth has any dropout friends. The reference group includes youths with no dropout friends.

Turning to protective factors, the first category pertains to parental authority and management. I measure parental trust with youth responses to this statement: "My parents/guardians trust me to do what they expect without checking up on me." To measure obedience of parental authority, I use youths' responses to the following statement: "I often do not know why I am to do what my parents/guardians tell me to do." Response options for both are (1) false to (6) true. I reverse-code the parental trust variable so that larger numbers indicate that youths *do* know why they should obey their parents. Additionally, I include a measure of how often youths spend time talking with their parents. Responses range from (1) never/rarely to (4) almost every day.

I also include two additive scales that measure parent-child decision making.[27] The first scale represents authority in decisions relating to drinking (1) with parents and (2) at parties.[28] The second scale involves decisions about (1) how late the youth can stay out, (2) when he/she can use a car, (3) if he/she can have a job, and (4) how he/she spends money. Original response options for the two sets of items range across a five-point scale from (1) parents decide to (3) parents and youth decide together to (5) youth decides by him/herself.[29] Larger numbers, then, represent youths' greater authority.

In addition, I include an indicator of parent intervention at school based on Muller's (1995, 1998) work on education and parental involvement. I create an additive scale from the following survey items which ask parents how many times they or their partners have contacted their youths' schools in the last year about: (1) their youths' academic performance, (2) their youths' academic program for this year, and (3) their youths' behavior in school. Response options range from (0) none for all to (9) more than four times for all.[30] As with some of the other protective factors, it is possible that this item actually represents greater need for parents to contact the school because of youth discipline and/or academic problems. Greater contact with schools, in this case, may be associated with lower odds of upward economic mobility.

The second category involves measures of social capital or networks outside of the family, including peer influences. In their work on parental involvement using NELS data, Freese and Powell (1999) create counts of the number (up to five) of youths' friends and youth's friends' parents that the parent knows as measures of social capital. I create the same measures based on their work.[31] For models involving parents with more than a high school degree, this information is highly skewed; therefore, I use a dummy variable to indicate that parents know all of the youth's closest friends in these models. I also include a measure of how often youths spend time talking with adults other than their parents. Responses range from (1) never/rarely to (4) almost every day.

The remaining social capital measures deal with youths' friendship networks. I produce a scale from items asking youths how important (1) attending class, (2) studying, (3) getting good grades, (4) finishing high school, and (5) continuing education past high school are to their friends. The summed response options range from (0) not important for all to (10) very important for all.[32] I create another measure from similar items that ask respondents how important (1) participating in religious activities and (2) doing community work or volunteering are to their friends.[33] Summed responses to these items are rather skewed; therefore, I create a dummy variable out of these items indicating that religious activities or community service are of, at least, some importance to respondents' friends. The reference group includes those for whom religious activities and community service are of no importance. The final social capital variable about friends is a count of respondents' friends with college plans, ranging from (1) none to (5) all of them.

The last set of protective factors involves youths' economic expectations. I include a dummy variable indicating youths' educational expectations. In all models, except those for youths whose parents have less than a high school degree, the dummy indicates that youths expect to complete a college degree or more. The dummy for youths with low educational status parents indicates expectations of some college or more. The reference groups for these dummies are some college or less and a high school degree or less, respectively. I also include a dummy variable for high occupational expectations. The reference category includes those who expect less than high occupational status.

Missing Data: Multiple Imputation

As I noted above, there are problems with missing data for these variables, as is often the case when using longitudinal data. Missing data cause problems for researchers because almost all statistical methods are based on complete data (Allison 2002). There are various sources and causes of missing data and a number of different strategies that one can use to deal with them. Every method of dealing with missing data has its drawbacks. For example, two common ways of handling missing data, listwise deletion and mean substitution, do not make use of all available information and involve implausible assumptions.

I use multiple imputation to deal with missing data in this analysis. The idea behind multiple imputation is that one uses the available distribution of data to impute for the missing values of variables. One performs this step multiple times to create more than one imputed data set. One then analyzes these multiple data sets simultaneously, averaging coefficients across the data sets and using a correction to calculate appropriate standard errors.

According to Allison (2000), multiple imputation is a good way of dealing with missing data because, by introducing a random element into the process, it is "possible to get approximately unbiased estimates of all parameters" (301-302). Furthermore, performing the imputation multiple times allows me to calculate standard errors appropriately, especially in comparison with single imputation. There are three requirements that Allison states are necessary for multiple imputation. The first is that data must be missing at random, though not completely at random. Missing at random means that the probability of missing data on a particular variable is not related to that variable itself, after controlling for other variables. Although CILS and NELS data, particularly for certain variables, are not likely to be missing at random, inclusion of control variables helps make up for the possible lack of randomness. The second requirement is that the model used to create the imputed values must be appropriate for the analysis. It should contain all of the necessary variables and use the correct method of analysis. Finally, the model used for the imputation must match up with the model used for the final analysis. This requirement suggests that at least all variables used in the final analysis—dependent and independent—should also be used in the imputation (Allison 2000, 2002; Rubin 1996).

To perform the multiple imputation, I begin with my incomplete data sets. I then use a statistical model (one for NELS and one for CILS), incorporating an element of randomization and including all of the variables in my final regression models, to calculate the values for variables with missing information. I use Stata's "ice" command for multiple chained equations (Royston 2005) to perform this imputation five times for a result of five complete data sets. Then I use Stata's "micombine" command to combine these data sets in my regression analysis with a correction for the standard errors.

Analytical Methods

I use bivariate methods to examine the distributions of the paths of mobility and assimilation and test for statistically significant differences by gender, generational status, and life course stage. I then perform logistic regression—both binomial and multinomial—to examine the factors that predict mobility and assimilation paths. I use the appropriate weights for the NELS data to deal with issues of study design. For the CILS data, weights are not publicly available; however, I use Rumbaut's (2005) method of including variables that predict dropping out of the sample, specifically, family structure, parent socioeconomic status, and youth grades, to deal with sample selection bias. I perform a number of different logistic regressions depending on the path of mobility and assimilation I am studying and the starting point on which I am focusing. Where the sample size allows, I perform these analyses separately by gender. In general, for NELS, I aim to have more than 350 cases for each category of the dependent variable before analyzing the outcomes separately by gender. For CILS, I want approximately 250 cases for each category of the dependent variable before dividing it by gender. I require more cases for the NELS analysis because the distribution of individuals in the different ethnic groups is more highly skewed. For each indicator, I begin with a baseline model including my demographic characteristics, to which I add the downward leveling characteristics, and finally the protective factors in a third, full model.

In the last few decades, there has been much discussion about how best to analyze change at the individual level, particularly in the psychological literature (see Gottman and Rushe 1993, for a review). Most methods for analyzing change, including difference scores and autoregressors, are best for changes in quantitative measures. Moreover, they do not fully take into account the limits that starting points place upon the direction of change. I want to capture qualitative changes (or the lack thereof) in economic and cultural indicators of mobility and assimilation by their different starting points; therefore, I define the pathways in this manner and analyze them with logistic regression. Although I have not found previous research that has made use of this particular method of defining pathways, its conceptualization is simple and straightforward. It allows me to speak only to the direction rather than the size of any change.

Descriptive Results

Educational Mobility

The descriptive results for educational mobility show that positive forms of mobility are common across the board. They reveal greater success among children of immigrants than later generation youths from low and intermediate starting points (see Table 2.4, above[34]). However, these differences fade among youths whose parents have college degrees. There are more gender differences in educational mobility among third and later generation youths than among children of immigrants.

Among youths whose parents have less than a high school degree, the upward path of mobility is especially common. Statistically significantly more CILS youths (about 94 percent) experience upward mobility than NELS youths (about 80 percent).[35] A larger proportion of third and later generation young women exceed their parents' low levels of education than their male counterparts; however, gender differences are not statistically significant among children of immigrants.

Among youths whose parents have an intermediate level of education—a high school degree or some college—a smaller proportion experience upward educational mobility. Of course, for these youths upward mobility requires a higher level of education than youths with low-education parents. Children of immigrants are also statistically significantly more upwardly mobile than the third and later generation from this starting point. Within both the CILS and NELS data, young women are more upwardly mobile than their male counterparts.

Downward mobility is quite uncommon among young adults with intermediate-education parents. The proportion of individuals experiencing downward educational mobility ranges from about 10 percent among CILS females to about 17 percent among NELS males. A larger proportion of NELS males than NELS and CILS females experiences downward educational mobility; however, other group comparisons are not statistically significant.

Most young adults with highly educated parents (college degree or more) hold on to their parents' levels of education. In this case, the group with the largest proportion of young adults experiencing horizontal mobility is NELS females (about 70 percent). This group is statistically significantly larger than NELS and CILS males, though it does not differ statistically significantly from CILS females. Differences between the other groups are not statistically significant.

Occupational Mobility

As expected, positive forms of occupational mobility are much less common than positive forms of educational mobility. Also in contrast to educational mobility, gender differences from low and intermediate starting points are highly associated with occupational mobility (see Table 2.5, above). In this case, as expected, young men have more positive mobility outcomes than young women. At the highest parental occupational starting point, immigrant status factors in more. In this case, children of non-immigrants experience more horizontal mobility than children of immigrants. However, this outcome may be related to differences between the NELS and CILS data. I discuss this matter further below.

Most youths with low occupational status parents experience upward mobility by the time they are in their mid-twenties. Differences between data sets as a whole are not statistically significant; however, a statistically significantly larger proportion of NELS males experiences upward mobility than NELS females.

Among youths with intermediate occupational status parents, upward mobility is the most common path for CILS youths while horizontal mobility is most common for NELS youths. A statistically significantly larger proportion of CILS respondents experiences downward occupational mobility than do NELS respondents. Within the NELS data, a statistically significantly larger proportion of females than males experience downward mobility. CILS gender differences are not statistically significant.

Among those with high occupational status parents, NELS youths have statistically significantly lower odds of downward mobility than CILS youths. This finding may be due to differences in my system of occupational rankings across the two data sets or the age of the two samples. CILS youths are younger, on average, than their NELS counterparts; therefore, they have had less time to achieve their parents' occupational status levels than the NELS participants.

Linguistic Assimilation

My examination of cultural assimilation using the CILS data reveals that, as previous research suggests, English use assimilation is quite rapid and commonplace (see Table 2.6, above). Not surprisingly, most youths whose parents do not use English mostly with them as high school seniors use English mostly with their friends in their mid-twenties. Almost all youths whose parents use English mostly with them do so with their friends in their mid-twenties. Gender differences are not statistically significant.

Identificational Assimilation

Table 2.7 (above) reveals how the distributions of directions of identificational assimilation differ by each ethnic identity starting point. Very few youths have parents with American identities; therefore, I do not discuss these results further. The general pattern of evidence reveals that intergenerational movement towards (or stability of) dual identities that encompass one's place of origin and one's new home is widespread. For example, the most common path of assimilation for youths whose parents have hyphenated identities is a stable path. In fact, across the different starting points, stable assimilation is most common for youths with hyphenated identity parents. For youths with national-origin-identified parents and racial/pan-ethnic-identified parents, the most common paths are linear and resurgent, respectively. In both cases, these paths can, and do, involve youths' adoption of hyphenated identities. In contrast to expectations, gender differences are not statistically significant.

Multivariate Results

The multivariate results reveal that the factors associated with pathways of educational and occupational mobility and linguistic and identificational assimilation differ by starting point, gender, and parental immigration status. However, there is neither a clear pattern to these different associations nor a cohesive story to tell. Below, I highlight some of the most consistent findings and the results that challenge segmented assimilation theory's claims.

Educational Mobility

Table 2.8A. Odds of Intergenerational Educational Mobility Paths among Children of Immigrants, By Parental Educational Status and Gender: Statistically Significant Demographic Characteristics

Demographic Characteristics	PARENTAL EDUCATIONAL STATUS		
	INTERMEDIATE: Up vs. Not Up		HIGH: Down vs. Stable
	MALES	FEMALES	FULL
Later year of birth (ref: earlier)	ns	ns	ns
West Indian	ns	Higher up	ns
Mexican origin	ns	ns	Higher down
Asian origin (Ref: other)	ns	SE Asians: Higher up	Filipinos: Higher down
2 parent family (Ref: other)	ns	ns	ns
Number of dependents	ns	Lower up	ns
Parent: some college (Ref: h.s. degree)	Lower up	Lower up	-
Parent: low occupational status (Ref: high status)	-	-	-
Parent: high income (Ref: not high)	ns	ns	ns

Source: Children of Immigrants Longitudinal Study

- indicates variable not included in model

Demographic variables not statistically significant: Cuban and Nicaraguan origin and gender

The educational mobility results reveal that friend and family attributes are generally important for predicting paths of educational mobility, regardless of starting point, gender, and immigrant generational status (see Tables 2.8A-F). Before discussing these results further, I will discuss associations between other demographic characteristics and educational mobility paths. Of the demographic characteristics, there are a few associations between race-ethnicity and educational mobility (see Tables 2.8A-B). Among children of immigrants, individuals of Mexican origin have higher odds of downward mobility than "other" immigrants, as segmented assimilation researchers have suggested. Surprisingly, however, this finding holds only among Mexicans with college-educated immigrant parents (a small proportion of all Mexican origin youths in the CILS data). There are no statistically significant differences among third and later generation Mexican origin individuals.

Table 2.8B. Odds of Intergenerational Educational Mobility Paths among Third and Later Generation Youths, By Parental Educational Status and Gender: Statistically Significant Demographic Characteristics

| *Demographic Characteristics* | PARENTAL EDUCATIONAL STATUS | | | |
| | INTERMEDIATE: Up vs. Stable vs. Down | | HIGH: Down vs. Stable | |
	Males	Females	Males	Females
Later year of birth (ref: earlier)	Lower down vs. up	Higher up vs. stable	ns	ns
Black (ref: whites)	ns	ns	ns	ns
Mexican origin	ns	ns	ns	ns
Asian origin	-	-	-	-
2 parent family (ref: other)	ns	ns	Lower down	Lower down
Number of dependents	Higher down vs. not	ns	ns	ns
Parent: some college (ref: h.s. degree)	Lower up vs. not	Lower up vs. not	-	-
Parent: low status occupation	Higher down vs. not	Lower up vs. stable	-	-
Parent: high income (ref: not high)	Lower down vs. up	Lower down vs. not	Lower down	ns

Source: National Educational Longitudinal Study

- indicates variable not included in model

Note: Low educational status not shown

Associations between ethnic group and educational mobility also provide mixed support for segmented assimilation's claims. Southeast Asian and West Indian females in CILS whose parents have intermediate levels of education have more positive mobility outcomes than others. However, Filipinos with college-educated parents have higher odds of downward mobility than "other" immigrants.

Table 2.8C. Odds of Intergenerational Educational Mobility Paths among Children of Immigrants, By Parental Educational Status and Gender: Statistically Significant Downward Leveling Factors

	PARENTAL EDUCATIONAL STATUS		
Downward Leveling Factors	INTERMEDIATE: Up vs. Not Up		HIGH: Down vs. Stable
	MALES	FEMALES	FULL
Count of problems at school	-	-	-
Scale: Racial problems in the US	Higher up	ns	ns
Dropout friends	ns	Lower up	ns
Scale: how different parent and peer views (not at all to very)	ns	ns	Higher down
Parent reports any neighborhood problems (ref: none)	ns	ns	Higher down

Source: Children of Immigrants Longitudinal Study
- indicates variable not included in model
Downward leveling factors not statistically significant: parents worry about negative peer influence, negative experiences at school, problem with drugs in neighborhood, ever discriminated against

Family structure and family socioeconomic status are quite consistent predictors of educational mobility. Living in a two biological parent family is protective of parents' high levels of education for third and later generation youths with college educated parents only; however, family size, specifically number of dependents, has some negative associations with mobility in both the CILS and NELS data sets, among females and males, respectively, for youths whose parents have a high school degree or some college. Due to the construction of the models, parental education level only comes into play for youths from intermediate levels of education, for whom it is more difficult to surpass the educational levels of parents with some college compared to parents with a high school degree only. Parental income predicts more positive mobility outcomes among third and later generation youths only.

Table 2.8D. Odds of Intergenerational Educational Mobility Paths among Third and Later Generation Youths, By Parental Educational Status and Gender: Statistically Significant Downward Leveling Factors

	PARENTAL EDUCATIONAL STATUS			
Downward Leveling Factors	INTERMEDIATE: Up vs. Not Up		HIGH: Down vs. Stable	
	Males	Females	Males	Females
Count of problems at school	Lower up vs. not	ns	ns	ns
Scale: Racial/gang problems at schl	ns	Higher down vs. not	ns	ns
Dropout friends	Higher down vs. not	Lower up vs. stable	ns	Higher down vs. stable
Scale: how different parent and peer views (not at all to 8=very)	-	-	-	-
Parent reports any neighborhood problems (ref: none)	-	-	-	-

Source: National Educational Longitudinal Study
- indicates variable not included in model
Downward leveling factors not statistically significant: urban neighborhood, school violence, school safety, negative peer influences

Of the downward leveling factors (see Tables 2.8C-D), having dropout friends is most consistently associated with negative mobility outcomes across the starting points and data sets. But the association holds more for females than males and for children of immigrants than children of non-immigrants. It also holds more often for youths whose parents have less than a college degree. Most of the few remaining statistically significant associations between downward leveling factors and educational mobility differ across the starting points. All but one association supports segmented assimilation theory's claims. I find one exception among sons of intermediate status immigrant parents: the more they agree that there are racial problems in the United States, the higher their odds of upward vs. other forms of educational mobility.

Table 2.8F. Odds of Intergenerational Educational Mobility Paths among Third and Later Generation Youths, By Parental Educational Status and Gender: Statistically Significant Protective Factors

Protective Factors	INTERMEDIATE: Up vs. Stable vs. Down		HIGH: Down vs. Stable	
	Males	Females	Males	Females
Frequency talk to parents	ns	Lower down vs. not	ns	ns
Family closeness	-	-	-	-
Count of friends' parents that parent knows	Higher up vs. not	Lower down vs. not	ns	Lower down vs. stable
Frequency parents contact school	Lower up vs. not	Lower up vs. not	Higher down vs. stable	Higher down vs. stable
Frequency talk to non-parent adults	ns	Lower up vs. stable	ns	ns
Scale: n'hood social capital (disagree to agree strongly)	-	-	-	-
Scale: importance of relatives	-	-	-	-
Community service important to friends (ref: not)	ns	Higher down vs. other	ns	ns
Friends with college plans	Higher up vs. not	Higher up vs. not	Lower down vs. stable	Lower down vs. stable
College expectations (ref: lower expect)	Higher up vs. not	Higher up vs. not	Lower down vs. stable	Lower down vs. stable
High occupational status expectations (ref: not high)	Higher up vs. not	ns	ns	ns

Source: National Educational Longitudinal Study

- indicates variable not included in model

Protective factors not statistically significant: parental trust, parent obedience, parents know friends, drinking decisions, positive peer influence

Table 2.8F. Odds of Intergenerational Educational Mobility Paths among Third and Later Generation Youths, By Parental Educational Status and Gender: Statistically Significant Protective Factors

Protective Factors	INTERMEDIATE: Up vs. Stable vs. Down		HIGH: Down vs. Stable	
	Males	Females	Males	Females
Frequency talk to parents	ns	Lower down vs. not	ns	ns
Family closeness	-	-	-	-
Count of friends' parents that parent knows	Higher up vs. not	Lower down vs. not	ns	Lower down vs. stable
Frequency parents contact school	Lower up vs. not	Lower up vs. not	Higher down vs. stable	Higher down vs. stable
Frequency talk to non-parent adults	ns	Lower up vs. stable	ns	ns
Scale: n'hood social capital (disagree to agree strongly)	-	-	-	-
Scale: importance of relatives	-	-	-	-
Community service important to friends (ref: not)	ns	Higher down vs. other	ns	ns
Friends with college plans	Higher up vs. not	Higher up vs. not	Lower down vs. stable	Lower down vs. stable
College expectations (ref: lower expect)	Higher up vs. not	Higher up vs. not	Lower down vs. stable	Lower down vs. stable
High occupational status expectations (ref: not high)	Higher up vs. not	ns	ns	ns

Source: National Educational Longitudinal Study
- indicates variable not included in model
Protective factors not statistically significant: parental trust, parent obedience, parents know friends, drinking decisions, positive peer influence

Of the protective factors, across almost all models, the more friends youths have with college plans, the more positive are their educational mobility outcomes (see Tables 2.8E-F). Children of immigrants whose parents have intermediate levels of education are the exception. The frequency with which parents have contacted the school and college expectations, two items only applicable to NELS youths, are consistently negatively and positively, respectively, associated with educational mobility. Connections between youths and parents generally produce positive educational mobility outcomes for youths, though the specific predictors vary somewhat by starting point, gender, and parent immigration status. Among third and later generation youths, parent connections with youths' friends' parents yield positive mobility outcomes for all youths when parents have intermediate levels of education and for young women only when parents have a college degree or more. Among youths whose parents have intermediate levels of education, third and later generation females and male children of immigrants have more positive mobility outcomes the more they talk with their parents, while female children of immigrants' odds of upward mobility increase as their family closeness increases.

In contrast to segmented assimilation theory's predictions, some social connections, including talking with non-parent adults and neighborhood social capital, have negative consequences. Furthermore, in the CILS data, the more important youths consider their relatives to be, the lower their odds of upward mobility. Interestingly, these results hold only for youths with intermediate-education parents. No measures of ethnic attachment prove to be statistically significantly protective of educational mobility.

Occupational Mobility

In the occupational mobility results, some racial-ethnic origin associations generally are in line with segmented assimilation's predictions, though there are some gender differences among third and later generation youths (see Tables 2.9A-B). Among youths whose parents have intermediate status occupations, those of Mexican origin have lower odds of upward mobility than others. However, this association holds only for males among third and later generation youths (there were not enough cases to split the CILS analysis by gender). Similarly, third and later generation black males have higher odds of downward mobility than their white counterparts; however, this finding holds only for blacks with high occupational status parents.

Findings for Southeast Asian and Filipino immigrants were less positive than segmented assimilation theory suggested.

Table 2.9A. Odds of Intergenerational Occupational Mobility Paths among Children of Immigrants, By Parental Occupational Status: Statistically Significant Demographic Characteristics and Downward Leveling Factors

	PARENTAL OCCUPATIONAL STATUS	
Demographic Characteristics	INTERMEDIATE: Up vs. Stable vs. Down	HIGH: Down vs. Stable
Later year of birth (Ref: earlier)	Lower up vs. not	ns
West Indian	ns	ns
Mexican origin	Lower up vs. stable	ns
Asian origin (Ref: other)	SE Asian: Lower up vs. stable	Filipinos: Higher down vs. stable
# of dependents	ns	ns
Parent: higher education (Ref: not high)	Lower down vs. stable	ns
Parent: higher occupational status (Ref: lower)	Lower odds up vs. not	-
Downward Leveling Factors		
Ever discriminated against	-	-
Scale: school problems	ns	ns

Source: Children of Immigrants Longitudinal Study
- indicates variable not included in model
Demographic variables not statistically significant: Cuban and Nicaraguan origin and gender
Downward leveling factors not statistically significant: dropout friends, parent worries about peer influences/differences from peers, negative experiences at school, neighborhood problems items, views of racial problems in the U.S.

Family demographic characteristics are not quite as consistently predictive of occupational mobility as they are with educational mobility. Family size is only related to occupational mobility among third and later generation youths with intermediate status parents; moreover, the association, unexpectedly, differs by gender. Living in a family with more dependents increases young men's odds and decreases young women's odds of downward occupational mobility. In contrast, parent education more consistently predicts more positive outcomes for youths across starting points (intermediate and higher), genders, and parental immigration status.

Table 2.9B. Odds of Intergenerational Occupational Mobility Paths among Third and Later Generation Youths, By Occupational Status and Gender: Statistically Significant Demographic Characteristics and Downward Leveling Factors

| Demographic Characteristics | PARENTAL OCCUPATIONAL STATUS | | | |
| | INTERMEDIATE: Up vs. Stable vs. Down | | HIGH: Down vs. Stable | |
	Males	Females	Males	Females
Later year of birth (Ref: earlier)	ns	ns	ns	ns
Black (Ref: white)	ns	ns	Higher down vs. stable	ns
Mexican origin	Lower up vs. not	ns	ns	ns
Asian origin	-	-	-	-
# of dependents	Higher down vs. up	Lower down vs. up	ns	ns
Parent: higher education (Ref: not high)	ns	Lower down vs. up	Lower down vs. stable	Lower down vs. stable
Parent: higher occup status (Ref: lower)	-	-	-	-
Downward Leveling Factors				
Ever discriminated against	-	-	-	-
Scale: school problems	Higher down vs. up	ns	ns	ns

Source: National Educational Longitudinal Study

- indicates variable not included in model

Demographic variables not statistically significant: parental income

Downward leveling factors not statistically significant: urban school, dropout friends, fighting/gangs at school, and school safety

There are few statistically significant associations between downward leveling factors and occupational mobility in the full models (see Tables 2.9A-B). Among NELS males with intermediate status parents or higher, the more negative of an influence youths' peers are, the higher their odds of downward mobility. However, contrary to segmented assimilation's predictions, CILS youths with intermediate status parents actually have *lower* odds of downward mobility if they report ever being discriminated against.

Many more statistically significant associations exist between protective factors and direction of occupational mobility (see Tables 2.9C-D). Educational and occupational expectations are consistent

Table 2.9C. Odds of Intergenerational Occupational Mobility Paths among Children of Immigrants, By Parental Occupational Status: Statistically Significant Protective Factors

	PARENTAL OCCUPATIONAL STATUS	
Protective Factors	INTERMEDIATE: Up vs. Stable vs. Down	HIGH: Down vs. Stable
Parent knows youths' closest friends (Ref: does not)	-	-
Parent friends mostly of co-ethnic group (Ref: not)	ns	Lower down vs. stable
Frequency parents contact school	-	-
Scale: neighborhood social capital (strongly disagree to strongly agree)	Lower up vs. stable	ns
Scale: importance of relatives	Higher down vs. up	ns
Community service important to friends (Ref: not)	-	-
Friends with college plans	ns	ns
College expectations (Ref: other)	-	-
High occupational status expectations (Ref: not high)	-	-

Source: Children of Immigrants Longitudinal Study

- indicates variable not included in model

Protective factors not statistically significant: friends w/ college plans, friends w/ foreign-born parents, get along w/ parents, family closeness, talk w/ parents, parents involved in school, family rules items, neighbor intervention, family moved, parent-youth ec attachment measures, grades

Table 2.9D. Odds of Intergenerational Occupational Mobility Paths among Third and Later Generation Youths, By Occupational Status and Gender: Statistically Significant Protective Factors

	PARENTAL OCCUPATIONAL STATUS			
	INTERMEDIATE: Up vs.		HIGH: Down vs.	
Protective Factors	Males	Females	Males	Females
Parent knows youths' closest friends (Ref:not)	ns	ns	ns	Lower down
Parent friends mostly of co-ethnic group (Ref: not)	-	-	-	-
Frequency parents contact school	ns	ns	ns	Higher down
Scale: neighborhood social capital	-	-	-	-
Scale: importance of relatives	-	-	-	-
Community service important to friends (Ref: not)	ns	Higher down vs. up	ns	ns
Friends with college plans	Higher up vs. not	ns	Lower down	ns
College expect. (Ref: not)	Higher up vs. not	Lower down vs. up	Lower down	Lower down
High occup. status expectations (Ref: not)	Higher up vs. stable	Higher up vs. stable	Lower down	ns

Source: National Educational Longitudinal Study

- indicates variable not included in model

Protective factors not statistically significant: parent trust, parent obedience, talk with parents, talk with other adults, parent knows friends' parents, and decision-making items

predictors of occupational mobility (though only applicable to third and later generation youths due to the uniformly high expectations reported by children of immigrants). Friends' characteristics are associated with occupational mobility for third and later generation youths only. Having friends with college plans and friends who are involved in community service are protective of these young men's occupational mobility from intermediate and higher starting points and all youths from low parental occupational starting points, respectively. The opposite association holds between friends who view community service as important and third and later generation females whose parents hold intermediate status occupations.

Social capital results are more mixed. When third and later generation young women's high occupational status parents know their friends, the young women are less likely to experience downward mobility. Similarly, children of immigrants whose parents' friends are mostly co-ethnics have lower odds of negative mobility, but only when their parents have high occupational status to begin with. Neighborhood social capital and importance of relatives, in contrast, are associated with poorer occupational mobility outcomes among children of immigrants, but only for those with intermediate status parents. I find this pattern of association for educational mobility as well. Finally, parental school involvement, as measured by the frequency with which parents contacted the school, is associated with more negative mobility outcomes, but only for NELS females with intermediate status parents.

Linguistic Assimilation

I am only able to examine linguistic assimilation multivariately for CILS youths whose parents do not use English mostly with them when they are in about the twelfth grade. There is not enough variation in the paths of assimilation for youths whose parents use English mostly. I am able to perform the analyses separately by gender; therefore, I focus on gender similarities and differences. Of the racial-ethnic origin categories, only Mexican females have higher odds of classical linguistic assimilation than "other" children of immigrants (see Table 2.10). The one relationship between downward leveling factors and linguistic assimilation in the full model also holds only for young women. More neighborhood problems are associated with lower odds of classical assimilation. In this case, the downward leveling factor is associated with maintenance of non-English use, an outcome that segmented assimilation theory generally views as having positive consequences for youths.

There are more protective factors related to linguistic assimilation. Unsurprisingly, among young men and young women, non-English language ability is associated with lower odds of classical assimilation.

Frequency of non-English use at home, however, is associated with lower odds of classical assimilation among young women. The remaining protective factor that is statistically significantly associated with linguistic assimilation, friends with college plans, predicts higher odds of classical assimilation among both young men and young women.

Table 2.10. Odds of Intergenerational Linguistic Assimilation Paths among Children of Immigrants Whose Parents Use a Non-English Language Mostly at Home, By Gender: Statistically Significant Logistic Regression Results

	MALES	FEMALES
Demographic Variables		
Born 1978/79 (Ref: born 75-77)	Higher classical	ns
Mexican origin (Ref: other)	ns	Lower classical
Downward Leveling Factors		
Parent reports any (non-drug related) neighborhood problems (Ref: none)	ns	Lower classical
Protective Factors		
Many friends with college plans (Ref: not many)	Higher classical	Higher classical
Non-English language ability	Lower classical	Lower classical
Frequency of non-English language use at home	ns	Lower classical

Source: Children of Immigrants Longitudinal Study

Not statistically significant:

Demographic characteristics: Cuban, Nicaraguan, West Indian, Filipino, and Southeast Asian origin, family structure and size, parent education and income

Downward leveling factors: dropout friends, parents worried about peers, negative experiences at school, neighborhood drug problems, experienced discrimination, and views of racial problems in U.S.

Protective factors: friends w/ foreign-born parents, get along w/ and talk w/ parents, family closeness, parents involved at school, family rules, neighborhood social capital, importance of relatives, parent attachment to country of origin, parent-youth ethnic attachment, grades

Identificational Assimilation

For my examination of identificational mobility, I have enough cases only to perform regression analysis for youths whose parents have national origin or racial/pan-ethnic identities. Furthermore, there are not enough cases of each of these starting points to perform the analyses by gender. I focus, then, on similarities and differences in relationships by starting point.

Racial-ethnic origin is an important predictor of identificational assimilation (see Table 2.11). Cubans, Mexicans, Filipinos, and Southeast Asians, compared with "other" immigrants, all have higher odds of resurgent assimilation from racial/pan-ethnic identified parental starting points and lower odds of racialized assimilation from national origin identified parental starting points. These results suggest that these groups are much less likely to maintain or take on racial or pan-ethnic identities than the primarily European, Canadian, and other groups who make up the "other" immigrant category. West Indians also have lower odds of racialized assimilation vs. other forms of assimilation when their parents have national origin identities. As was the case with linguistic assimilation, only one downward leveling factor is associated with identificational assimilation. In this case, it is associated with more classical forms of assimilation: youths with dropout friends have lower odds of resurgent identity from racial/pan-ethnic identified parental starting points than youths with no dropout friends.

Finally, a number of protective factors are associated with identificational assimilation paths; however, only one indicator is statistically significant for youths with racial/pan-ethnic identified parents. For these youths, the more they get along with their parents, the lower their odds of resurgent vs. other forms of assimilation; they are more likely to experience linear or stable assimilation. Since linear assimilation from this starting point is rare, odds are higher that youths hold onto their parents' racial/pan-ethnic identities. Among youths whose parents have national origin identities, talking regularly with parents about school and greater importance of relatives are associated with higher odds of linear vs. stable assimilation. The importance of relatives finding is unexpected since one's relatives may seem to support attachment to family ethnic origin, and this hypothesis does not play out in this case. Greater family closeness, in contrast, is associated with lower odds of racialized vs. stable assimilation. Perhaps type of

Table 2.11. Odds of Intergenerational Identificational Assimilation Paths among Children of Immigrants, by Parent Ethnic Identity: Statistically Significant Logistic Regression Results

	PARENT ETHNIC IDENTITY	
Demographic Variables	NATIONAL ORIGIN: Linear vs. Stable vs. Racialized	RACIAL/ PAN-ETHNIC: Resurgent vs. Not
Cuban (Ref: other)	Lower racialized vs. linear	Higher resurgent
Mexican	Lower racialized vs. stable	Higher resurgent
West Indian	Lower racialized vs. other	ns
Filipino	Lower racialized vs. other	Higher resurgent
Southeast Asian	Lower racialized vs. other	Higher resurgent
Downward Leveling Factors		
Any dropout friends (Ref: none)	ns	Lower resurgent
Protective Factors		
Scale: family closeness	Lower racialized vs. stable	ns
Scale: parents and R get along	ns	Lower resurgent
Talk regularly with parent about school (Ref: do not)	Higher linear vs. stable	ns
Neither youth nor parent prefers American ways (Ref: other)	Lower linear vs. stable	ns
Scale: importance of relatives	Higher linear vs. stable	ns

Source: Children of Immigrants Longitudinal Study

Variables not statistically significant: gender, year of birth, Nicaraguan origin, family structure and size, parent education, income, parents worried about peer influences/differences, negative experiences at school, neighborhood problems, experienced discrimination, views of racial problems in U.S., friends w/ college plans and foreign-born parents, parents involved at school, family rules, neighborhood social capital, parent attachment to country of origin, language ability and use, and grades family relationship (nuclear vs. extended) matters for predicting identificational outcomes. Finally, as expected, when neither parents nor their children prefer American ways most of the time, youths' odds of linear vs. stable assimilation are reduced.

Discussion and Conclusion

In general, although there are similarities in outcomes across starting point, gender, and parent immigration status, previous research has missed out on the full complexity of the factors influencing intergenerational mobility and assimilation by not considering paths separately by these elements. These results show how difficult it is to tease out a simple coherent story regarding these associations: immigrant incorporation is even more complicated than segmented assimilation suggests.

Educational Mobility

The results for educational mobility suggest that positive forms of intergenerational mobility are very common. In fact, downward mobility is quite rare, even among youths with college-educated parents. In this case, as other researchers have suggested (Boyd 2002; Hirschman 2001; Farley and Alba 2002; Kasinitz, Mollenkopf and Waters 2002; Smith 2003; Waldinger and Feliciano 2004; Waldinger and Reichl 2007; Kasinitz et al. 2008), segmented assimilation theory seems to have overstated the prevalence of downward mobility.

The story of educational mobility appears to be one of immigrant optimism at lower starting points on the economic ladder. While, as segmented assimilation theory suggests, children of immigrants have more positive mobility experiences than their third and later generation counterparts, children of immigrants from higher status origins do not have as much relative success. The immigrant optimism hypothesis (Kao and Tienda 1995) may partially explain children of immigrants' greater success from lower parental educational starting points. Because of their selectivity, lower socioeconomic status immigrant parents may be more motivated to help their children do well in school than non-immigrant parents of the same status. In contrast, more highly educated parents may be supportive of their children's educational achievement regardless of their immigrant status.

Young women generally have more positive educational mobility results than young men; however, within gender, there are differences by ethnic origin. I discuss patterns of economic mobility, both educational and occupational, by ethnic origin further below. These findings are in line with recent educational literature indicating that young women are having greater success in schools than young men, perhaps because women are more accomplished at the kinds of behaviors that get rewarded in schools (Kimmel 2004). Moreover, men generally receive greater economic and occupational rewards at each level of education. Perhaps they have less motivation than women to reach higher levels of education since they receive greater economic rewards for less educational effort.

Several factors influence mobility similarly for young men and women. Males and females share more associations in common when their parents do not have a college degree. Although the differences in associations by gender do not follow a clear pattern, parent-youth relations may be particularly important for young women's educational success. For example, among young women only, family closeness and the number of friends that parents know are associated with more positive mobility outcomes.

For all youths, parent characteristics are important predictors of educational mobility. Parents with more resources can often promote more positive forms of mobility in their children. In addition, various measures of the quality and strength of the parent-child relationship appear to promote more positive educational mobility across the board. These finding suggests that segmented assimilation theory should consider parent-child relationships beyond differences or similarities in acculturation.

In contrast, non-parent connections, including connections to other relatives, do not appear to lead to positive educational mobility outcomes among youths with intermediate status parents. Segmented assimilation theory suggests that, in many circumstances, social capital and social ties—particularly those that are ethnically-based—will have a positive influence on later generations' achievements, although Portes and colleagues suggest that social capital can have negative consequences for the less well off, particularly among immigrants with poor, native minority counterparts living in the inner-cities. I find that some forms of social capital have negative influences for youths starting out from the middle of the educational distribution.

Apparently, even intermediate status networks can lack the resources, information, and role models that help support upward mobility.

Occupational Mobility

Downward intergenerational mobility is far more common in terms of occupational status than educational status. As I mentioned above, this result is due in part to the young age of the NELS and CILS samples: while many youths have attained their highest level of education by their mid-twenties, most have not attained their highest occupational status, unlike their parents whose occupational reports come from ages at which they are closer to the summits of their occupational trajectories.

The occupational mobility results do not accord with the immigrant optimism hypothesis. From intermediate and lower occupational starting points, there are no statistically significant differences between children of immigrants and non-immigrants in terms of upward mobility; however, fewer third and later generation youths experience downward mobility than children of immigrants. Third and later generation youths also experience more positive intergenerational occupational mobility outcomes from high parental occupational starting points. These results, however, should not be taken as solid evidence against the immigrant optimism hypothesis because they are at least in part the result of data artifacts. For example, paths of occupational mobility are not totally comparable across the two data sets because the CILS and NELS different occupational categories lend to different occupational classification and ranking schemes. Perhaps more importantly, CILS children of immigrant participants are younger than the NELS third and later generation respondents on average; therefore, they have had less time to achieve their parents' levels of occupational status. This explanation seems especially plausible since children of immigrants have (slightly but not statistically significantly) better mobility outcomes compared to third and later generation young adults when their parents have lower levels of occupational status. High occupational status usually requires more time to achieve; therefore, the young CILS respondents with high status parents necessarily have a relatively poor showing in terms of occupational mobility.

Also unlike the educational mobility results, for cases in which there are statistically significant gender differences, young men tend to have an advantage over young women. These results are consistent with studies that reveal that women's educational successes have not been matched by their occupational successes (Jacobs 1996; Sewell, Hauser, and Wolf 1980). Participating in the work force is a very different experience for young men and young women, and there are different paths to occupational attainment for women and men (Warren , Sheridan, and Hauser 2002; Sewell, Hauser, and Wolf 1980; Marini 1980). In addition to choosing lower status fields of study and career paths (Kimmel 2004), women's occupational goals and career trajectories are more likely to be changed or interrupted by life events such as marriage and childbearing than men's, inhibiting their occupational mobility (and perhaps explaining the lack of statistically significant association between occupational expectations and mobility for women).

While parental education and youth expectations are associated with mobility outcomes across starting points, most factors associated with occupational mobility differ by parental occupational status. In general, I find evidence that high occupational status parents' friendship networks among children of immigrants are better predictors of youths' occupational mobility than lower status parents' networks. High occupational status parents and their friends are likely to have information on similarly high status jobs for their children. Youths who are able to tap into these networks gain occupational advantages from them. In contrast, no matter how many connections lower status parents have, the kinds of information and resources that they provide to their members are not particularly useful for youths attempting to move up the occupational ladder. This outcome suggests, as segmented assimilation theory predicts, an interaction between socioeconomic status and social capital. Better off individuals can make better use of their social capital than those who are worse off.

In contrast, among intermediate status immigrant parents, measures of social capital are associated with worse outcomes among their children. These results are similar to those found for educational mobility and, again, contrast with segmented assimilation theory's predictions; segmented assimilation theory has not suggested that intermediate status individuals will have negative consequences from their social capital. These results suggest that social capital is only helpful to high status individuals—and not just detrimental to those of the very lowest status.

Economic Mobility by Ethnic Origin

Associations between ethnic origin and economic mobility differ by starting point, gender, and immigrant generational status. Once we take into account demographic, downward leveling, and protective factors, results for Mexicans suggest that segmented assimilation's claims about this group miss some of its complexity. First, although I find higher odds of downward intergenerational educational mobility among children of Mexican immigrants than other children of immigrants, surprisingly, this result holds only among youths with college-educated parents. This finding is quite a puzzle because there has been very little research on the small, well-educated Mexican immigrant group. Because the parental educational starting point was so high, this form of downward mobility is not highly likely to be associated with eventual underclass membership. Controlling for the characteristics in my analyses, Mexican origin youths, both children of immigrants and non-immigrants, do not have statistically significantly different odds of downward mobility or stagnation at low levels of parental education than other groups.

Second, occupational mobility outcomes for Mexicans are negative but only for youths whose parents have intermediate occupational status. Third and later generation males and children of immigrants (for whom the analysis could not be separated by gender) are less likely to experience upward mobility and more likely to experience horizontal than upward mobility. These results suggest that Mexicans experience more occupational than educational challenges. There appears to be more variation in the Mexican experience than often gets discussed in the assimilation literature. I find variability in intergenerational economic mobility across economic indicators (education vs. occupation), parental starting points, gender, and parental immigration status.

Southeast Asians have somewhat more positive intergenerational mobility outcomes. They experience a pattern of greater educational mobility but lower occupational mobility from intermediate starting points. Previous research reveals quite positive educational outcomes among Southeast Asian groups (Bankston and Zhou 1995; Zhou and Bankston 1994, 1998; Portes and Rumbaut 2001a). However, in this case, positive educational outcomes do not translate into positive occupational mobility. Again, this finding may be due to the young age of the sample. It is also possible that, in this case, the relative recency of Southeast Asian immigration leads to less developed occupational networks that are not helpful for those starting out at a lower position. These findings support segmented assimilation theory's claims about Asian immigrants' educational success but question whether the rosy picture that the theory paints for these groups applies to occupational mobility as well.

Filipinos starting off from high economic status positions have consistently negative outcomes. These findings contrast with the general predictions of segmented assimilation theory regarding Asians and suggest that even groups whose modes of incorporation are considered most positive (see Rumbaut 2008) can still experience challenges of incorporation. In their research, Zhou and Xiong (2005) also find negative outcomes among Filipinos. They suggest that downward mobility of these Filipinos is of no real consequence; it is just regression to the mean because Filipino parents start off with such high economic status. In this book, however, I examine economic mobility among high status parents and find that Filipinos have a harder time maintaining that status than "other" immigrants with high status parents. It is unclear why this is the case. Segmented assimilation theory's discussion of downward mobility into the underclass does not seem to be at play here because Filipinos with college educated parent are not likely to be at risk of assimilating into the underclass. Also, there is not a significantly large native Filipino group in poverty into which they could incorporate. Segmented assimilation theory thus fails to provide an explanation of Filipinos' downward mobility experience. Future research on this population would benefit from further examination of these negative mobility outcomes among children of Filipino immigrants.

Finally, mobility experiences for West Indian children of immigrants contrast with those of third and later generation blacks. These results differ by economic indicator (education vs. occupation), starting point, and gender. West Indian female children of immigrants with intermediate educational status parents have more positive mobility outcomes than their "other" immigrant counterparts while (primarily third and later generation) black males with high occupational status parents have negative mobility outcomes compared with their white counterparts. These results, again, suggest that immigrant optimism has some effect on educational outcomes, particularly among some ethnic groups of intermediate educational status.

Segmented assimilation theory suggests that one's ethnic origin is more likely to be a positive force for mobility at higher status levels. West Indians' success from intermediate status and blacks' lack of success from high status conflict with this prediction. Young black men with high status parents have lower odds of maintaining this status than whites, which may be due to labor market constraints or discrimination. Perhaps high occupational status black parents lack the density of social network ties or have a more difficult time translating them into high status jobs for their sons. That this association holds for black men only is easier to explain: black men have lower labor force attachment than black females (Bianchi and Spain 1996). This outcome may just be one more example of this growing occupational gap between black men and women, particularly in comparison to whites.

West Indian women's positive educational outcomes are in line with the research (Foner 2009) that suggests that a significant proportion of West Indian immigrant women (more so than men) have come as economic immigrants, to fill certain occupations, rather than through family reunification visas. They have filled highly feminized occupations in the domestic sphere and services occupations, including food service and health care (Foner 2009; Waters 1999). Perhaps these women, who relatively easily found their places in the labor market, may be able to pass on their feminized occupational successes to their daughters.

Linguistic Assimilation

As previous research has shown, the transition to English use is quite rapid among immigrants and children of immigrants (Alba et al. 2002; Portes and Schauffler 1994). Once English use is established in a family, it is very likely to be maintained. In fact, this path of assimilation is so common among youths whose parents use mostly English with them that there are not enough cases for regression analysis.

Segmented assimilation theory suggests that stronger cultural ties help maintain non-English language ability and use. Only two factors are associated with these paths of linguistic assimilation for both young men and women whose parents do not use mostly English with them: having friends with college plans and non-English language ability. Friends with college plans are likely to have good English skills because these skills are necessary to get into and succeed in college; therefore, having more of these kinds of friends provides greater opportunities for English use. Non-English ability, of course, influences one's assimilation path because it is necessary for non-English communication and may indicate stronger attachment to one's culture of origin.

More factors are associated with female assimilation than male assimilation. For young women alone, Mexican origin is associated with lower odds of classical assimilation. This finding is supported by previous research (Alba et al. 2002) that suggests that Spanish speakers, particularly Mexicans, have a slower path to English-only use because the large size and continual immigration of this group constantly renew opportunities for Spanish use. That this result holds only for Mexican women is consistent with Stevens' (1986) claims that women maintain their native language more than men because of "closer kinship ties, a stronger sense of cultural and ethnic heritage...and stronger identification with the minority language community..." (34). The other statistically significant factors for women only, frequency of non-English language use at home and neighborhood safety, also suggest that family and home ties are important for influencing women's linguistic assimilation (Stevens 1986; Portes and Rumbaut 2001a). These forces do not appear to play out similarly for young men.

Identificational Assimilation

In my examination of identificational assimilation, I do not find any statistically significant gender differences and am unable to examine differences in associations between young men and women in multivariate models because of the small number of cases in my analyses. These results provide no support for the idea that women function as "carriers of culture." I also find that movement to American identities is extremely rare and racial or pan-ethnic identities are quite uncommon.

I find that youths are more likely to hold on to their parents' identities when they are already partially U.S.-based; that is, when they are hyphenated or pan-ethnic rather than just national origin. Otherwise, youths tend to report more American identities than their parents, particularly hyphenated identities. Perhaps because they have a foot in two worlds, children of immigrants seem to show attachment to their parents' past as well as to their current living situation.

Parents' original ethnic identities are likely to indicate something about the degree to which parents are attached to or involved in their own ethnic communities compared with larger American society. Their children's experiences of identificational assimilation differ, then, based on these distinct starting points. Nonetheless, I find that ethnic origin matters in very similar ways across the two different starting points. All in all, Cuban, Mexican, West Indian, Filipino, and Southeast Asian youths whose parents have national origin or racial/pan-ethnic identities seem averse to racial/pan-ethnic identities. They are more likely to maintain their parents' national origin identities or adopt identities tied more closely to their families' places of origin. For these groups, pan-ethnic, made-in-America identities may not suit them, due to the great diversity masked by these group labels. Furthermore, pan-ethnic identities represent a step further away from one's immigrant origins. Children of immigrants from these groups are numerous enough for their hyphenated identities to have sufficient communal support not to have to take that step yet, compared with "other" groups, who include smaller Asian and Latino groups plus European and Canadian immigrants.

Contrary to segmented assimilation theory's claims, downward leveling factors, such as experiencing discrimination, do not result in youths' return to their parents' national origin identities or adoption of racial/pan-ethnic ones. Instead, family relationships are important for predicting intergenerational paths of assimilation. Closer family ties and shared values tend to promote the retention of parents' identities.

Paths of intergenerational assimilation and the factors associated with them differ by starting point, gender, and immigrant generation. Family characteristics are very important for predicting assimilation outcomes. Networks are also very important and function differently depending again on starting point, gender, and immigrant generation. I also find that paths of assimilation are not so clear-cut or consistent even within ethnic groups. For example, some groups experience different paths of educational and occupational mobility. In terms of cultural assimilation, while linguistic assimilation is extremely commonplace for all groups, there is evidence of greater retention of ethnic identities among youths from larger ethnic groups.

NOTES

[1] These associations can differ depending on how one measures occupational status. Most commonly, researchers measure occupational status by prestige, social standing, or economic position in society. I discuss my methods for classifying occupational status below.

[2] English use is also associated with individuals' language skills. Those who use English mostly have reasonably good English skills. English use among these individuals, however, does not allow one to make inferences about one's non-English skills. In contrast, those who do not use English mostly may or may not have good English skills; however, they are likely to have maintained minimal non-English skills—skills good enough to maintain communication. Good English skills permit exposure to American cultural values; moreover, they increase an immigrant's ability to gather information in American societal and cultural institutions. In contrast, those who maintain non-English language skills in the United States preserve some connections to their cultures of origin.

[3] Portes and Rumbaut (2001a) also classify the term "Chicano" as racial or pan-ethnic even though it applies only to individuals of Mexican descent. I classified "Chicanos" similarly because it is a made-in-America identity like other racial and pan-ethnic identities.

[4] It is an anti-classical path under certain conditions, however, as I illustrate below.

[5] In both CILS and NELS, home-schooled youths and those who dropped out prior to eighth grade were also excluded from the samples. There is some evidence that very early dropouts are more likely to be Hispanic (see Frase 1989); therefore, the Latinos remaining in the samples may have more positive economic consequences than the Latino population living in the United States as a whole.

[6] All tables include information after multiple imputation. I will discuss imputation as a means of dealing with missing data below.

[7] I include all respondents in this analysis of linguistic assimilation because there is no clear way to determine for whom English is truly one's only native language option.

[8] I had originally planned to include an indicator of original survey setting (Miami vs. San Diego); however, this variable is too closely associated with ethnic origin. I therefore leave it out of the analyses.

[9] Post-imputation factor analyses suggest for this and all scales used in this analysis that these items measure the same underlying concept. The Cronbach's alpha for this scale is .81.

[10] The Cronbach's alpha for this scale is .72.

[11] The post-imputation alpha is .60. Of course, these questions only applied to youths who were still in school at the time of the second interview; however, I decided to include it in the analysis because the vast majority of dropouts actually provided this information.

[12] Factor analysis reveals that the neighborhood problems represent two underlying concepts—one related to drugs and gangs and the other relating to different problems. The alphas for these scales are .88 and .76, respectively.

[13] No specific reason or explanation is included for the discrimination in this question.

[14] The Cronbach's alpha for this scale is .60.

[15] The Cronbach's alpha is .71.

[16] The Cronbach's alpha for this scale is .84.

[17] The Cronbach's alpha for this scale is .63.

[18] The alpha for this scale is .86.

[19] The alpha for this scale is .54.

[20] The alpha for this scale is .93.

[21] In most cases, youths prefer American ways most of the time while parents do not. There are few cases in which only parents prefer American ways.

[22] The alpha for the scale is .60.

[23] I had intended to include indicators of grades and educational expectations. However, many youths, particularly in the NELS data, are missing grade information in this wave. This information is not valid for dropout students. Therefore, I exclude the variable from both CILS and NELS analyses. For educational expectations, the vast majority of students report college expectations. There is not enough variation to include this variable.

[24] The alpha for this scale is .52.

[25] The alpha for this scale is .84.

[26] The alpha for this scale is .64.

[27] I had originally planned to create one decision-making scale, but factor analysis suggests that these items represent two different underlying concepts.

[28] The alpha for this scale is .58.

[29] The alpha for this scale is .60.

[30] The alpha for this scale is .65.

[31] Of course, the number of friends and the number of parents of friends that the parent reports knowing are highly associated; however, inclusion of both variables in the models does not greatly increase standard errors compared to inclusion of just one of the variables.

[32] The alpha for the scale is .83.

[33] I had originally intended to create one variable out of these items; however, factor analysis suggests that they measure two underlying concepts.

[34] I use data from just one of the imputed data sets when presenting distributions and cross-tabulations.

[35] I consider statistical significance at the $p < .05$ level, unless noted otherwise.

CHAPTER 3

Intragenerational Paths of Assimilation

In this chapter, I examine paths of mobility and assimilation intragenerationally over the life course of individuals. Specifically, I examine educational mobility, linguistic assimilation (non-English language ability and English use), and identificational assimilation among youths during adolescence and the transition from adolescence to emerging adulthood. In doing so, I examine trajectories of mobility and assimilation during particular life course stages rather than static levels of mobility and assimilation indicators at one point in time. I analyze these patterns of assimilation separately depending on where the youth "started out" his or her path of assimilation or mobility in about eighth grade. Moreover, as with the intergenerational analysis, I examine paths by parental immigrant status and gender, where possible. I use this methodology to analyze if, and how, youths' experiences of mobility and assimilation differ depending on their starting point, gender, and parental immigrant status.

Theoretical Framework

As I discussed in the introductory chapter, segmented assimilation and other theories of assimilation have failed to take into account the life course in their explications of immigrant incorporation. Life course studies, however, suggest that experiences and the factors associated with them change across different stages in individuals' lives; therefore, it seems likely that immigrants' experiences of integration are also likely to differ over the life course. Two important stages in the life course are adolescence and the transition to emerging adulthood.

Recent scholars have typically defined adolescence as the life stage from 10 to 18 years of age (Arnett 2000). Adolescence is a time of important developmental and social changes. It involves distancing oneself from one's childhood dependence and movement towards the responsibilities of adulthood. In the United States, during this life stage, most youths live with their parents and attend school. In such a living situation, "a school-based peer culture" has great importance in the lives of youths (Arnett 2000, 476). At the same time, however, the vast majority of youths are financially and emotionally dependent on their parents or guardians, and daily interactions between parents and children greatly influence youths' outcomes (Hao and Bonstead-Bruns 1998; Muller 1993, 1995, 1998; Astone and McLanahan 1991; Sui-Chu and Willms 1996).

In the past few decades, researchers have found that adolescents' transition to adulthood, marked by indicators such as school leaving, home leaving, and marriage, has been delayed. Arnett (2000) argues that this delay has led to a new stage in the life cycle, one that is neither adolescence nor adulthood. He coins the term "emerging adulthood" to describe this life stage, occurring from the late teenage years until the mid-twenties. According to Arnett (2000), emerging adulthood involves a great deal of exploration, change, and increasing independence.

During the emerging adulthood period, youths are more focused on their eventual adult roles. For example, they may enter into higher education. They also make choices about the kinds of careers they wish to pursue, whether by selecting a field of study or by applying for jobs. Youths also begin to make their own decisions about cultural attachments when they live outside of their parents' homes. Identity formation is particularly important during this period. In fact, Arnett (2000) notes that while many researchers focus on adolescence as the most important period for identity formation, evidence suggests that most youths have not achieved a solid identity by the end of high school (Waterman 1982). Instead, identity formation continues during the emerging adulthood years (Valde 1996; Whitbourne and Tesch 1985).

Although the life course literature suggests that important developmental and social differences exist across the life course, segmented assimilation theory, like the assimilation literature in general, has not discussed how assimilation may differ across the life course. Consequently, assimilation researchers have not analyzed empirically if or how assimilation differs across the life course. It is not clear if intragenerational assimilation findings are specific to certain life course stages or if some findings may hold temporarily but not over the longer term. Vermeulen (2010) suggests that failing to consider changes over the life course may reify outcomes found during certain life stages as *the* story of assimilation for immigrants and their children. Instead, if we examine how individuals experience mobility and assimilation over the life course, we can get a better experience of the process and the bumps along the paths.

Educational Mobility Indicators

In this chapter, I examine intragenerational paths of mobility and assimilation across adolescence and emerging adulthood to examine if these paths and the factors associated with them are consistent across the life course or change over time. I focus on educational measures across the two time periods: (1) expectations over adolescence (from eighth grade to twelfth grade) and (2) expectations in adolescence to attainment in emerging adulthood (from eighth grade to the mid-twenties). As I noted in the previous chapter, individuals can experience three patterns of educational mobility over time: downward, horizontal or stable, or upward. During adolescence, then, youths whose expectations decrease over time experience downward mobility; those whose expectations increase over time experience upward mobility. During emerging adulthood, youths who meet their educational expectations experience horizontal mobility; those who fail to meet them experience downward mobility; and those who surpass them experience upward mobility.

As is the case with intergenerational mobility, starting point matters for understanding intragenerational mobility. In this case, youths' initial educational expectations influence the paths of mobility that they experience. Youths with high educational expectations can only experience stable or downward mobility; those with very low expectations can only experience upward or stable mobility. In addition, the meaning of the forms of mobility differs depending on youths' initial expectations. Upward mobility is likely to mark a more positive outcome for youths from higher starting points. Downward mobility is likely to have more negative consequences for youths from lower starting points.

Life course stage has an important influence on intragenerational educational mobility in this analysis because of the way in which it is associated with the potential paths. Because of changes in education across the life course, the adolescent time period is associated with shifts in educational expectations only. The transitional period from adolescence to emerging adulthood involves attainment of expectations (or lack thereof). There are important differences between expectations and attainment. Educational expectations are beliefs about one's future attainment (Morgan 1998; 2005). Unlike aspirations, educational expectations—as they are measured in CILS and NELS, at least—require that individuals make realistic assessments about their likelihood of educational success, perhaps taking into account their own situations and abilities as well as the costs of following through on these expectations. Educational expectations are generally highly associated with educational attainment (Sewell and Hauser 1975; Alexander, Eckland, and Griffin 1975; Morgan 1998; Schneider and Stevenson 2000); however, they are not perfect predictors of attainment (Morgan 1998). Indeed, the degree to which expectations predict educational outcomes differs by race-ethnicity and gender (Morgan 1996, 1998, 2005; Marini and Greenberger 1978; Mickelson 1990). The distribution of the paths of mobility are likely to differ across the life course because changes (or lack thereof) in expectations are distinct from attainment (or lack thereof) of expectations. Youths can raise or lower their expectations without too much cognitive difficulty; however, actually following through on one's expectations and attaining a certain level of education requires effort, resources, and time. For these reasons, I expect to find very different patterns in intragenerational educational mobility across these two time periods.

Along with differences by life course stage, experiences of intragenerational educational mobility are likely to differ by gender. The literature reveals gender differences in both educational expectations and attainment. Previous research suggests that boys tend to have higher educational expectations than girls (Crowley and Shapiro 1982; Marini 1978). There is also evidence that young women are more likely than young men to reduce their educational expectations over time (Haggstrom, Kanouse, and Morrison 1986; Marini 1984; Randour, Strasburg, and Lipman-Blumen 1982). However, recent research reveals that female children of immigrants have higher educational expectations than their male counterparts (Portes and Rumbaut 2001a; Zhou and Bankston 2001). Trusty and

Harris (1999) and others (Marini and Greenberger 1978) also find that different factors are associated with expectations for male and female adolescents.

In terms of educational attainment, in recent years, young women have surpassed young men. For example, young women have higher college attendance and graduation rates (Morgan 2005; Planty et al. 2008). Rumbaut (2005) finds that second generation immigrant women have higher educational attainment than their male counterparts. Hanson (1994) finds that the process leading to unrealized educational expectations differs for young men and women. In particular, young women's failures to attain their expectations are influenced more by family, individual, and school resources than are young men's failures.

Segmented assimilation researchers have recently begun to take into account how gender influences intragenerational educational mobility. Using the San Diego CILS data for a descriptive analysis, Feliciano and Rumbaut (2005) find that males have lower educational expectations on average and are less able to achieve high expectations than females. In their multivariate analysis, they also find that predictors of educational attainment differed by gender. Feliciano and Rumbaut (2005) propose that these more positive educational outcomes for young women may be a result of the greater restrictions that their parents place on them. Female children of immigrants may have stronger attachments to their homes and families that protect them from negative outside influences and prop up their parents' hopes and expectations compared with their male counterparts.

Alternatively, non-cognitive skills may best explain females' success, regardless of their immigrant status. Mickelson (1989) suggests that socialization is key: girls do better in school because being feminine involves obeying rules and authority, characteristics that are rewarded in schools, while masculinity involves challenging authority, a behavior not always welcome in educational settings. In high school, teachers consistently rate girls more positively than boys in terms of effort expended and lower in terms of disruption (Downey and Yuan 2005). Studies show that adolescent girls also are more attentive and organized (Farkas, Sheehan, and Grobe 1990; Jacob 2002), and they show more self-discipline than boys (Silverman 2003; Duckworth and Seligman 2006). I examine paths by gender, then, to take into account these differences and uncover whether they are associated with educational mobility. I predict that young women will have more positive educational mobility across the life course than young men and that different factors will be associated with educational mobility for young women and men (see Table 3.1 for my hypotheses).

Table 3.1. Intragenerational Mobility and Assimilation Hypotheses

1. Youths will experience all possible forms of mobility and assimilation.
2. Resurgent assimilation will be the most common form of identificational assimilation.
3. The distributions of paths of mobility and assimilation and the factors associated with them will differ by starting point, gender, life course stage, and parental immigration status.
   a. Starting point:
      i. By definition, the possible paths of mobility and assimilation differ from each starting point.
      ii. Upward mobility is more likely from lower starting points; downward mobility is more likely from higher starting
      iii. Classical assimilation is more likely from less acculturated starting points. Anti-classical assimilation is more likely from more acculturated starting points.
   b. Gender:
      i. Females will be more likely to experience positive forms of educational mobility than males.
      ii. Females will be less classical in terms of cultural assimilation than males, especially linguistic assimilation.
   c. Life course stage:
      i. There will be more positive forms of educational mobility in adolescence than emerging adulthood.
      ii. More classical forms of linguistic assimilation will be more common over emerging adulthood period than adolescence.
      iii. There will be greater variability in identificational assimilation paths, particularly more anti-classical assimilation types, than in linguistic assimilation.
      iv. There will be more shifts in ethnic identity over emerging adulthood than adolescence.
   d. Parental immigration status: Children of immigrants will be more likely to experience positive forms of educational mobility than third and later generation youths.
   e. Gendered life course: women will be more likely than men to hold on to their ethnic identities during adolescence. This association will not hold over emerging adulthood.

As with the intergenerational analysis, I analyze paths of educational mobility by parental immigration status, comparing a sample of children of immigrants (CILS) to a sample of third and later generation youths (NELS). As I noted in the previous chapter, segmented assimilation theorists suggest that children of immigrants will outperform children of non-immigrants. They propose that immigrants' cultural connections protect them from negative outside influences. The immigrant optimism hypothesis (Kao and Tienda 1995), discussed in detail in the previous chapter, also suggests that children of immigrants, particularly the second generation, will outperform later generation youths due to their parents' selectivity and high expectations for their children.

Most previous empirical work has not examined the experiences of children of immigrants and non-immigrants in this way. Feliciano and Rumbaut (2005) compare the educational expectations of CILS youths with Hanson's (1994) High School and Beyond study and find that more children of immigrants fail to meet their expectations than later generation youths. They explain that this finding is partly a result of children of immigrants' higher educational expectations, on average; however, they do not take into account the fact that those in Hanson's sample included only high-achieving students who were more likely to meet their high expectations. I predict that children of immigrants will have more positive educational mobility across adolescence and emerging adulthood than later generation youths, due to the immigrant optimism hypothesis, and that there will be differences in the factors that predict these mobility paths for the two groups.

Indicators of Cultural Assimilation

The indicators of cultural assimilation that I analyze are non-English language ability, English use, and ethnic identification. As I noted in the previous chapter, there are a number of differences between the analysis of economic mobility and cultural assimilation. First, like the intergenerational analysis, I am unable to include later generation individuals in my acculturation analysis. Second, paths of economic mobility and cultural assimilation differ. I base acculturation paths not on downward or upward mobility but, instead, on anti-classical or classical forms of assimilation. Finally, for the intragenerational analysis, the acculturation indicators allow for more consistent comparisons across the time periods than the education measures because questions about non-English language ability, English use, and ethnic identity are the same across the life course, unlike questions about educational expectations and attainment.

Acculturation Indicators: Non-English Ability Linguistic Assimilation

Language is an important cultural indicator of assimilation. Research suggests that non-English language ability deteriorates quite rapidly in the United States, especially among those who come to the United States at young ages and those born in the United States. (Alba et al. 2002; Portes and Hao 1998). Those who are able to maintain their non-English language ability appear to be more immersed in their cultures of origin and/or have sufficient opportunities to make use of these languages (and, in some cases, are making concerted efforts to maintain linguistic connections to their places of origin) (Alba et al. 2002). Segmented assimilation theory suggests that non-English language ability can have positive consequences for youths because it helps maintain ethnic group solidarity and keeps communication channels open between immigrant parents and their children. Youths may be protected from negative influences outside their immigrant community when they maintain their non-English language skills. This is especially the case when non-English language ability is accompanied by English skills.

There are three possible paths of non-English ability assimilation that youths can follow: they can (1) lose their non-English language skills over time (classical assimilation), (2) maintain them (stable or horizontal assimilation), or (3) improve upon them (anti-classical assimilation). Of course, the paths that immigrants can experience depend on their level of non-English skills at a designated starting point, eighth grade in this analysis. Some children of immigrants and their families come to the United States highly skilled in English (or, in some cases, with English as their only language). Many of these individuals have few, or no, non-English language skills. These individuals, according to my methods of classification, can only experience no change or anti-classical non-English ability assimilation. Those with the highest levels of non-English ability cannot experience anti-classical assimilation; they can only experience horizontal assimilation or classical assimilation (losing their non-English skills over time). Only those who start out with an intermediate level of non-English skills can experience all three patterns of assimilation.

The meanings of the paths of non-English language skills assimilation are also likely to differ depending on starting point. For example, the horizontal path may indicate greater attachment to home cultures for high non-English language ability immigrants than a similar path does for those with intermediate or low levels of non-English ability. A drop in non-English language skills, classical acculturation, may not indicate much of a departure from one's cultural attachment when one starts out at a very high level of non-English ability; however, it may be associated with a greater loss of cultural attachment for those who started out with middling non-English language ability.

As I noted above, many scholars suggest that age or developmental stage is related to the ease of acquisition of language skills (Lenneberg 1967; Laponce 1987; Bialystok and Hakuta 1994; Stevens 1999), although there is some disagreement as to the extent to which age matters (Bialystok 1997; Singleton and Ryan 2004). If these claims hold true, youths will be able to pick up non-English language skills more easily in adolescence than in emerging adulthood. Consequently, maintenance or improvement of non-English skills may require less cognitive effort and social support at younger ages. Segmented assimilation theory generally involves no predictions relating to life course stage and language ability, although Rumbaut (1997a) supports the idea that the ease of language acquisition changes over time. For these reasons, I predict that anti-classical forms of assimilation will be more common over adolescence than the longer emerging adulthood. More classical patterns of linguistic assimilation will be more common over the longer transition to emerging adulthood period.

Although segmented assimilation theory does not discuss it, gender is likely to be associated with non-English language ability. Some research suggests that girls have greater verbal aptitude than boys in general (Kleinfeld 1999). Portes and Rumbaut (2001a) and Portes and Hao (2002) find that, among CILS youths in twelfth grade, girls are statistically significantly more likely to be fluent bilinguals (have high English and non-English language skills) than boys. Portes and Schauffler (1994) find that CILS girls are significantly more likely to retain their language of origin than CILS boys. Lutz (2006) finds that Latino girls are more likely to have high Spanish ability than boys. These researchers suggest that, because young women of immigrant origin are more often tied to their homes than young men, they are more likely to maintain cultural attachments, such as language ability.

Similarly, as I noted in the first chapter, some authors consider that young women are, conventionally, "keepers of the culture" (Billson 1995) or more likely to maintain cultural ties or perform important cultural maintenance within families (Waters 1996; Das Gupta 1997; Valenzuela 1999; Dion and Dion 2001; Espiritu 1999; Ginorio and Huston 2001; Williams et al. 2002; Suárez-Orozco and Qin 2006). For these reasons, girls may be more likely to maintain (or improve upon) their non-English language skills than boys. Because of these gendered patterns of language ability, it also seems likely that young women will have more anti-classical patterns of linguistic assimilation than young men and that different factors will predict paths of this form of linguistic assimilation for girls and boys.

Acculturation Indicators: English Use Linguistic Assimilation

In addition to my examination of non-English ability over time, I study a second indicator of linguistic assimilation: English use with friends. English use, as I described in the previous chapter, shows the degree of participation in an English-speaking social sphere. Regardless of the ethnic make-up of this social sphere, immigrants' greater English use connotes, in most cases, lesser attachment to one's culture of origin and greater exposure to the norms and values of American society. Although context matters in both cases, individuals generally have more choice in terms of their language use—given a minimal level of ability—than their language ability, particularly in the case of English use with friends.

For my analysis of English use assimilation, I am only able to distinguish those who use English only with their friends from those who did not use English only. Those who use English only can either maintain that level of English use (stable or horizontal assimilation) or use it less over time (anti-classical acculturation); those who do not use English only either maintain their level of use or use English more over time (classical acculturation). Again, it is clear that the same path (stable or horizontal) has very different meanings depending on the starting point.[1]

Paths of English use assimilation are likely to vary from adolescence to emerging adulthood. Immigrants tend to settle near their co-ethnics, particularly when they are new or relatively new to this country (Portes and Rumbaut 1996). Children of immigrants, then, are likely to be exposed to relatively large numbers of their co-ethnics, who are likely to have similar non-English language skills. Opportunities for using a language other than English with their friends are likely to be plentiful. As children of immigrants enter emerging adulthood, they have greater opportunities to move away from home and, possibly, from communities with high concentrations of their co-ethnics. It is likely, then, that their opportunities for non-English language use with friends diminish over time. In other words, I expect to find greater classical assimilation of this linguistic form during emerging adulthood than during adolescence. I also expect to find lower levels of anti-classical assimilation during young adulthood than during adolescence.

These paths of linguistic assimilation and the factors associated with them may also differ by gender. Again, female immigrants (and children of immigrants), across the life course, may have stronger attachment to their cultures of origin and are likely to spend more time in the home than male immigrants (Portes and Rumbaut 2001a; Dion and Dion 2001; Espiritu 1999; Valenzuela 1999; Williams et al. 2002; Suárez-Orozco and Qin 2006). If these claims hold true, it is likely that, over the adolescent period, girls have less exposure to the English language and fewer English skills. For these reasons, girls may be more likely to make use of a non-English language with their friends than boys over different life course stages. Additionally, over the emerging adulthood period, there is evidence that young immigrant men are more likely to leave the home for work or school than immigrant women (Gee, Mitchell, and Wister 2003). Leaving home is likely to expose boys to greater numbers of non-co-ethnics and, therefore, increased opportunities for English use. Boys, then, may be more likely to experience classical linguistic assimilation, particularly over the emerging adulthood period, than girls.

Acculturation Indicators: Identificational Assimilation

I also examine paths of identificational assimilation over adolescence and the transition to emerging adulthood. As I discussed in the previous chapter, ethnic identification is a form of self-categorization. It involves "not only a claim to membership in a group or category but also a contrast of one's group or category with other groups of categories" (Portes and Rumbaut 2001a, 151). Shifts in identities over time may reveal changes in one's view of oneself and one's group membership.

As in the previous chapter, I use the four types of ethnic identities identified by Portes and Rumbaut (2001a): (1) plain American, (2) racial/pan-ethnic, (3) hyphenated American, and (4) national origin. They define shifts from one of these identities to another by three patterns of identificational assimilation: (1) a linear path, involving acquisition of a more "American" identity over time (classical-type assimilation); (2) a racialized path, in which one adopts a made-in-America identity that is associated with minority group status (classical-type variant in most cases); and (3) a resurgent path, involving acquisition of a more national origin identity over time (anti-classical assimilation). I once again add a fourth path of stability, i.e., no change over time.

Paths of identificational assimilation open to individuals depend on their initial ethnic identities. Table 3.2 shows the possible identificational assimilation paths open to individuals who initially hold each of the four ethnic identities. It reveals that not all paths are open to all ethnic identities. Youths' identificational assimilation paths' meanings are also likely to differ depending on their initial ethnic identities.

Table 3.2. Possible Paths of Intragenerational Identificational Assimilation

Youth Identity at T1	Youth Identity at T2			
	American	Hyphenated	National origin	Racial/pan-ethnic
American	Stable	Resurgent	Resurgent	Racialized
Hyphenated	Linear	Stable	Resurgent	Racialized
National origin	Linear	Linear	Stable	Racialized
Racial/ pan-ethnic	Linear	Resurgent	Resurgent	Stable

In their research, Portes and Rumbaut (2001a) find that, during adolescence, youths more commonly experience resurgent than linear identificational assimilation. Moreover, those youths who hold national origin identities report stronger connections to these identities than youths with more American identities. I expect to find that resurgent assimilation (or maintenance of a national origin identity) is the most common form of assimilation, although its likelihood will depend on youths' starting points. Youths whose identities provide more "room" for resurgent assimilation—those with American or racial/pan-ethnic identities—will be more likely to experience resurgent assimilation than youths with less "room" for resurgent assimilation— those with hyphenated identities.

Just as considering youths' initial ethnic identities is important for understanding their identificational assimilation, so too is it important to take into account how shifts in identities may vary across different life course stages. Some researchers suggest that adolescence is the most important time of identity formation (Côté and Allahar 1996; Erikson 1950, 1968; Marcia 1980; Suarez-Orozco and Suarez-Orozco 2001); however, many researchers, including Erikson (1950, 1968), view identity formation as part of a prolonged adolescence extending beyond age 18. As Arnett (2000) observes, "If adolescence is the period from ages 10 to 18 and emerging adulthood is the period from (roughly) ages 18 to 25, most identity exploration takes place in emerging adulthood rather than adolescence" (473). It is also likely, then, that there will be greater shifts in ethnic identity over emerging adulthood than adolescence. The factors associated with identity formation are likely to change across the life course, as well.

Gender may also be associated with identificational assimilation. As I discussed in the previous chapter, many scholars, including segmented assimilation theorists, suggest that females have stronger associations with their ethnic attachments, including ethnic identity, than males (Phinney 1990; Portes and Rumbaut 2001a; Bankston 1995; Gibson 1988; Lopez 2002; Warikoo 2005). Young women thus will be less likely to experience more classical forms of identificational assimilation than young men.

Additionally, some empirical evidence suggests that the association between gender and identificational assimilation may vary over the life course. Previous research findings provide some support for this claim. For example, Portes and Rumbaut (2001a) find, at the bivariate level, that gender is closely related to ethnic identity at younger ages (eighth or ninth grade) but not at older ages (twelfth grade). Moreover, they discover that girls are more likely than males to have stable identities over time. While I am able to examine gender differences in identificational assimilation at a bivariate level in this analysis, data restrictions prevent me from investigating regression models predicting paths of assimilation separately for boys and girls. I predict that young women will be more likely to hold on to their ethnic identities during adolescence than young men but that this association will not hold over the longer emerging adulthood period.

Data

As in the previous chapter, I use CILS and NELS data for my analysis, although the inter- and intragenerational samples are not exactly equivalent. For the CILS intragenerational analysis, I do not limit the sample to those youths for whom parent survey data is available because I do not require the same detailed parent information. Instead, my sample includes those youths for whom survey information is available from all three waves of data collection: 1992, when youths were in eighth or ninth grade; 1995-1996, when most were in twelfth grade; and 2001-2003, when youths were in their early-to-mid twenties.

Like the intergenerational sample, I limit the NELS intragenerational sample to white, black, and Mexican-origin third and later generation youths (U.S.-born youths with two U.S.-born parents). The NELS sample includes those respondents who participated in all waves of the survey, including both parent surveys. My intragenerational NELS analysis makes use of three points in time: baseline survey information when youths were in eighth grade (1988), information from the second follow-up when youths were in twelfth grade (1992), and fourth follow-up information when youths were in their mid-twenties (2000). I make two comparisons—during adolescence (eighth grade to twelfth grade) and the transition to emerging adulthood (from eighth grade to mid-twenties)—to determine the patterns of educational mobility for NELS youths.

Again, both the CILS and NELS data sets allow me to examine patterns of mobility and assimilation longitudinally. They each have the same advantages and disadvantages for the intragenerational analyses as they do for the intergenerational analyses. However, because I no longer restrict the CILS sample to those for whom parental surveys are available, the intragenerational CILS sample is substantially larger.

Dependent Variables

Educational Mobility Indicators

I compare educational expectations in eighth grade to those in twelfth grade and educational expectations in eighth grade to attainment by the mid-twenties to determine if educational mobility over these two time periods is downward, stable, or upward. With the CILS data, I categorize educational expectations/attainment into the following four categories: (1) less than high school degree, (2) high school degree, (3) some college, and (4) college degree or more. The NELS data have greater detail about educational expectations and attainment; therefore, I classify educational expectations and attainment into five categories for comparison: (1) less than high school, (2) high school only, (3) vocational/technical schooling or degree, (4) some four-year college, and (5) a four-year college degree or more. See Table 3.3 for the post-imputation distribution of these variables that comprise my measures of intragenerational educational mobility. The distributions of the CILS and NELS educational mobility variables by starting point, gender are in Table 3.4A, for adolescence, and Table 3.4B, for the transition to emerging adulthood.

Indicators of Cultural Assimilation

I examine three forms of intragenerational cultural assimilation using the CILS data: (1) non-English language ability, (2) English use, and (3) ethnic identification. I compare non-English language ability scores in eighth grade to twelfth grade and in eighth grade to the mid-twenties to determine if the direction of assimilation in each case is anti-classical (greater non-English ability over time), stable, or classical (less non-English ability over time). To create these non-English ability scores, I average responses to CILS survey items regarding how well youths speak, understand, read, and write a non-English language at each of the three waves of data collection. Response options are (1) very little, (2) not well, (3) well, and (4) very well. I code individuals as having no non-English language ability (0) if they report having no knowledge of a language other than English on another survey item. The scale, then, ranges from zero (no ability) to four (high ability on all four language items). See Table 3.3 for the post-imputation distributions of this variable across the waves of data collection. Table 3.5 contains the distribution of directions of non-English ability assimilation for the two time periods by starting point and gender.

Table 3.3. Post-Imputation Percentage of Indicators Used to Create Intragenerational Mobility and Assimilation Dependent Variables

Economic indicator	NELS: 3rd and later generation			CILS: Children of immigrants		
Educational status	T1	T2	T3	T1	T2	T3
Less than high school	1	2	4	0	0	3
High school degree	9	6	16	7	4	12
Some college	21	26	44	11	10	38
College degree or more	69	66	36	82	86	48
Total	100	100	100	100	100	100

Acculturation indicators for CILS: Children of immigrants

Rounded non-English ability score	T1	T2	T3
No ability	8	9	12
Very little	3	3	2
Not well	22	22	15
Well	40	38	35
Very well	26	29	36
Total	100	100	100
English use	T1	T2	T3
English only with friends	35	38	46
Not English only with friends	65	62	54
Total	100	100	100
Ethnic identity	T1	T2	T3
National origin	29	35	25
Hyphenated	45	35	41
Racial/pan-ethnic	15	27	29
American	12	3	4
Total	100	100	100

Table 3.4A. Distribution of Intragenerational Educational Mobility Paths during Adolescence among NELS and CILS Youths by Educational Expectations in 8th Grade and Gender

	NELS: 3RD AND LATER GENERATION			CILS: CHILDREN OF IMMIGRANTS		
	Males	Females	Total	Males	Females	Total
Youths with low educational expectations						
Stable	5	6	11	0	0	0
Up	35	33	68	6	1	7
Total	40	39	79	6	1	7
% Up	87.5%	84.6%	86.1%	100.0%	100.0%	100.0%
Youths with intermediate educational expectations						
Down	212	209	421	21	10	31
Stable	318	293	611	56	63	119
Up	610	646	1256	197	193	390
Total	1140	1148	2288	274	266	540
% Down	18.6%	18.2%	18.4%	7.7%	3.8%	5.7%
% Up	53.5%	56.3%	54.9%	71.9%	72.6%	72.2%
Youths with high educational expectations						
Down	509	574	1083	118	106	224
Stable	1882	2210	4092	969	1,277	2246
Total	2391	2784	5175	1,087	1,383	2470
% Down	21.3%	20.6%	20.9%	10.9%	7.7%	9.1%

Table 3.4B. Distribution of Intragenerational Educational Mobility Paths during the Transition to Emerging Adulthood among NELS and CILS Youths by Educational Expectations in 8th Grade and Gender

	NELS: 3RD AND LATER GENERATION			CILS: CHILDREN OF IMMIGRANTS		
	Males	Females	Total	Males	Females	Total
Youths with low educational expectations						
Stable	13	11	24	2	0	2
Up	27	28	55	4	1	5
Total	40	39	79	6	1	7
% Up	67.5%	71.8%	69.6%	66.7%	100.0%	71.4%
Youths with intermediate educational expectations						
Down	471	494	965	51	39	90
Stable	394	344	738	115	124	239
Up	275	310	585	108	103	211
Total	1140	1148	2288	274	266	540
% Down	41.3%	43.0%	42.2%	18.6%	14.7%	16.7%
% Up	24.1%	27.0%	25.6%	39.4%	38.7%	39.1%
Youths with high educational expectations						
Down	1,270	1,404	2674	523	630	1153
Stable	1,121	1,380	2501	564	753	1317
Total	2391	2784	5175	1,087	1,383	2470
% Down	53.1%	50.4%	51.7%	48.1%	45.6%	46.7%

Table 3.5. Distribution of Intragenerational Non-English Ability Assimilation Paths among Children of Immigrants by Non-English Ability in 8th Grade, Life Course Stage, and Gender

Youths with High Non-English Ability

	ADOLESCENCE			EMERGING ADULTHOOD		
	Males	Females	Total	Males	Females	Total
Stable	187	354	541	218	362	580
Classical	124	119	243	93	111	204
Total	311	473	784	311	473	784
% Classical	39.9%	25.2%	31.0%	29.9%	23.5%	26.0%

Youths with Intermediate Non-English Ability

	Males	Females	Total	Males	Females	Total
Anti-classical	276	316	592	393	423	816
Stable	487	561	1048	366	444	810
Classical	168	179	347	172	189	361
Total	931	1056	1987	931	1056	1987
% Anti-classical	29.6%	29.9%	29.8%	42.2%	40.1%	41.1%
% Classical	18.0%	17.0%	17.5%	18.5%	17.9%	18.2%

Youths with No Non-English Ability

	Males	Females	Total	Males	Females	Total
Anti-classical	49	48	97	40	41	81
Stable	76	73	149	85	80	165
Total	125	121	246	125	121	246
% Anti-classical	39.2%	39.7%	39.4%	32.0%	33.9%	32.9%

Source: Children of Immigrants Longitudinal Study

I also create a set of indicators for English language use assimilation. Although the CILS English language use variables differ across waves, it is possible to identify respondents who use only English with their friends. For wave one and two, I consider those who report that they do not use a language other than English with friends as English only users. For wave three, youths who report that they use English only with their closest friends are English only users. See Table 3.3 (above) for the post-imputation distribution of this variable across the waves of data collection. I classify those who maintain their English only use status over time as experiencing stable assimilation. Those who start out as English only users but report using another language with friends at the second time point experience anti-classical assimilation. Those who start out as non-English only users but become English only users over time experience classical assimilation.

The distributions of the assimilation paths, by starting point, are in Table 3.6.

Table 3.6. Distribution of Intragenerational English Use Assimilation Paths among Children of Immigrants by Level of English Use with Friends in 8th Grade, Life Course Stage, and Gender

Youths Who Did Not Use English Only with Friends

	Adolescence			Emerging Adulthood		
	Males	Females	Total	Males	Females	Total
Stable	668	910	1578	574	783	1357
Classical	164	230	394	258	357	615
Total	832	1140	1972	832	1140	1972
% Classical	19.7%	20.2%	20.0%	31.0%	31.3%	31.2%

Youths Who Used English Only with Friends

	Adolescence			Emerging Adulthood		
	Males	Females	Total	Males	Females	Total
Stable	368	397	765	378	403	781
Anti-classical	167	113	280	157	107	264
Total	535	510	1045	535	510	1045
% Anti-classical	31.2%	22.2%	26.8%	29.3%	21.0%	25.3%

Source: Children of Immigrants Longitudinal Study

Information on ethnic identity comes from a survey question at each wave that asks respondents how they identify themselves. The survey question lists a series of possible options including examples of national origin, hyphenated, racial/pan-ethnic, and plain American identities. I code this raw data into four categories for comparison: American, racial/pan-ethnic, hyphenated, and national origin (see Table 3.3 for the distribution at each data collection wave). I compare the ethnic identities at the different points in time to determine path of identificational assimilation. Table 3.7 shows the distribution of the paths of identificational assimilation by starting point and gender.

Table 3.7. Distribution of Intragenerational Identificational Assimilation Paths among Children of Immigrants by Ethnic Identity in 8th Grade, Life Course Stage, and Gender

	ADOLESCENCE			EMERGING ADULTHOOD		
Youths with American Identities in 8th Grade						
	MALE	FEMALE	TOTAL	MALE	FEMALE	TOTAL
Resurgent	123	54	177	113	47	160
Stable	26	18	44	30	16	46
Racialized	86	53	139	92	62	154
Total	235	125	360	235	125	360
% Resurgent	52.3%	43.2%	49.2%	48.1%	37.6%	44.4%
% Racialized	36.6%	42.4%	38.6%	39.1%	49.6%	42.8%
Youths with Racial/Pan-ethnic Identities in 8th Grade						
Resurgent	90	139	229	83	122	205
Stable	83	134	217	83	148	231
Linear	1	2	3	8	5	13
Total	174	275	449	174	275	449
% Resurgent	51.7%	50.5%	51.0%	47.7%	44.4%	45.7%
% Linear	0.6%	0.7%	0.7%	4.6%	1.8%	2.9%
Youths with Hyphenated Americans in 8th Grade						
Resurgent	187	197	384	128	140	268
Stable	269	375	644	309	410	719
Linear	17	21	38	17	27	44
Racialized	110	171	281	129	187	316
Total	583	764	1347	583	764	1347
% Resurgent	32.1%	25.8%	28.5%	22.0%	18.3%	19.9%
% Linear	2.9%	2.7%	2.8%	2.9%	3.5%	3.3%
% Racialized	18.9%	22.4%	20.9%	22.1%	24.5%	23.5%
Youths with National Origin Identities in 8th Grade						
Stable	208	280	488	154	198	352
Linear	92	96	188	142	179	321
Racialized	75	110	185	79	109	188
Total	375	486	861	375	486	861
% Linear	24.5%	19.8%	21.8%	37.9%	36.8%	37.3%
% Racialized	20.0%	22.6%	21.5%	21.1%	22.4%	21.8%

Source: Children of Immigrants Longitudinal Study

Independent Variables: CILS

I create three groups of independent variables from the first wave of the CILS data: demographic characteristics, downward leveling factors, and protective factors. The demographic measures are primarily the same as those used in the intergenerational analysis, including gender, year of birth, family structure, parental education, number of siblings, and ethnic origin. The sample is approximately 23 percent Cuban, 13 percent Mexican, 6 percent Nicaraguan, 7 percent West Indian, 18 percent Filipino, 12 percent Southeast Asian, and 21 percent other. I still do not divide these groups by generational status, however, because there are not enough cases to do so given my analytical methods, and, as I noted in the previous chapter, ethnic group membership and generational status are highly associated. I add an additional dummy variable indicating home ownership (non-ownership is the reference group) because I lack measures of parental occupational status and income from the youth surveys.

Although they come from the first wave of data collection, two of the downward leveling factors in the CILS intragenerational analysis are equivalent to those used in the intergenerational analysis. One is a dummy indicating that youths had reported ever being discriminated against. The other is an additive scale concerning the respondents' views of racial problems in America.[2] The remaining downward leveling factors are specific to the intragenerational analysis. These items pertain to school characteristics, specifically the proportion of (1) black students, (2) Latino students, and (3) students eligible for subsidized lunch in the school, and (4) whether the school is located in the inner city (outside of the inner city is the reference group).

I create several sets of protective factors. The first set involves parent-child relationship measures. I construct a measure of parental warmth from youth reports of the truthfulness of the following two statements: (1) "My parents don't like me very much," and (2) "My parents are usually not very interested in what I say." I code those youths who report that these statements are not true at all as one and all other youths as zero. This measure taps only into relationship quality.

I also construct a dummy variable indicating that youths do not find their parents embarrassing because they do not know American ways. The reference category is that youths *do* find their parents embarrassing because of their lack of knowledge of American ways. Additionally, I create an item measuring how often youths get in trouble because they do things differently from their parents, reverse-coded from (1) all the time to (4) never. Finally, as in the intergenerational analysis, I create two dummy variables measuring parent-youth preferences for American ways. The first variable indicates that neither parent nor child prefers American ways. The second indicates that either parent or child prefers American ways. The reference group includes those cases in which both parents and their children prefer American ways.

The second set of protective factors represents ethnic attachments. I construct a scale indicating the youth's perception of the importance of relatives, equivalent to that used in the intergenerational analysis.[3] Another item indicates the extent to which youths agree that the American way of life weakens the family. Responses range from (1) disagree a lot to (4) agree a lot. For another variable, youths reported the extent to which they disagree with this statement: "There is no better country to live in than the U.S." I reverse-code the responses so that higher numbers reveal less attachment to the United States, from (1) agree a lot to (4) disagree a lot. I also include a dummy variable indicating that many or most of the youths' friends were born abroad. The reference group represents that some or fewer friends were born abroad.

The remaining two ethnic connections variables relate to language. I first include an indicator of frequency of non-English use in the home. Responses range from (0) never to (4) always. I also construct an English ability measure. Of course, English ability not only represents cultural attachments; it is also associated with educational success. However, other variables in my models, particularly expectations, grades, and test scores, should explain away most of that association. Because high English skills are very common, I create a dummy indicating that youths understand, speak, read, and write English very well. The omitted category includes those with lower levels of English ability.

The third set of protective factors includes respondents' educational characteristics. I control for educational expectations, where applicable, using a dummy variable indicating college expectations. The reference category includes those with lower expectations. I also include measures of the respondents' grade point average and reading and math test score percentiles.

Independent Variables: NELS

As with the CILS data, I include demographic variables, downward leveling factors, and protective factors in my NELS analysis. All of these variables come from the third and later generation youths' 1988 base-year data when respondents were in eighth grade, with one exception as noted below. The demographic characteristics in my models are gender, year of birth, family structure, number dependent upon parents, parent educational and occupational status, and race-ethnicity. As I noted above, I separate the NELS respondents into the follow groups: whites, blacks, and Mexicans. I described these variables in more detail in the previous chapter.

I construct downward leveling variables related to youths' schools. I include a dummy variable indicating that the youth's school in eighth grade is in an urban area. The omitted category includes those schools in non-urban (rural or suburban) areas. I also create dummy variables to represent school composition. I measure school minority composition with a dummy variable indicating that 40 to 100 percent of a school's students are members of minority groups. The reference group includes youths attending schools that are less than 40 percent minority. I measure school poverty with two dummy variables indicating that 5 to 30 percent and 30 to 100 percent of students receive free lunch. The reference group includes youths attending schools where fewer than 5 percent of students receive free lunch.

I also include two dummies indicating that youths have had something stolen at school or have been threatened with physical harm. In both cases, the reference group includes those who have not had the particular negative experience at school. I use students' level of agreement with the following statement to gauge school safety: "I don't feel safe at school." Responses range from (1) strongly disagree to (4) strongly agree. Finally, I include two additive scales measuring school environment issues.[4] The first indicates the degree to which the following problems are serious at the youth's school: (1) tardiness, (2) absenteeism, and (3) cutting class. The second deals with more serious problems: (1) physical conflict among students, (2) robbery or theft, (3) vandalism of school property, (4) alcohol use, (5) drug use, (6) weapons possession, (7) physical abuse of teachers, and (8) verbal abuse of teachers. [5] Response options for the individual items (before summing them) range from (1) not a problem to (4) a serious problem.

Most of the protective factors represent the quality of the parent-child relationship. I include a dummy indicating that parents trust youths to do what they expect. The reference group indicates a lack of parental trust. Another dummy indicates that youths know why they should obey their parents. The reference group includes those who do not know why they should obey. I operationalize parental supervision with a variable indicating the amount of time youths spend after school unsupervised, based on Muller's (1998) measure in her study of parental involvement in academic achievement. I reverse-code the item to represent supervision rather than a lack of it; therefore, responses range from (1) greater than 3 hours unsupervised to (5) no time unsupervised.

Two measures count family rules. The first counts rules related to television, specifically (1) programs the youth is allowed to watch, (2) how early or late he/she may watch, and (3) how many hours he/she may watch. The second counts other rules: (1) maintaining a grade point average, (2) doing homework, and (3) doing household chores.[6]

I base my parental monitoring scale, the only variable from the 1990 wave of NELS, when youths were in 10th grade, on Freese and Powell's (1999) analysis of parental involvement. Youths report how much their parents try to find out about (1) who their friends are, (2) where they go at night, (3) how much money they spend, (4) what they do with their free time, and (5) where they are most afternoons after school. Responses range from (0) not at all for all to (15) a lot for all. I also create a parental strictness scale from items indicating how often parents (1) check on homework, (2) require that chores be done, (3) limit television watching, and (4) limit time with friends on week nights. Response options (pre-additive scale) range from (1) often to (4) never.[7]

I also include three measures of parent intervention at school. I base the first measure on Muller's work on education and parental involvement (1998, 1995). I construct a scale of the frequency with which parents contact school about: (1) their youths' academic performance, (2) their youths' academic program for this year, and (3) their youths' behavior in school. Responses range from (0) none for all to (9) more than four times for all. The other parent intervention items are based on the work of Freese and Powell (1999). The parental involvement in school score counts, since the beginning of the school year, if parents have (1) attended a school meeting, (2) phoned or spoken to a teacher or counselor, (3) visited their classes, and (4) attended a school event. The parent-teacher organization involvement score counts if parents (1) belong to the PTO, (2) have ever attended a meeting, and (3) have taken part in PTO activities. [8]   While these parental involvement measures may be protective, they may also be a sign of a child's behavioral or academic problems.

The next set of protective factors represents social capital. The first two variables are counts of the number of (1) youth's friends and (2) youth's friends' parents that the parent knows, based on Freese and Powell's work (1999).   Of course, the number of friends and the number of parents of friends that the parent reports knowing are highly associated, but their simultaneous inclusion in the analysis does not change the pattern of results.

The final set of protective factors captures youths' educational characteristics, specifically, grade point average, test scores, and educational expectations. Grade information comes from a NELS-constructed variable averaging self-reported grades in English, math, science, and social studies. [9] The test score variable is the standardized composite reading and math test score included in the NELS data collection. In my economic mobility analyses, I contrast high school educational expectations to expectations for some college among youths with intermediate educational expectations. In my acculturation analyses, I include a dummy variable indicating college or higher expectations.

Missing Data: Multiple Imputation

As with the intergenerational analysis, I use multiple imputation for CILS and NELS separately to deal with missing values. Because my intragenerational and intergenerational samples differ, I performed separate imputations for them.   My regression results include information from all five of the data sets that I create with the imputations with corrections for standard errors.

Analytical Methods

Like the intergenerational analysis, I perform both bivariate and multivariate analyses of the intragenerational paths of mobility and assimilation. For the bivariate analyses, I examine paths of mobility and assimilation by starting point.   I perform statistical tests to determine if there are statistically significant associations between these paths and life course stage, gender, and immigrant generational status.

For the multivariate analysis, I perform binomial and multinomial logistic regression to examine the associations between my predictor variables and the pathways of (1) economic mobility, (2) non-English ability assimilation, (3) English use assimilation, and (4) identificational assimilation. I analyze these various paths by their respective starting points. I also perform these analyses for both the adolescent and emerging adulthood time periods and separately for young men and young women, where possible. I use the appropriate NELS weights to deal with the study design. As with the intergenerational CILS analysis, I include variables that predict dropping out of the sample to deal with sample selection bias. I perform multivariate analyses for a particular starting point/gender/parent immigration status category when I have approximately 350 or more NELS cases and 250 or more CILS cases for that category.

For each of these comparisons, I examine three models. For example, I analyze economic mobility during adolescence for boys who had college expectations in eighth grade. I start with a baseline model that includes youths' demographic characteristics. In the second model, I add downward leveling characteristics. In the third model, I add protective factors. I do the same for girls with college expectations in eighth grade as well.

Descriptive Results

Educational Mobility

Youths with low educational expectations in eighth grade only have two paths of mobility open to them: horizontal and upward (see Tables 3.4A-B, above[10]). Very few youths expect to complete less than a high school education in eighth grade in the NELS and CILS data. Among NELS youths, statistically significantly more raise their expectations during adolescence than attain a higher level of education by their mid-twenties. All CILS youths raise their expectations between eighth and twelfth grade, and most attain a higher level of education by their mid-twenties. Because so few youths have this low level of educational expectations in both NELS and CILS, I am not able to study them further in the multivariate analyses.

All three paths of mobility are open to youths with intermediate educational expectations in eighth grade. From eighth to twelfth grade, few youths lower their educational expectations, and most youths increase them. During the emerging adulthood stage, statistically significantly more youths experience downward mobility and fail to achieve upward mobility than during adolescence. Of course, during adolescence, I examine only educational expectations; in emerging adulthood, I examine youths' attainment of those expectations. From this intermediate starting point, mobility is statistically significantly more positive for children of immigrants than non-immigrants in both life course stages; that is, children of immigrants are more likely to raise their educational expectations over adolescence and exceed their eighth grade expectations by their mid-twenties than third and later generation youths. Third and later generation youths are more likely to lower their expectations over adolescence and fail to meet their eighth grade expectations by their mid-twenties than children of immigrants. Gender differences are not statistically significant.

College expectations are more stable than lower educational expectations during adolescence. They are statistically significantly more stable among children of immigrants than third and later generation youths. While gender differences are not statistically significant among third and later generation youths in adolescence, female children of immigrants maintain their college expectations more than their male counterparts. Far fewer youths attain a college degree by their mid-twenties than maintain college expectations between eighth and twelfth grade regardless of gender or parental immigration status. Children of immigrants maintain their advantage over this longer time period as well: a statistically significantly larger proportion of CILS youths vs. NELS youths attain their eighth grade college expectations by their mid-twenties. While the difference between third and later generation young men's and women's attainment of their college expectations falls just short of statistical significance (at $p<.05$, two-tailed test), a statistically significantly lower proportion of NELS boys attain their expected college education by their mid-twenties compared with CILS youths, regardless of gender.

Linguistic Assimilation: Non-English Ability

I next discuss cultural assimilation, applicable only to the CILS data. Of the few youths who report having no non-English language ability (see Table 3.5, above), most maintain this level of ability over time. Differences by gender and life course stage are not statistically significant. Most youths with intermediate non-English skills maintain this level of ability over adolescence, although more youths' skills improve rather than worsen over this time period. Statistically significantly more youths experience anti-classical assimilation over the longer emerging adulthood period than during adolescence only, regardless of gender. Most youths with high non-English skills maintain them over both adolescence and emerging adulthood; however, statistically significantly more females than males maintain their high levels of non-English ability in adolescence. This association loses statistical significance over the longer transition to emerging adulthood period. Differences between the two time periods, however, are not statistically significant.

Linguistic Assimilation: English Use with Friends

Turning to English use assimilation, the majority of youths do not use English only with their friends in eighth grade. Most of these youths experience horizontal assimilation over both adolescence and emerging adulthood; however, classical assimilation is more common over the longer emerging adulthood period than during adolescence, regardless of gender (see Table 3.6, above). Among youths who use English only with their friends in eighth grade, most experience horizontal assimilation. Differences by life course stage and gender are not statistically significant.

Identificational Assimilation

The likelihood of following different paths of assimilation differs by youths' identities in eighth or ninth grades. In many cases, as expected, the more "room" a youth has to follow a path, the more common that path is (see Table 3.7, above). For example, resurgent assimilation during adolescence and emerging adulthood is more common among youths with American or racial/pan-ethnic identities in eighth grade than youths with hyphenated identities, regardless of gender. Youths with American or racial/pan-ethnic identities can follow the resurgent path by adopting hyphenated or national origin identities; hyphenated-identified youths must adopt national origin identities to experience this path. Similarly, linear assimilation is generally more common among youths with national origin identities in eighth grade compared to other identities.   Youths with American identities are most likely to experience racialized assimilation. Moreover, American identities are the least stable of all initial identities, regardless of gender or life course stage. National origin identities are most stable in adolescence, but hyphenated identities are most stable across the longer emerging adulthood period, regardless of gender.

Among those surveyed in eighth or ninth grade, few have American and racial/pan-ethnic identities. Most of these youths change their identities over time—both through adolescence and continuing on to emerging adulthood. Gender and life course stage differences are not statistically significant in either case.

For those with hyphenated identities in eighth grade, the stable path is quite common, followed by the resurgent and racialized paths. In adolescence, boys are more likely to experience resurgent assimilation than girls (one-tailed test). No gender differences remain statistically significant continuing into the emerging adulthood period. Both boys and girls experience resurgent assimilation more often in adolescence than emerging adulthood. At least some youths, then, who acquire a more national origin identity during adolescence, give up that identity by the time they reach their mid-twenties. For boys, the stable path is more common over the longer emerging adulthood period than during adolescence. For those with national origin identities, stable assimilation is most common. Gender differences are not statistically significant; however, both boys and girls are less likely to experience stable assimilation and more likely to experience linear assimilation during adolescence than emerging adulthood.   In this case, linear assimilation usually involves the adoption of a hyphenated identity. The results for those with hyphenated and national origin identities suggest that the hyphenated American identity is quite commonly adopted over the long haul among children of immigrants. Perhaps it best incorporates elements of their parents' places of origin and their new home.

Multivariate Results

As with the intergenerational analysis, the associations between directions of assimilation and mobility vary by starting point, gender, life course stage, and parental immigration status. Again, there is no simple story to tell. I highlight the most consistent results and challenges to segmented assimilation theory.

Educational Mobility

As I noted above, too few youths expect to complete less than high school expectations in eighth or ninth grade to perform a multivariate analysis of their paths of mobility; therefore, I focus on youths with higher educational expectations. In Tables 3.8A-G, I present those factors that are statistically significantly associated with educational mobility by gender and generational status for youths who have intermediate educational expectations and high (college) educational expectations in eighth grade.

Of the demographic characteristics (see Tables 3.8A-D), different racial/ethnic groups are statistically significant predictors of educational mobility across the two life course stages and starting points. These results provide mixed support for segmented assimilation theory. For example, CILS Mexican females have higher odds of failing to meet their expectations than "other" children of immigrants, but only when they have college expectations or more. Filipinos with intermediate educational expectations have higher odds of raising their expectations over the course of adolescence grade than "other" children of immigrants, but they do not have higher odds of surpassing their expectations by their mid-twenties. Furthermore, Filipino females with college expectations have higher odds of failing to attain them than "other" children of immigrants. Zhou and Xiong (2005), as I noted in the previous chapter, argue that Filipinos' downward mobility is just regression to the mean; however, these results reveal that Filipino young women have a harder time of reaching their educational expectations than other young women.

The findings for blacks conflict in most cases with segmented assimilation theory's predictions. Third and later generation black males and females with intermediate educational expectations have lower odds of failing to meet their expectations by their mid-twenties than comparable whites. Black females with high expectations are less likely to reduce these expectations by twelfth grade than white females, but this statistically significant association does not carry over to educational attainment in emerging adulthood. West Indian female children of immigrants, however, have higher odds of maintaining their

Table 3.8A. Odds of Intragenerational Educational Mobility Paths among Third and Later Generation Youths with Intermediate 8th Grade Educational Expectations, by Life Course Stage and Gender: Statistically Significant Demographic and Downward Leveling Variables

| | INTERMEDIATE EXPECTATIONS | | | |
| | ADOLESCENCE: Up vs. Not | | EMERGING ADULTHOOD: Up vs. Stable vs. Down | |
	MALE	FEMALE	MALE	FEMALE
Demographic Variables				
Later year of birth (ref: earlier)	ns	ns	Lower down v. not	Lower down vs. not
Blacks (ref: whites)	ns	ns	Lower down vs. not	Lower down vs. up
High parent education (ref: other)	Higher up	Higher up	Lower down vs. up	ns
H.S. expectations (ref: trade schl)	ns	Higher up	Lower down vs. up	Lower down vs. not
Some college expect. (ref: not)	ns	ns	Higher down	Higher down
Downward leveling factors				
not)	Higher up	ns	Higher stable	ns
School poor (ref: not)	ns	ns	Higher down vs. up	ns
Threatened at school (ref: never)	ns	ns	Lower up vs. stable	ns
Unsafe school	ns	ns	Higher up vs. stable	ns

Source: National Educational Longitudinal Study
- indicates variable not included in model
Demographic and downward leveling variables not shown: Mexican origin, family structure/size, high parent occupation, school location and composition, negative experiences at school, school saftey and problems

college expectations by their mid-twenties than "other" children of immigrants. Under some circumstances, segmented assimilation theory makes positive predictions about West Indians assimilation. However, segmented assimilation theory does not predict positive results for native black Americans.

Table 3.8B. Odds of Intragenerational Educational Mobility Paths among Children of Immigrants with Intermediate 8th Grade Educational Expectations, by Life Course Stage: Statistically Significant Demographic and Downward Leveling Variables

	INTERMEDIATE EXPECTATIONS	
	ADOLESCENCE: Up vs. Not	EMERGING ADULTHOOD: Up vs. Not
	FULL	FULL
Demographic Variables		
Later year of birth (ref: earlier)	Higher up	ns
West Indians (CILS ref: other)	ns	ns
Filipinos (ref: other)	Higher up	ns
High parent education (ref: other)	ns	ns
H.S. expectations (ref: trade schl)	-	-
Some college expect.	ns	ns
Downward Leveling Variables		
Urban school (ref: not)	ns	ns
School poor (ref: not)	ns	ns
Threatened at school (ref: never)	-	-
Unsafe school	-	-

Source: Children of Immigrants Longitudinal Study
- indicates variable not included in model
Demographic and downward leveling variables not shown: gender, Cuban, Nicaraguan, and Southeast Asian origin, family size, discrimination, racial problems in the US, and school location and composition

As segmented assimilation theory predicts, another demographic characteristic, parental education, is quite consistently positively associated with intragenerational educational mobility. However, these associations do not hold for children of immigrants with intermediate educational expectations in adolescence or emerging adulthood. Moreover, over emerging adulthood, regardless of starting point, the association is statistically significant for males only.

Table 3.8C. Odds of Intragenerational Educational Mobility Paths among Third and Later Generation Youths with High 8th Grade Educational Expectations, by Life Course Stage and Gender: Statistically Significant Demographic and Downward Leveling Variables

| | HIGH EDUCATIONAL EXPECTATIONS: Down vs. Stable | | | |
| | ADOLESCENCE | | EMERGING ADULTHOOD | |
	MALE	FEMALE	MALE	FEMALE
Demographic Variables				
Blacks (ref: whites)	ns	Lower down	ns	ns
Mexicans	ns	ns	ns	ns
Two parent family (ref: other)	ns	Lower down	Lower down	Lower down
High parent education (ref: other)	Lower down	Lower down	Lower down	ns
High parent occupation status (ref: not high)	ns	ns	Lower down	ns
Parents own home (ref: do not own)	-	-	-	-
Downward Leveling Factors				
School poor (ref: not)	ns	ns	Higher down	ns

Source: National Educational Longitudinal Study
- indicates variable not included in model
Demographic and downward leveling variables not shown: year of birth, family size, school location and composition, negative experiences at school, school saftey and problems

Coming from a two-parent family is consistently associated with more positive educational mobility among youths with high college expectations over the emerging adulthood life stage. It is not statistically significantly associated with mobility outcomes among youths with lower educational expectations. Other parental status indicators, including home ownership and parental occupational status, are statistically significant for youths with college expectations over emerging adulthood only.

Associations between downward leveling factors and educational mobility hold for third and later generation males only and are primarily found over the longer time period from adolescence to emerging adulthood (see Tables 3.8A-D). Third and later generation young men with intermediate educational expectations who attend schools that are poor and in which they have been personally threatened with physical harm are less likely to attain their eighth grade educational expectations than other young men. School poverty also has a negative association with educational mobility for young men with college expectations over the emerging adulthood period. Two

Table 3.8D. Odds of Intragenerational Educational Mobility Paths among Children of Immigrants with High 8th Grade Educational Expectations, by Life Course Stage and Gender: Statistically Significant Demographic and Downward Leveling Variables

	HIGH EDUCATIONAL EXPECTATIONS: Down vs. Stable		
	ADOLESCENCE	EMERGING ADULTHOOD	
	FULL	MALE	FEMALE
Demographic Variables			
West Indians	ns	ns	Lower down
Mexicans (ref: other)	ns	ns	Higher down
Filipinos	ns	ns	Higher down
Two parent family (ref: other)	ns	Lower down	ns
High parent education (ref: other)	Lower down	Lower down	ns
High parent occupation status (ref: not high)	-	ns	-
Parents own home (ref: do not own)	ns	ns	Lower down
Downward Leveling Factors			
School poor (ref: not)	ns	ns	ns

Source: Children of Immigrants Longitudinal Study
- indicates variable not included in model
Demographic and downward leveling variables not shown: gender, Cuban, Nicaraguan, and Southeast Asian origin, family size, discrimination, racial problems in the US, and school location and composition

Table 3.8E. Odds of Intragenerational Educational Mobility Paths among Children of Immigrants (CILS) and Third and Later Generation Youths (NELS) with Intermediate 8th Grade Educational Expectations, by Life Course Stage and Gender: Statistically Significant Protective Factors

	INTERMEDIATE EDUCATIONAL EXPECTATIONS					
	ADOLESCENCE			EMERGING ADULTHOOD		
	NELS: Up vs. Stable vs. Down		CILS: Up vs. Not	NELS: Up vs. Stable vs. Down		CILS: Up vs. Not
	MALE	FEMALE	FULL	MALE	FEMALE	FULL
Protective Factors						
Parental trust	ns	ns	-	Lower up vs. not	ns	-
Parental strictness	ns	ns	-	Higher up vs. stable	Higher down vs. up	-
Grades	Higher up	ns	Higher up	Lower down vs. not	Lower down vs. not	Higher up
Test scores	ns	ns	ns	Higher up vs. stable	Lower down vs. up	ns

Sources: Children of Immigrants Longitudinal Study and National Educational Longitudinal Study

- indicates variable not included in model

Protective factors not shown: parental warmth and obedience, parental supervision and monitoring, family rules, parents know friends and friends' parents, parents involved in PTO, talking with parents about school (NELS); parents embarrass youths, importance of relatives, American ways weaken family, either parent or child prefers American ways, and language-related items (CILS)

Table 3.8F. Odds of Intragenerational Educational Mobility Paths among Children of Immigrants with High 8th Grade Educational Expectations, by Life Course Stage and Gender: Statistically Significant Protective Factors

	HIGH EDUCATIONAL EXPECTATIONS: Down vs. Stable		
	ADOLESCENCE	EMERGING ADULTHOOD	
	FULL	MALE	FEMALE
Protective Factors			
Parental warmth	Lower down	ns	ns
Parent involvement at school (PTO)	ns	ns	ns
Parents contact school	-	-	-
Not in trouble for doing this different from parents (ref: other)	Lower down	ns	ns
Neither parent nor child prefers American ways (ref: other)	Lower down	ns	ns
US not best country (ref: disagree)	ns	ns	Lower down
American identity (ref: national origin)	ns	Lower down	ns
Racial/pan-ethnic identity	ns	ns	Higher down
Grades	Lower down	Lower down	Lower down
Test scores	Lower down	Lower down	Lower down

Source: Children of Immigrants Longitudinal Study
- indicates variable not included in model

Protective factors not shown: parents embarrass youths, importance of relatives, American ways weaken family, either parent or child prefers American ways, and language-related items

factors that I predicted to have negative influences are unexpectedly more positively associated with intragenerational educational mobility among third and later generation males with intermediate educational expectations. Over both adolescence and emerging adulthood, young men who attend urban schools have higher odds of upward and stable

Table 3.8G. Odds of Intragenerational Educational Mobility Paths among Third and Later Generation Youths with High 8th Grade Educational Expectations, by Life Course Stage and Gender: Statistically Significant Protective Factors

| | HIGH EDUCATIONAL EXPECTATIONS: Down vs. Stable | | | |
| | ADOLESCENCE | | EMERGING ADULTHOOD | |
Protective Factors	MALE	FEMALE	MALE	FEMALE
Parental warmth	-	-	-	-
Parent involvement at school (PTO)	ns	ns	ns	Lower down
Parents contact school	ns	ns	ns	Higher down
Not in trouble for doing things different from parents (ref: trouble)	-	-	-	-
Neither parent nor child prefers American ways	-	-	-	-
US not best country (ref: disagree)	-	-	-	-
American identity (ref: national origin)	-	-	-	-
Racial/pan-ethnic identity	-	-	-	-
Grades	Lower down	Lower down	Lower down	Lower down
Test scores	Lower down	ns	ns	Lower down

Source: National Educational Longitudinal Study
- indicates variable not included in model
Not statistically significant: parental obedience, parental supervision and monitoring, family rules, parents know friends and friends' parents, parents involved in PTO, talk w/ parents about school

mobility, respectively, than other young men. Finally, young men who rate their schools as unsafe actually have higher odds of surpassing vs. attaining their educational expectations. Most of the other items relating to school environment had to do with youths' physical and material well-being. It is possible that after controlling for these measures, the perception of school safety measure tapped into more emotional forms of safety. Considering the wider culture of mediocrity in the United States (Tyson, Darity, and Castellino 2005), it is possible that issues of emotional well-being and safety are more salient for high-achieving students.

Protective factors are more widely associated with educational mobility paths (see Tables 3.8E-G). Grades and test scores are quite consistently associated with educational mobility across starting points, life course stages, gender, and parental immigration status. Parent-child relationships, as with intergenerational mobility, prove to have significance in predicting intragenerational educational mobility. Surprisingly, among NELS youths with intermediate educational expectations, parental trust (for males) and parental strictness (for females) are negatively associated with educational mobility over emerging adulthood. However, parental strictness is associated with higher odds of positive educational mobility over this same period for young men. Parental warmth also appears protective of expectations for a college degree among children of immigrants over adolescence. Other findings regarding parent-child relationship quality, specifically parent-child acculturation, are more mixed and only hold for children of immigrants with college expectations over adolescence.

Associations between other measures of cultural attachments and intragenerational educational mobility vary in direction and are only statistically significant for youths with college expectations over the longer emerging adulthood time period. There are also gender differences in these patterns of associations. Stronger American cultural attachments are associated with more positive educational mobility outcomes for young men than young women. Young men who report American—as opposed to national origin—identities have higher odds of attaining their eighth grade college expectations by their mid-twenties. In contrast, young women with more American identities, specifically racial or pan-ethnic ones, have higher odds of failing to attain their eighth grade college expectations by their mid-twenties. Similarly, females who believe that the United States is not the best country, exhibiting somewhat weaker American cultural attachments, are more likely to meet their college expectations by their mid-twenties. The findings for young women support segmented assimilation theory's claims while the findings for young men challenge them.

Linguistic Assimilation: Non-English Language Ability

I now turn to linguistic assimilation in terms of non-English language ability (see Tables 3.9A-F). Although I present results by gender for those who have intermediate non-English language abilities, I do not focus on these results because the number of cases following the classical path for males and females separately leads to small cell sizes. I do not attach too much weight, then, to differences by gender.

Examining the results in Tables 3.9A-B, I find some consistency in results across racial/ethnic groups that follows the predictions of segmented assimilation theory. Cubans with intermediate non-English skills, for example, have higher odds of stable vs. classical assimilation than "other" children of immigrants in both adolescence and emerging adulthood. In contrast, Mexicans, almost across the board, have higher odds of anti-classical assimilation and lower odds of classical assimilation than "other" children of immigrants. Given that the Cuban and Mexican children of immigrants reside in large co-ethnic communities in Miami and San Diego, respectively, in which the Spanish language is highly represented, it is logical that these youths would be able to hold on to their language capabilities more so than other immigrants whose languages are less likely to find wider communal and societal supports. Alba et al. (1999) find similarly in their research on language retention. West Indians, Filipinos, and Southeast Asians with intermediate non-English skills all have higher odds of classical vs. other forms of assimilation compared with "other" immigrants. For West Indians and Filipinos, this outcome is likely the result of the high English skills and use in their home countries. Southeast Asians, in contrast, may lack a sizeable community to support their language maintenance.

Of the remaining demographic characteristics, gender is statistically significantly associated with non-English ability assimilation among youths with high non-English skills only. Females have lower odds of classical assimilation in both adolescence and emerging adulthood than males. These findings are in line with claims that girls have stronger cultural attachments than boys (Portes and Rumbaut 2001a).

Additional parent characteristics are more often statistically significant in adolescence than emerging adulthood, though their effects on assimilation pathways are mixed. For example, as Portes and Rumbaut (2001a) suggest, living in a two parent family is associated

Table 3.9A. Odds of Intragenerational Non-English Ability Assimilation Paths among Children of Immigrants during Adolescence, By 8th Grade Non-English Ability and Gender: Statistically Significant Demographic Variables

	INTERMEDIATE: Classical vs. stable vs. anti-classical			HIGH: Classical vs. stable
	FULL	MALE	FEMALE	FULL
Demographic Variables				
Female (ref: male)	ns	-	-	Lower classical
Cubans (ref: other)	Higher stable vs. classical	ns	Higher stable vs. classical	ns
Mexicans	Higher anti vs. not	ns	ns	ns
West Indians	Higher classical vs. not	ns	ns	ns
Filipinos	Higher classical vs. anti	ns	Higher classical vs. anti	ns
Southeast Asians	Higher stable vs. anti	Higher stable vs. anti	ns	ns
Two parent family (ref: other)	ns	Higher stable vs. anti	ns	Lower classical
Parent college education (ref: h.s.)	Higher stable vs. anti	Higher classical vs. not	Higher stable vs. anti	ns
Parents own home (ref: do not)	Higher classical vs. anti	Higher classical vs. anti	ns	Higher classical

Source: Children of Immigrants Longitudinal Study

Demographic variables in the models not shown: year of birth, Nicaraguan origin, and family size

Table 3.9B. Odds of Intragenerational Non-English Ability Assimilation Paths among Children of Immigrants during the Transition to Emerging Adulthood, By 8th Grade Non-English Ability and Gender: Statistically Significant Demographic Variables

| | FULL | INTERMEDIATE: Classical vs. stable vs. anti-classical | | HIGH: Classical vs. stable |
		MALE	FEMALE	FULL
Downward Leveling Factors				
Female (ref: male)	ns	-	-	Lower classical
Cubans (ref: other)	Higher stable vs. classical	ns	ns	ns
Mexicans	Higher anti vs not	ns	ns	Lower classical
West Indians	Higher classical vs. not	Higher classical vs. not	Higher classical vs. not	ns
Filipinos	Higher classical vs. not	Higher classical vs. not	Higher classical vs. not	ns
Southeast Asians	Higher stable vs. not	Higher stable vs. not	Higher stable vs. not	ns
Two parent family (ref: other)	ns	ns	ns	ns
Parent college education (ref: h.s.)	ns	ns	ns	ns
Parents own home (ref: do not)	Lower anti vs. not	Lower anti vs. not	Lower anti vs. not	ns

Source: Children of Immigrants Longitudinal Study

Demographic variables in the models not shown: year of birth, Nicaraguan origin, and family size
Protective variables not shown: embarrassed by parents, friends from abroad, English ability

with language retention for youths of both intermediate and high abilities in adolescence only. Parental education is also associated with higher odds of language ability retention among intermediate ability youths in adolescence only. Home ownership is associated with higher odds of classical assimilation/lower odds of anti-classical assimilation in both adolescence and over the emerging for intermediate ability youths but during adolescence only for high ability youths.

Several downward leveling factors are also associated with this form of linguistic assimilation (see Tables 3.9C-D). Views of racial problems and experiences of discrimination are associated with more classical/less anti-classical trajectories of assimilation. For youths with intermediate non-English ability in eighth/ninth grade, views of racial problems are statistically significant across both life course stages. Experiences of discrimination are more important for youths with high non-English ability, but this association is statistically significant in adolescence only.

School composition measures are consistent predictors of non-English assimilation for intermediate ability youths. The more blacks and Latinos in the youths' schools, regardless of life course stage, the higher are youths' odds of less classical/more anti-classical assimilation. Greater minority school composition is associated, then, with anti-classical assimilation. However, higher school poverty is associated with more classical linguistic assimilation for youths during their adolescence only. While not a school composition measure per se, youths with high non-English ability who attended schools in the inner city in eighth grade have higher odds of classical assimilation than other youths during their transition to emerging adulthood. These associations yield mixed support for segmented assimilation's claims.

The protective factors' associations with linguistic assimilation suggest that some parent-child relationship qualities promote youths' language retention (see Tables 3.9C-F). For example, parental warmth is associated with lower odds of classical assimilation for high ability youths through the transition to emerging adulthood only. Also, youths who do not find their parents' lack of American ways embarrassing have higher odds of anti-classical assimilation from intermediate starting points during adolescence, especially boys. Odds of classical vs. stable assimilation lower when either the youth or his/her parent prefers American ways, compared to when both prefer American ways. In contrast, youths who do not get in trouble for doing things

Table 3.9C. Odds of Intragenerational Non-English Ability Assimilation Paths among Children of Immigrants during Adolescence, By 8th Grade Non-English Ability and Gender: Statistically Significant Downward Leveling and Protective Variables

	INTERMEDIATE: Classical vs. Stable vs. Anti-classical			HIGH: Classical vs. Stable
	FULL	MALE	FEMALE	FULL
Downward Leveling Variables				
Ever discriminated against (ref: never)	ns	ns	ns	Higher classical
Believes more racial problems in US	Higher classical vs. stable	ns	Higher classical vs. stable	ns
% black in school	Higher anti vs. classical	Lower classical vs. not	ns	ns
% Latino in school	Higher anti vs. not	Higher anti vs. not	Higher anti vs. not	ns
% poor in school	Lower anti vs. not	Higher classical vs. not	ns	ns
Inner city school (ref: other)	ns	ns	ns	ns
Protective Factors				
Parental warmth	ns	ns	ns	ns
U.S. not best country (ref: best)	ns	ns	ns	ns
American way weakens family (ref: does not)	ns	ns	ns	Lower classical

Source: Children of Immigrants Longitudinal Study
Protective variables not shown: embarrassed by parents, friends from abroad, English ability

Table 3.9D. Odds of Intragenerational Non-English Ability Assimilation Paths among Children of Immigrants during Adolescence, By 8th Grade Non-English Ability and Gender: Statistically Significant Protective Variables (cont'd)

Protective Factors	INTERMEDIATE: Classical vs. Stable vs. Anti-classical			HIGH: Classical vs. Stable
	FULL	MALE	FEMALE	FULL
Parent's non-American ways not embarrassing (ref: embarrassing)	Higher anti vs. classical	Higher anti vs. classical	ns	ns
Not in trouble for doing things different from parents (ref: in trouble)	Lower anti vs. classical	Higher classical vs. not	Lower anti vs. stable	ns
Importance of relatives	Higher anti vs. stable	Higher anti vs. stable	ns	Lower classical
Either parent/child prefers American ways (ref: other)	ns	ns	Higher stable vs. classical	ns
Extent non-English language used at home	Lower classical vs. not	Lower classical vs. not	Lower classical vs. not	Lower classical
Use English only with friends (ref: other)	Higher classical vs. not	Higher classical vs. not	Higher classical vs. not	ns
Hyphenated identity (ref: national origin)	ns	Lower anti vs. classical	ns	ns
College expectations (ref: other)	Higher anti vs. stable	ns	ns	ns
GPA	Lower classical vs. stable	ns	Lower classical vs. stable	ns

Source: Children of Immigrants Longitudinal Study

Table 3.9E. Odds of Intragenerational Non-English Ability Assimilation Paths among Children of Immigrants during the Transition to Adulthood, By 8th Grade Non-English Ability and Gender: Statistically Significant Downward Leveling and Protective Variables

	INTERMEDIATE: Classical vs. Stable vs. Anti-classical			HIGH: Classical vs. Stable
	FULL	MALE	FEMALE	FULL
Downward Leveling Variables				
Ever discriminated against (ref: never)	ns	ns	ns	ns
Believes more racial problems in US	Lower anti vs. stable	ns	Lower anti vs. stable	ns
% black in school	Lower classical vs. not	Lower classical vs. not	ns	ns
% Latino in school	Higher anti vs. not	Higher anti vs. not	Higher anti vs. not	ns
% poor in school	ns	ns	ns	ns
Inner city school (ref: other)	ns	ns	ns	Higher classical
Protective Factors				
Parental warmth	ns	ns	ns	Lower classical
U.S. not best country (ref: US best)	Lower classical vs. not	Lower classical vs. not	ns	ns
American way weakens family (ref: does not)	ns	ns	ns	ns

Source: Children of Immigrants Longitudinal Study

Protective variables not shown: embarrassed by parents, friends from abroad, English ability

Table 3.9F. Odds of Intragenerational Non-English Ability Assimilation Paths among Children of Immigrants during the Transition to Emerging Adulthood, By 8th Grade Non-English Ability and Gender: Statistically Significant Protective Variables (cont'd)

	INTERMEDIATE: Classical vs. Stable vs. Anti-classical			HIGH: Classical vs. Stable
Protective Factors	FULL	MALE	FEMALE	FULL
Parent's non-American ways not embarrassing (ref: embarrassing)	ns	ns	ns	ns
Not in trouble for doing things different from parents (ref: in trouble)	ns	ns	ns	ns
Importance of relatives	ns	ns	ns	ns
Either parent/child prefers American ways (ref: other)	ns	ns	ns	ns
Extent non-English language used at home	Higher anti vs. not	Higher anti vs. not	Higher anti vs. not	Lower classical
Use English only with friends (ref: other)	Higher classical vs. anti	ns	Higher classical vs. anti	ns
Hyphenated identity (ref: national origin)	ns	ns	ns	ns
College expectations (ref: other)	ns	ns	ns	ns
GPA	Lower classical vs. stable	ns	Lower classical vs. stable	ns

Source: Children of Immigrants Longitudinal Study

differently from their parents have higher odds classical/lower odds anti-classical assimilation.

As Portes and Rumbaut (2001a) assert, other cultural factors influence this form of linguistic assimilation, as well. More negative views of the United States—including that the United States is not the best country and the American way weakens the family—are associated with lower odds of classical linguistic assimilation from different starting points in different life course stages. Greater importance of relatives is also associated with lower odds of classical assimilation for youths from different starting points; however, in this case, the association holds during adolescence only.

Unsurprisingly, other language characteristics influence linguistic assimilation. Youths who used a non-English language at home in eighth grade have lower odds of classical assimilation across starting point, life course stage, and gender. Those who used English only with their friends in eighth grade have higher odds of classical assimilation from intermediate starting points, regardless of life course stage and gender, than those who did not use English only.

Finally, GPA is associated with lower odds of classical assimilation among youths with intermediate non-English skills. This association holds across life course stage and gender. Though Portes and colleagues focus on the positive influence that non-English language ability, particularly bilingualism, may have on educational outcomes, they discuss somewhat less the inverse of this relationship: higher grades may promote non-English language use, perhaps due to grades' association with cognitive capacity or educational motivation.

Linguistic Assimilation: English Use with Friends

For English use assimilation, I also present findings by gender (see Tables 3.10A-D); however, I do not focus on those results here because of cell size issues. Several demographic variables are associated with linguistic assimilation regardless of starting point (see Tables 3.10A-B). Spanish speakers tend to have lower odds of classical assimilation and higher odds of anti-classical assimilation than "other" immigrants regardless of life course stage, gender, and starting point. In contrast, Asians, Filipinos especially, experience the opposite pattern of association. In addition, in general, the greater families' status or resources are, the higher are youths' odds of classical assimilation from

Table 3.10A. Odds of Intragenerational English Use Assimilation Paths among Children of Immigrants during Adolescence, By 8th Grade English Use and Gender: Statistically Significant Demographic and Downward Leveling Variables

| | NON-ENGLISH ONLY USERS: Classical vs. Stable | | | ENGLISH ONLY USERS: Anti-classical vs. Stable |
	FULL	MALE	FEMALE	FULL
Demographic Variables				
Female (ref: male)	ns		ns	Lower anti
Cuban (ref: "other")	Lower classical	Lower classical	Lower classical	Higher anti
Mexican	Lower classical	Lower classical	Lower classical	Higher anti
Nicaraguan	Lower classical	ns	ns	ns
West Indian	ns	ns	ns	ns
Filipino	Higher classical	Higher classical	Higher classical	Higher anti
Southeast Asian	ns	ns	ns	ns
Two parent family (ref: other)	ns	ns	ns	ns
Number of siblings	Lower classical	Lower classical	ns	ns
Parent college education (ref: lower)	Higher classical	Higher classical	ns	ns
Parents own home (ref: do not)	ns	ns	ns	ns
Downward Leveling Factors				
% Latino in school	ns	ns	ns	ns
Inner city school (ref: other)	ns	ns	ns	ns
Views of racial problems in U.S.	ns	ns	ns	Lower anti

Source: Children of Immigrants Longitudinal Study

Table 3.10B. Odds of Intragenerational English Use Assimilation Paths among Children of Immigrants during the Transition to Emerging Adulthood, By 8th Grade English Use and Gender: Statistically Significant Demographic and Downward Leveling Variables

	NON-ENGLISH ONLY USERS: Classical vs. Stable			ENGLISH ONLY USERS: Anti-classical vs. Stable
	FULL	MALE	FEMALE	FULL
Demographic Variables				
Female (ref: male)	ns			ns
Cuban (ref: "other")	Lower classical	Lower classical	ns	ns
Mexican	Lower classical	ns	Lower classical	ns
Nicaraguan	ns	ns	ns	ns
West Indian	ns	ns	Higher classical	ns
Filipino	Higher classical	Higher classical	Higher classical	Lower anti
Southeast Asian	ns	ns	ns	ns
Two parent family (ref: other)	ns	ns	ns	Lower anti
Number of siblings	ns	ns	ns	ns
Parent college education (ref: not)	ns	ns	ns	ns
Parents own home (ref: do not)	ns	Higher classical	ns	ns
Downward Leveling Factors				
% Latino in school	Lower classical	ns	Lower classical	Higher anti
Inner city school (ref: other)	ns	ns	Higher classical	ns
Views of racial problems in U.S.	ns	ns	ns	ns

Source: Children of Immigrants Longitudinal Study

Table 3.10C. Odds of Intragenerational English Use Assimilation Paths among Children of Immigrants during Adolescence, By 8th Grade English Use and Gender: Statistically Significant Protective Factors

Protective Factors	NON-ENGLISH ONLY USERS: Classical vs. Stable			ENGLISH ONLY USERS: Anti-classical vs. Stable
	FULL	MALE	FEMALE	FULL
Neither parent nor child prefers American ways (ref: both prefer)	ns	ns	Lower classical	ns
Most friends from abroad (ref: other)	Lower classical	Lower classical	ns	Higher anti-classical
Extent non-English language used at home	ns	ns	Lower classical	Higher anti-classical
High English ability (ref: not high)	Higher classical	Higher classical	Higher classical	ns
Non-English ability	Lower classical	ns	Lower classical	Higher anti-classical
Hyphenated identity (ref: national origin)	ns	Higher classical	ns	ns
Racial/pan-ethnic identity	ns	ns	ns	Higher anti-classical
College expectations (ref: lower)	ns	ns	ns	ns
Math test score	ns	Higher classical	ns	ns

Source: Children of Immigrants Longitudinal Study

Demographic variables in the models not shown: year of birth

Downward leveling variables not shown: experienced discrimination, school composition (% black and % poor)

Protective variables not shown: embarrassed by parents, parental warmth, trouble for doing things different from parents, importance of relatives, American way weakens family, U.S. not best country, test score, and grades

Table 3.10D. Odds of Intragenerational English Use Assimilation Paths among Children of Immigrants during the Transition to Emerging Adulthood, By 8th Grade English Use and Gender: Statistically Significant Protective Factors

Protective Factors	NON-ENGLISH ONLY USERS: Classical vs. Stable			ENGLISH ONLY USERS: Anti-classical vs. Stable
	FULL	MALE	FEMALE	FULL
Neither parent nor child prefers American ways (ref: both prefer)	Lower classical	ns	Lower classical	ns
Most friends from abroad (ref: other)	ns	ns	ns	Higher anti-classical
Extent non-English language used at home	Lower classical	ns	Lower classical	ns
High English ability (ref: not high)	Higher classical	ns	ns	ns
Non-English ability	Lower classical	ns	Lower classical	Higher anti-classical
Hyphenated identity (ref: national origin)	ns	ns	ns	ns
Racial/pan-ethnic identity	ns	ns	ns	ns
College expectations (ref: lower)	ns	ns	ns	Lower anti-classical
Math test score	ns	ns	ns	ns

Source: Children of Immigrants Longitudinal Study

Demographic variables in the models not shown: year of birth

Downward leveling variables not shown: experienced discrimination, school composition (% black and % poor)

Protective variables not shown: embarrassed by parents, parental warmth, trouble for doing things different from parents, importance of relatives, American way weakens family, U.S. not best country, test score, and grades a non-English-only starting point and the lower are their odds of anti-classical assimilation from an English-only starting point.

As with non-English ability, school composition is associated with English use assimilation (see Tables 3.10A-B). In this case, however, the proportion of students who are Latino is associated with English use assimilation over the longer emerging adulthood period and not during adolescence alone. As the proportion of Latino students in the youth's school increases, the odds of using English more decrease for non-English only users and the odds of using a language other than English with friends increase for English only users. Other downward leveling factors are related to this form of linguistic assimilation for certain starting points and life course stages only.

Turning to the protective factors (see Tables 3.10C-D), when neither parents nor their children prefer American ways vs. when they both prefer American ways, non-English only youths have lower odds of classical assimilation in emerging adulthood (and adolescence, for females). Cultural characteristics generally are consistent predictors of linguistic assimilation, as expected. Non-English language ability is associated with higher odds of anti-classical assimilation and lower odds of classical assimilation, depending on starting points. These associations hold regardless of life course stage. Similarly, youths who use a non-English language at home have lower odds of classical assimilation and higher odds of anti-classical assimilation, depending on their starting points. However, the associations differ across life course stage and, for non-English only youths, hold only for females among non-English only users. Greater English skills are associated with higher odds of classical assimilation among non-English only users regardless of life course stage. There are no consistent associations with ethnic self-identification. The relationships between linguistic assimilation and educational characteristics differ across starting points and life course stages also but suggest that more positive educational characteristics are associated with more classical/less anti-classical forms of English use assimilation.

Identificational Assimilation

There are four different starting points for identificational assimilation: American identity, hyphenated identity, national origin identity, and racial/pan-ethnic identity. Across each of these different starting points, various factors are associated with identificational assimilation

Table 3.11A. Odds of Intragenerational Identificational Assimilation Paths among Children of Immigrants during Adolescence, By 8th Grade Ethnic Identity and Gender: Statistically Significant Demographic Variables

	AMERICAN: Resurgent vs. Not	RACIAL/PAN-ETHNIC: Resurgent vs. Not	HYPHENATED: Resurgent vs. Stable vs. Linear/Racialized	NATIONAL ORIGIN: Linear vs. Stable vs. Racialized
Demographic Variables				
Later year of birth (ref: earlier)	ns	ns	ns	Higher racialized vs. stable
Female (ref: male)	ns	ns	ns	ns
Cuban (ref: "other")	Higher resurgent	ns	Higher resurgent vs. not	Lower racialized vs. not
Mexican	ns	Higher resurgent	Lower linear/ racialized vs. stable	Lower racialized vs. not
Nicaraguan	ns	Higher resurgent	ns	Lower racialized vs. not
West Indian	Higher resurgent		Lower linear/ racialized vs. not	Higher stable vs. not
Filipino	ns	ns	Lower lin/rac vs. not	ns
Southeast Asian	ns	ns	Lower lin/rac vs. not	Lower rac vs. not
Parent less than high school (ref: h.s.)	ns	ns	Higher linear/ racialized vs. resurgent	ns
Parents own home (ref: do not)	ns	ns	Lower lin/rac vs. resurgent	Higher linear vs. stable

Source: Children of Immigrants Longitudinal Study
Demographic variables in the models not shown: family structure and family size

Table 3.11B. Odds of Intragenerational Identificational Assimilation Paths among Children of Immigrants during the Transition to Emerging Adulthood, By 8th Grade Ethnic Identity and Gender: Statistically Significant Demographic Variables

	AMERICAN: Resurgent vs. Not	RACIAL/PAN-ETHNIC: Resurgent vs. Not	HYPHENATED: Resurgent vs. Stable vs. Linear/Racialized	NATIONAL ORIGIN: Linear vs. Stable vs. Racialized
Demographic Variables				
Later year of birth (ref: earlier)	ns	ns	ns	Higher racialized vs. stable
Female (ref: male)	ns	ns	Lower resurgent vs. stable	ns
Cuban (ref: "other")	Higher resurgent	Higher resurgent	Higher resurgent vs. not	Lower racialized vs. not
Mexican	ns	ns	ns	Lower racialized vs. not
Nicaraguan	ns	Higher resurgent	ns	Higher odds stable vs. not
West Indian	Higher resurgent	ns	Lower linear/racialized vs. not	Higher stable vs. not
Filipino	ns	ns	Lower lin/rac vs. not	ns
Southeast Asian	ns	ns	Lower lin/rac vs. not	ns
Parent less than high school (ref: h.s.)	ns	ns	Lower odds linear/racialized vs. stable	ns
Parents own home (ref: do not)	ns	ns	ns	Higher racialized vs. not

Source: Children of Immigrants Longitudinal Study
Demographic variables in the models not shown: family structure and family size

paths (see Tables 3.11A-E). I am unable to examine identificational assimilation by gender because of the limits of my sample size; therefore, I focus on differences by starting point and life course stage.

Ethnic origin is associated with assimilation paths across a variety of starting points (see Tables 3.11A-B). Cubans seem particularly likely to experience anti-classical forms of assimilation and unlikely to experience racialized assimilation, regardless of life course stage and starting point, compared with "other" immigrants. Similarly, West Indians and Mexicans have lower odds of linear or racialized assimilation from American and racial/pan-ethnic identities, respectively, than "other" immigrants, regardless of life course stage, for the most part. Filipinos and Southeast Asians also have lower odds of linear or racialized assimilation from hyphenated identities, regardless of life course stage. Only Southeast Asian adolescents, however, have lower odds of racialized assimilation from national origin identities. Outcomes for Nicaraguans are more mixed, though they typically move away from racial/pan-ethnic identities over time.

Family socioeconomic status variables, when statistically significant, are positively associated with return to national origin identities from hyphenated starting points, regardless of life course stage. However, among youths with national origin identities in eighth grade, the opposite pattern holds. Home ownership is associated with higher odds of more classical (linear and racialized) forms of assimilation.

Of the downward leveling factors (see Table 3.11C), school composition and location are most consistently associated with pathways of identificational assimilation. Among youths with hyphenated identities, the larger the proportions of black, Latino, and poor students are in their schools, the higher are their odds of linear or racialized assimilation compared with other forms of assimilation. These associations hold over the adolescent period only and do not continue into the emerging adulthood life stage. Also among youths with hyphenated identities in eighth grade, attending inner-city schools raises one's odds of resurgent vs. linear or racialized assimilation. This relationship holds both in adolescence and over the entire transition to emerging adulthood period. I find, similarly, that youths with American identities have lower odds of resurgent assimilation as the proportion of Latinos students in their schools increases. This finding does not appear in adolescence only but surfaces over the longer emerging adulthood life stage. In contrast to the previous findings,

Table 3.11C. Odds of Intragenerational Identificational Assimilation Paths among Children of Immigrants, By 8th Grade Ethnic Identity, Life Course Stage, and Gender: Statistically Significant Downward Leveling Variables

	AMERICAN: Resurgent vs. Not	RACIAL/PAN-ETHNIC: Resurgent vs. Not	HYPHENATED: Resurgent vs. Stable vs. Linear/Racialized	NATIONAL ORIGIN: Linear vs. Stable vs. Racialized
Adolescence				
% black in school	ns	ns	Higher linear/racialized vs. resurgent	ns
% Latino in school	ns	ns	Higher linear/racialized vs. not	ns
% poor in school	ns	ns	Higher linear/racialized vs. stable	ns
Inner city school (ref: other)	ns	ns	Lower linear/racialized vs. resurgent	ns
Transition to Emerging Adulthood				
% black in school	ns	ns	ns	
% Latino in school	Lower resurgent	ns	ns	
% poor in school	ns	ns	ns	
Inner city school (ref: other)	ns	ns	Lower linear/racialized vs. resurgent	Lower odds racialized vs. linear

Source: Children of Immigrants Longitudinal Study

Downward leveling variables not shown: experienced discrimination and views of racial problems in the U.S.

Table 3.11D. Odds of Intragenerational Identificational Assimilation Paths among Children of Immigrants during Adolescence, By 8th Grade Ethnic Identity and Gender: Statistically Significant Protective Factors

Protective Factors	AMERICAN: Resurgent vs. Not	RACIAL/ PAN-ETHNIC: Resurgent vs. Not	HYPHENATED: Resurgent vs. Stable vs. Linear/ Racialized	NATIONAL ORIGIN: Linear vs. Stable vs. Racialized
Parents un-American ways do not embarrass (ref: embarrass)	ns	ns	ns	ns
Neither parent/child prefers American ways (ref: both prefer)	ns	ns	Higher resurgent vs. not	Lower linear vs. stable
Either parent or child prefers American ways	ns	Higher resurgent		ns
Extent non-English language used at home	ns	ns	Lower lin/rac vs. not	ns
Non-English ability		ns	ns	Lower linear vs. stable
Use English only with friends (ref: other)	ns	ns	ns	ns
High English ability (ref: not high)	ns	ns	ns	Higher linear vs. stable
College expectations (ref: lower)	ns	ns	ns	ns
Reading test score	ns	ns	ns	Lower linear vs. stable

Source: Children of Immigrants Longitudinal Study

Protective variables not shown: parental warmth, trouble for doing things different from parents, importance of relatives, American way weakens family, U.S. not best country, friends from abroad, reading test score, and grades

Table 3.11E. Odds of Intragenerational Identificational Assimilation Paths among Children of Immigrants during the Transition to Emerging Adulthood, By 8th Grade Ethnic Identity and Gender: Statistically Significant Protective Factors

Protective Factors	AMERICAN: Resurgent vs. Not	RACIAL/ PAN-ETHNIC: Resurgent vs. Not	HYPHENATED: Resurgent vs. Stable vs. Linear/ Racialized	NATIONAL ORIGIN: Linear vs. Stable vs. Racialized
Parents un-American ways do not embarrass (ref: embarrass)	ns	ns	Higher linear/ racialized vs. stable	ns
Neither parent/child prefers American ways (ref: both prefer)	Higher resurgent	ns	ns	ns
Either parent or child prefers American ways	ns	Higher resurgent	Higher resurgent vs. stable	ns
Extent non-English language used at home	ns	ns	Lower linear/racialized vs. not	ns
Non-English ability	ns	ns		ns
Use English only with friends (ref: other)	ns	ns	Higher resurgent vs. stable	ns
High English ability (ref: not high)	Lower resurgent	ns	ns	ns
College expectations (ref: lower)	ns	ns	ns	Higher linear vs. racialized
Reading test score	ns	ns	ns	ns

Source: Children of Immigrants Longitudinal Study

Protective variables not shown: parental warmth, trouble for doing things different from parents, importance of relatives, American way weakens family, U.S. not best country, friends from abroad, reading test score, and grades

youths with national origin identities have lower odds of racialized vs. linear assimilation as the proportion of poor students in their schools increases.

A few parent-child relationship variables are also associated with identificational assimilation paths (see Tables 3.11D-E). Hyphenated identity youths who are not embarrassed by their parents' lack of American ways have higher odds of linear or racialized assimilation compared with stable assimilation during the transition to emerging adulthood. More consistently related to identificational assimilation paths are the measures of parent-child preferences for American ways. Cases in which neither or either parent or child prefers American ways are associated with higher odds of resurgent assimilation or higher odds of national origin maintenance regardless of starting point and life course stage.

Language variables are also related to identificational assimilation paths, particularly among youths with hyphenated and national origin identities. Youths with these identities in eighth grade who use a language other than English at home have higher odds of retaining their language or, in the case of hyphenated identity youths, experiencing resurgent assimilation than youths who use English only at home. This finding holds across the entire transition to emerging adulthood for hyphenated American identified youths but in adolescence only for national origin identified youths. I find a similar association among youths with hyphenated identities for English only use with friends; however, this relationship surfaces only over the transition to emerging adulthood period and not during adolescence alone. In addition, high English skills are associated with more classical/less anti-classical forms of assimilation among youths with national origin identities and American identities, though over different life course stages.

Finally, there are statistically significant associations between identificational assimilation and educational characteristics for youths with national origin identities only. However, the directions of the associations differ by characteristic. Higher reading scores are associated with lower odds of linear vs. stable assimilation, and college expectations are associated with higher odds of linear vs. racialized assimilation.

Discussion and Conclusion

My analysis of intragenerational mobility and assimilation among youths during adolescence and emerging adulthood reveals that youths experience all possible paths of assimilation for each indicator during adolescence and during emerging adulthood, though, of course, some paths are more common than others. These results reveal that there are differences in mobility and assimilation experiences by starting point, life course stage, gender, and parental immigration status, although these differences are not always consistent.

Because of these inconsistencies, in order to discuss differences in outcomes by starting point, life course stage, gender, and parental immigration status, I would have to focus on minor details. Although I do comment on some additional patterns, for clarity of presentation, I choose to focus on differences in life course, the major innovation of this chapter, and to discuss patterns of associations between the demographic, downward leveling, and protective factors and the assimilation paths.

I find that individuals do not always follow the same assimilation paths at different points in the life course. In some cases, for example, with identificational assimilation, classical assimilation is more common over the longer, emerging adulthood period than during the shorter adolescent period. In other cases, such as non-English ability assimilation, classical assimilation is more common during the adolescent than emerging adulthood period, suggesting that some youths experience what Gans (1992) calls a "bumpy-line" path of assimilation. I also find that factors associated with the paths of mobility and assimilation vary across the life course stages, though they follow no consistent patterns. Examining assimilation outcomes over one period alone does not provide a full picture of assimilation outcomes. Below I discuss the implications of my analyses on segmented assimilation theory by each indicator of mobility or assimilation.

Educational Mobility

Although youths follow only three possible pathways of educational mobility, the factors associated with these paths differ by starting point, life course stage, gender, and parental immigration status in ways that segmented assimilation theory does not suggest. For educational mobility, life course stage is important because path definitions differ in adolescence and emerging adulthood. Over adolescence only, educational mobility refers to changes, or lack thereof, in expectations. Over the longer time period, the transition to emerging adulthood, mobility involves one's attainment, or lack thereof, of expectations. Unsurprisingly, actual attainment of educational expectations is much more difficult for youths than their maintenance. Starting point is also related to educational mobility, as expected. Furthermore, children of immigrants, regardless of gender, and females overall are generally more likely to hold on to or increase their expectations over adolescence and attain or surpass them during the transition to emerging adulthood than third and later generation youths and males, respectively. These results generally support segmented assimilation theory's claims, although segmented assimilation theory places very little attention on issues of gender.

Associations between predictors and paths of educational mobility provide mixed support for segmented assimilation theory's claims. For example, while segmented assimilation theory predicts negative educational outcomes for individuals of Mexican origin, particularly those of later generations with more American cultural attachments, I only find more negative intragenerational educational outcomes for daughters of Mexican immigrants with college expectations over emerging adulthood. Other groups for whom segmented assimilation theory predicts more negative outcomes, including third and later generation blacks, actually have more positive educational mobility outcomes. Among the other demographic variables, parental and family status variables are consistently related to educational mobility paths as segmented assimilation theory and, for that matter, classical assimilation theory predict.

Segmented assimilation theory focuses on the challenges that children of immigrants face as they integrate into American society. My analysis suggests that children of immigrants are more insulated from these challenges than third and later generation youths. More specifically, I find that (some) downward leveling factors are impediments to third and later generation young *men's* achievement of their educational expectations, from intermediate and higher starting points. These results provide support for the immigrant optimism hypothesis. Immigrant parents' high motivations and expectations for their children may help to insulate them from problems in their school environments. Third and later generation young men appear to lack this protection.

These results also support the literature that argues that matters of masculinity (and femininity) are at play in educational settings (see, for example, Thorne 1993; Dumais 2002; Skelton 2001). Regardless of school setting, research suggests that boys are more likely to encounter disciplinary action than girls (Gregory 1995; Lietz and Gregory 1978; McFadden et al. 1992; Shaw and Braden 1990; Skiba et al. 1997; Taylor and Foster 1986). Negotiating a difficult or problematic school environment may be more challenging for boys than girls because of gendered expectations of masculinity. Boys in unsafe school settings—in which violence, or the threat of it, is common—may have more opportunities to enact their masculinity in ways that can get them into trouble. These behavioral responses may lead to disciplinary responses—such as detentions, suspensions, or expulsions—that could inhibit boys' educational achievement.

Research also suggests that men and women—and perhaps boys and girls—experience poverty differently. Poverty may be more threatening to masculinity than femininity. For example, Fodor (2006) found that conditions of poverty intensified the need for conventional feminine performances of care work. In contrast, men living in poverty seemed to experience a crisis of masculinity for failing to live up to their expectations as breadwinners. In some cases, men appear to act in aggressive and self-destructive ways that shore up their threatened masculinities to the detriment of their economic, physical, and emotional well-being (see, for example, Bourgois 1996; Nonn 1995).

This process may function similarly for school-aged boys and girls. For example, in her study of middle and high school students, Carter (2006) finds that peers police poor boys of color who perform well in school—and present themselves in ways identified as "white"—with gay slurs and other taunts. Some of these boys then reject school success because it threatens their gender status. In contrast, peers challenged the racial and ethnic identities of high-achieving, low-income minority girls but their gender identities remained unscathed, with fewer negative consequences for girls' educational attainment. This research suggests that the class- and class-and-race-based versions of oppositionality to school success that Tyson, Darity, and Castellino (2005) discuss may also be gendered oppositionalities. Rejection of school success may not be just a "black thing" or a "poor thing."

Instead, gender—particularly masculinity—is implicated in attitudes antithetical to school success.

This intersection of gender and poverty may also result from outsiders' constructions of poor (and minority) masculinities. A whole body of research, including works by Chambliss (1973), Carter (2006), and Ferguson (2000), suggests that teachers and school officials tend to interpret (and label) performances of masculinity differently among poor (and minority) and non-poor (and white) boys, with more negative consequences for (minority) poor with few economic resources. Girls' feminine performances do not seem to elicit the same kinds of judgments.

Protective factor results provide mixed support for segmented assimilation theory. Parent-child relationship quality measures do not always lead to more positive educational outcomes. Moreover, segmented assimilation theory's claims that cultural attachments are associated with more positive assimilation outcomes are supported only among children of immigrants with college expectations. More importantly, these factors are only protective of youths' expectations during adolescence; they are not associated with actual attainment of college education.[11] These results suggest that ethnic attachments may be useful in spurring high educational expectations and motivations but less helpful in helping students actually get through all of the hurdles to attain or succeed their educational goals. Unsurprisingly, the most consistent indicators of educational mobility across starting point, life course stage, gender, and generational status are grades and test scores.

Non-English Ability Assimilation

Portes and Rumbaut (2001a) suggest that children of immigrants experience a form of "forced-march acculturation," whereby they are forced into English monolingualism and lose their languages of origin. They associate this language loss with problems for youths as they lose their connection to the co-ethnics in their community and also, more importantly, possibly lose the ability to communicate with their own parents. However, inclusion of the life course perspective in the examination of non-English ability assimilation reveals an increase in anti-classical assimilation from adolescence to emerging adulthood. While stability of non-English ability is most common during adolescence and the transition to emerging adulthood, the anti-classical path is more common than the classical trajectory. While it is likely that language loss still occurs over the long term—particularly intergenerational, as many researchers have found (Alba et al. 2002; Veltman 1988; Portes and Hao 2002), these results suggest that, at youthful stages in the life course, rapid native language loss is not the most common path of assimilation and is, to some extent, reversible.

While starting point is highly associated with possible paths of linguistic assimilation, gender generally is not. The one exception, among high non-English ability youths, provides support for researchers' claims that females have stronger ethnic connections than males. However, this finding is only statistically significant during adolescence. Girls may be more tied to their homes and families than boys as adolescents, where they are better able to maintain their non-English language skills; however, as they enter into young adulthood, these connections may be disrupted more equally, regardless of gender.

Demographic factors are important predictors of non-English ability linguistic assimilation. Spanish speakers, particularly those who live with a large co-ethnic population, are more likely to maintain or increase their Spanish ability over time than others. These results hold quite consistently across starting point, life course stage, and gender. Youths with greater opportunities to practice their language skills are more likely to be able to maintain or improve them. The Spanish language population, particularly in the Miami and San Diego areas, provides many opportunities for youths to practice their language skills. Furthermore, there are more common outlets for the Spanish language in the United States than other non-English languages. There are multiple television networks in Spanish, as well as numerous radio stations and newspapers. These resources can help Spanish speakers maintain or improve their abilities. Individuals of other language backgrounds lack such a wide variety of supports for their native languages.

Of the family status variables, there is no clear pattern of association. Some socioeconomic status variables are associated with higher odds of classical assimilation. Others are associated with higher odds of anti-classical assimilation. On the one hand, parents with economic resources, then, may be able to support their children's cultural connections by providing them additional language instruction or sending them to their countries of origin for language improvement. On the other hand, parents with fewer resources, while unable to provide the aforementioned accommodations, may have more limited social spheres, which provide greater support for native language

maintenance and even improvement. These results conflict somewhat
with Portes and Rumbaut's (2001a) findings that higher parental
socioeconomic status is associated with higher levels of non-English
ability, specifically, fluent bilingualism.

Associations between linguistic assimilation paths and downward
leveling and protective factors are generally more predictable.
Segmented assimilation theory suggests that downward leveling factors
will lead to native language loss while more positive factors will lead to
language maintenance. Accordingly, I find that negative racial
views/experiences in the United States (especially for females with
intermediate non-English skills) and greater school poverty (among
intermediate ability youths during adolescence only) are associated
with more classical forms of assimilation. Youths with negative racial
views or experiences in the United States may be more incorporated
into native minority cultures and, therefore, lose their languages of
origin. The school poverty finding is more puzzling. Poor schools
generally have fewer resources to promote English ability, but youths'
non-English ability may not be replaced by English skills. Poor
schools may have detrimental effects on youths' language skills across
the board. Poor schools are likely to have few resources to support
language ability of any kind.

In contrast, the proportion of Latino and black students in schools
is associated with higher odds of anti-classical assimilation, except
among youths with very good non-English skills. The proportion of
Latino students in a school is likely to support greater non-English
retention because it provides more opportunities for youths to speak a
non-English language (Portes and Rumbaut 2001a). It may also be
associated with an environment that is friendlier towards, and therefore
more conducive to, non-English languages. The proportion of black
students is also associated with anti-classical forms of assimilation.
This finding is unexpected, as segmented assimilation theory suggests
that native black minorities put children of immigrants at risk of
downward assimilation rather than greater cultural retention. One
possible explanation is that children of immigrants may react to larger
proportions of black students in their schools with fear. They may
enclose their ethnic circles more tightly by holding onto or improving
their non-English language skills to draw a stronger line between
themselves and blacks.

There are more consistent associations between protective factors
and language assimilation. First, I find, predictably, that stronger

homeland cultural connections and more negative views of American society are associated with higher odds of maintaining or increasing one's non-English skills during both adolescence and the longer emerging adulthood period, regardless of gender. Cultural values and characteristics thus appear to be supportive of one another. Second, I find that grades are associated with non-English maintenance and improvement among youths who have intermediate language skills in eighth grade, particularly females. Grades may provide some indication of cognitive skills (although test scores, which are not statistically significant, are generally considered a better indicator of cognitive skills). Youths with better grades may have the cognitive skills necessary to enable them to retain or improve their language skills. Moreover, youths with better grades may be more willing and able to put in the effort to maintain or increase their non-English language ability. Grades may, then, represent aptitude as well as attitude toward putting the effort into one's language skills.

English Language Use Assimilation

English language use assimilation follows the pattern that classical assimilation theory predicts and assimilation research has found (Portes and Rumbaut 2001a; Alba et al. 2002; Veltman 1990; Stevens 1985, 1992). Although most youths who do not use English only with their friends in eighth grade continue to do so in twelfth grade and in their mid-twenties, more youths experience classical assimilation from eighth grade to their mid-twenties than during adolescence alone. This outcome indicates a (perhaps slow but) straight-line path towards greater English use among children of immigrants, regardless of gender. Among youths who use English only with their friends in eighth grade, few experience anti-classical assimilation. According to the full multivariate model, boys are actually more likely to experience anti-classical assimilation than girls. This finding holds in adolescence only and contradicts predictions of Portes and Rumbaut (2001a) and others suggesting that females have greater cultural attachments than males.

I find that members of Spanish-speaking groups, particularly groups represented in large numbers in the two metropolitan areas under study, have lower odds of classical assimilation across both life stages. English language use assimilation is dependent on youths' language abilities. A minimum level of English language skills is necessary for English use with friends. Conversely, youths who do not use English mostly with their friends must have some minimum capabilities in another language. Level of English use also depends on youths' friends' language skills. As I discussed above, Spanish ability is propped by Spanish-language media outlets and greater opportunities to practice Spanish skills. Moreover, Spanish-speaking youths are likely to have many opportunities for Spanish use because of the sizes of their groups and because the Spanish language is common to other groups as well.

Spanish-speaking youths also have higher odds of anti-classical assimilation, although this association is statistically significant in adolescence only. The immigrant generation is likely to live near other immigrant co-ethnics; therefore, the pools from which children of Spanish-speaking immigrants choose friends in adolescence, both in schools and in their neighborhoods, are likely to involve many other Spanish speakers. However, when these youths enter into the emerging adulthood period and leave their parents' homes, their potential friends may come from more diverse backgrounds with fewer Spanish speakers, thereby limiting their opportunities for Spanish use.

Filipinos, conversely, have higher odds of classical assimilation than "other" immigrants. Filipinos typically arrive in the United States with good English skills. Moreover, there are not large numbers of individuals in the United States who speak Tagalog and other languages native to the Philippines. Filipino children of immigrants, then, may be lacking in non-English skills and have few opportunities to use them.

Associations between parental and family socioeconomic status variables and English use assimilation are also likely to be related to opportunities for non-English use. Higher socioeconomic status is associated with higher odds of classical assimilation and lower odds of anti-classical assimilation. These associations hold especially for boys. Higher socioeconomic status families are more likely to live outside of immigrant neighborhoods (Alba et al. 1999). Therefore, youths' possible friendship pools, both in their neighborhoods and at school, are likely to include fewer individuals of the same native language backgrounds. This finding may not hold as strongly for girls because of their closer connections to their homes and families. More of girls' friends may come from their families or extended family connections, thereby increasing the likelihood that they also speak the same non-English language. Furthermore, girls may spend more time with their friends in their homes or with their families. These closer home and family connections may raise girls' odds of speaking a non-English language with their friends regardless of their families' economic circumstances.

Of the downward leveling factors, proportion of students in school who are Latino is, unsurprisingly, most consistently associated with linguistic assimilation. As the proportion of Latino students increases, the odds of classical assimilation decrease and the odds of anti-classical assimilation increase. These associations, however, hold only over the longer emerging adulthood period and not the shorter adolescent one. Changes in living arrangements over these time periods may help explain this association. Almost all youths live with their parents in adolescence. Immigrant parents are likely to live alongside other co-ethnics; therefore, their children have more opportunities to make co-ethnic friends who also speak the same language. Proportions of minority students, then, may not have as much of an effect when most youth have many opportunities to make friends who share a similar native language. As youths enter emerging adulthood and leave their parents' homes, they are more likely to move away from their immigrant neighborhoods. However, their school environment may have something of a carry-over effect in their lives, affecting values and attitudes towards language use or the composition of their friendship networks later in life.

The other two downward leveling factors, inner city school and views of racial problems in the United States, are associated with higher odds of classical and lower odds of anti-classical English use assimilation. These findings support claims of segmented assimilation theory suggesting that greater connections to poor, inner city minorities and their cultural values are likely to lead to diminished attachment to immigrants' home culture (Portes and Rumbaut 2001a).

Finally, of the protective factors, measures of cultural attachment, including language ability, language use, and friends' ethnic backgrounds, are most consistently predictive of linguistic assimilation paths. However, parent-child preferences for American ways are statistically significantly associated with English use assimilation for girls only. Girls who, along with their parents, do not prefer American ways in eighth grade have higher odds of anti-classical assimilation than girls who share preferences for American ways with their parents. Again, these findings support researchers' claims that girls' stronger ties to their homes and families promote stronger cultural connections in them.

Identificational Assimilation

Children of immigrants experience every possible form of identificational assimilation. The results of this analysis reveal that the likelihood of these paths and the characteristics associated with them differ by starting point, gender, and life course stage.[12] In their book, *Legacies*, Portes and Rumbaut (2001a) claim that identificational assimilation among CILS respondents from eighth to twelfth grade "has not been toward mainstream identities but toward a more militant reaffirmation of the immigrant identity for some groups (notably Mexicans and Filipinos in California and Haitians and Nicaraguans in Florida) and toward pan-ethnic minority-group identities for others" (157). I find similarly that anti-classical paths of assimilation are more common than classical paths during both adolescence and the transition to emerging adulthood. Identities with obvious connections to national origin, particularly hyphenated identities, are very common over the entire time period, as Portes and Rumbaut (2001a) suggest.

However, the most common path of identificational assimilation in both periods is a stable one. Moreover, the life course approach provides a somewhat different view of identificational assimilation among children of immigrants in the long-term. Overall, anti-classical forms of assimilation are statistically significantly less common and classical forms of assimilation are more common over the longer emerging adulthood period than during adolescence alone. In other words, the longer period provides less evidence for Portes and Rumbaut's (2001a) claims than the shorter time span. The increase in classical assimilation from adolescence to emerging adulthood suggests that assimilation, in many cases, does not involve a straight line march into the (white) middle class or mainstream. Instead, it may involve a more bumpy-line pattern (Gans 1992) in which longer term outcomes reveal classical assimilation trends but shorter term outcomes may not, providing support for Vermeulen's (2010) contentions that researchers consider life course trajectories. Intragenerational analysis over a longer time frame still is necessary to determine if the pattern continues in a bumpy fashion or trends towards more classical assimilation outcomes.

Lower rates of anti-classical assimilation over the longer emerging adulthood period than during adolescence may be due to period effects. For example, as Portes and Rumbaut (2001a) suggest, children of immigrants might have reacted to the passing of Proposition 187 in California in 1994 by reclaiming their ethnic immigrant identities. During the period between the second and third survey follow-ups, the U.S. District Court ruled the law to be unconstitutional. Perhaps children of immigrants felt more welcomed by the country and more willing to take on more American identities with the overturning of this anti-immigrant law.

Theorists (Erikson 1950, 1968; Arnett 2000, 2004) suggest that adolescence and emerging adulthood are particularly important times of identity development. Arnett (2000, 2004) argues that identities are consolidated during the emerging adulthood years. Perhaps for this reason, we see bumps in the path. Youths may just be trying out identities during adolescence and may continue to do so until they reach young adulthood. Moreover, as youths move away from their homes, they may be less likely to subscribe to identities tied closely to their parents. Greater interactions with those outside of their families and ethnic groups may lead to lower likelihoods of anti-classical assimilation.

Along with the association with life course stage, the distributions of paths of assimilation are highly related to starting point. As I noted above, hyphenated identities are very common in adolescence and emerging adulthood. Therefore, paths that lead to this identity are quite common. In contrast, I find few differences by gender. Portes and Rumbaut's (2001a) and others' suggestions that females are more connected to their cultures of origin than males certainly do not play out in terms of ethnic identity.

Segmented assimilation theory implies that linear and racialized paths of assimilation are likely to have more negative consequences for youths' lives than resurgent ones. Portes, Rumbaut, and Zhou (Portes and Zhou 1993; Portes 1995; Zhou 1997; Portes and Rumbaut 2001a; Portes and Rumbaut 2001b) associate linear and racialized paths with the loss of protective cultural attachments. At worst, segmented assimilation theorists link the racialized path to acculturation into the underclass. At best, they relate racialized assimilation with membership in stigmatized groups and make no reference to possible positive associations, such as involvement in minority cultures of mobility (Neckerman, Carter, and Lee 1999). My analyses reveal mixed support for these claims. I find that some, downward leveling factors, particularly minority and poverty school composition, are associated with higher odds of linear or racialized vs. resurgent assimilation, but only during adolescence for youths who have hyphenated identities in eighth grade. In contrast, for youths with hyphenated identities, attending an inner city school is actually associated with lower odds of linear or racialized assimilation. Furthermore, while cultural attachments tend to promote non-linear/non-racialized paths of identificational assimilation, other protective factors are not consistently associated with lower odds of racialized or linear assimilation. These paths do not seem to hold the negative associations that segmented assimilation theory suggests nor do racial/pan-ethnic or more American identities have consistently negative associations with intragenerational educational mobility.

Like Portes and Rumbaut (2001a), I find that Cubans, Mexicans, and West Indians have consistently lower odds of classical forms of assimilation than "other" immigrants. Filipinos, Southeast Asians, and Nicaraguans also follow a similar pattern. This lack of classical identificational assimilation may mean different things for members of these different ethnic groups. Cuban origin youths in the CILS data reside in Miami (or at least did so during the first wave of data collection). They are part of a large and successful ethnic community for whom their Cuban identities shape significant portions of their lives. It may be easier for these children of immigrants to maintain or affirm their and their parents' connections to a more specifically Cuban or Cuban American identity under these conditions.

Mexican origin youths in the CILS data resided almost exclusively in San Diego in the first wave of data collection. Like the Cubans, this group has a very large ethnic presence in its community, although Mexicans have not experienced the entrepreneurial successes and lack the political clout of individuals of Cuban origin. Mexican cultural attachments and connections are also likely to shape Mexicans' daily experiences, making them more likely to espouse some form of a Mexican identity. Massey (2009) and Rumbaut (2009)[13] also suggest that the Mexican identity itself has become increasingly racialized. Children of Mexican immigrants may have low odds of racialized assimilation, as it is measured by acceptance of a pan-ethnic identity such as Latino or Hispanic; nonetheless, they may experience racialized assimilation (and its effects) because their national origin and hyphenated identities already place them in a (newly) racialized category. Further research can help shed light on the extent to which Mexican identities are lived as racialized identities.

While it appears that Mexicans have very few options but to accept their racialized national origin identities in some form, West Indians appear to hold on to the ethnic options that they, as children of immigrants, have. Children of West Indian immigrants have higher odds of maintaining or asserting national origin and hyphenated identities over time. These patterns may be part of a strategy of distancing themselves from the native black population and the stereotypes and prejudices associated with them (see, for example, Waters 1999).

The lack of classical assimilation among all of these groups, including Filipinos, Southeast Asians, and Nicaraguans, can be explained in part due to the group against which they are compared. The omitted category, composed primarily of Canadians, Europeans and Latino and Asian groups lacking in sufficient numbers to be adequately represented separately in the analysis, influences these outcomes. With their ethnic, cultural, and (likely) racial similarities to the white middle class in the United States, Canadian and European immigrants may more rapidly take on more assimilated identities than other groups. In the case of the smaller Latino and Asian groups, they may not have been represented in large enough numbers to maintain their own national origin identities. Instead, they may have more rapidly experienced classical assimilation by taking on pan-ethnic identities. These pan-ethnic identities may allow smaller immigrant groups to express their cultural attachments to some extent. It is also likely that these group members, because of their racial and cultural differences, feel separate from mainstream American society and therefore take on these more recognizable pan-ethnic identities rather than holding on to their national origin ones.

Members of smaller ethnic groups, then, may be less likely to experience resurgent assimilation. Smaller immigrant groups have fewer opportunities to speak their languages and fewer co-ethnics with whom they can practice their customs in the United States. Therefore, they may have fewer opportunities to renew their ethnic attachments. Furthermore, when responding to a survey question on ethnic identity, individuals may be less likely to define themselves by a group identity that is uncommon. They may consider their identity too unusual to be considered a possible response option for the survey. In this case, youths may take on a more common identity—whether plain American or racial/pan-ethnic—that places them in a larger group.

By neglecting to examine intragenerational paths of assimilation and experiences of assimilation by life course stage, gender, and generational status, segmented assimilation researchers do not have a full picture of immigrants' incorporation experiences. Overall, I find that youths experience every possible path of mobility and assimilation. Paths, and their distributions, are dependent upon individuals' starting points. Life course stage, gender, and generational status are all associated with direction of assimilation. Furthermore, there are differences in associations between assimilation trajectories and demographic, downward leveling, and protective factors by starting point, life course stage, gender, and generational status.

Segmented assimilation theory claims, in contrast to classical assimilation theory, that immigrants experience different paths of assimilation, incorporating into different segments of American society. It does not, however, suggest that outcomes themselves vary at different stages in individuals' lives. Conversely, I find that, for individuals in the study, patterns of assimilation vary with stages in the life course. Life course effects differ by the indicator under study. Educational mobility, for example, is more positive in adolescence than emerging adulthood. In contrast, non-English ability assimilation is more anti-classical over the longer emerging adulthood period than during adolescence. Further, for identificational assimilation, I find some evidence of bumpy line assimilation (Gans 1992), a form of assimilation that segmented assimilation theory neglects. There are also some consistent gender differences. In accordance with recent research, females have more positive educational mobility outcomes than males, for example. Also, girls appear to have stronger ties to their homes and families that play out in terms of stronger cultural connections overall. This finding is in line with segmented assimilation theory's claims, although they have rarely been sufficiently examined.

Generational status outcomes generally follow the predictions of segmented assimilation theory. Children of immigrants have more positive educational mobility outcomes than the NELS respondents, who are dominated by third and later generation youths. Of course, these outcomes do not indicate that the grandchildren of immigrants generally will follow a downward trajectory. The intergenerational analysis speaks to that claim. Instead, the intragenerational results reveal that children of immigrants are generally more likely to experience positive educational mobility than (primarily) third and later generation youths in the NELS data, who are largely white. Downward economic assimilation, then, is less common among children of immigrants than among the general U.S. population. This result begs the question of whether it is fair to discuss "downward mobility" as specific to immigrants' assimilation experiences when it is common among non-immigrants as well.

Finally, findings regarding ethnic origin provide mixed support for segmented assimilation theory's claims. My examination of cultural assimilation generally shows that Spanish-speaking groups, particularly Mexicans and Cubans, have stronger cultural attachments than "other" immigrants. This outcome is expected in terms of language assimilation. However, for identificational assimilation, segmented assimilation theory suggests that Mexicans, along with West Indians, have a large (poor) native minority population into which they can incorporate. These groups, then, should be more likely to take on racialized identities. However, results generally show that these groups are more likely to hold on to hyphenated or national origin identities than others and, in some cases, may even experience resurgent identificational assimilation.

There are some unexpected associations between educational mobility and ethnic origin as well. First, Mexicans as a whole do not have higher odds of negative mobility than the reference groups in CILS and NELS, although segmented assimilation theory argues that the large, poor third and later generation Mexican population in the United States places Mexicans at great risk for downward mobility (into the underclass). This prediction of downward mobility only holds for Mexican girls with college expectations. In this case, downward mobility would have to be quite drastic for these girls to experience the kind of downward mobility that is associated with the underclass. Second, in the NELS data, (primarily third and later generation) blacks with intermediate educational expectations, regardless of gender, and black girls with college expectations have more positive educational mobility than (primarily third and later generation) whites, after controlling for other factors. Segmented assimilation theory generally focuses on negative repercussions for immigrants attending schools or living in neighborhoods with third and later generation blacks, whom they assume to be poor. My results suggest that segmented assimilation theory fails to take into account blacks' positive influences, including, as Neckerman, Carter, and Lee (1999) propose, their minority cultures of mobility.

NOTES

[1] Of course, immigrants who come from countries in which English is the only language are not likely to begin using another language; however, many immigrants from countries where English is predominant also have some exposure to non-English languages in their home countries that, under some circumstances, they possibly use more often in the United States over time.

[2] As is the case in the intergenerational analysis, factor analyses of all scale items suggest that the scales represent the same underlying concept. For this scale, the alpha is .59.

[3] The alpha for this scale is .58.

[4] I do not use one scale for all of these items because factor analysis suggests that the items measure two underlying factors.

[5] The alphas for these scales are .79 and .90, respectively.

[6] I do not include these measures in one scale because factor analysis suggests that they represent two different underlying concepts. The alphas of the scales are .70 and .56, respectively.

[7] The alphas for these scales are .75 and .41, respectively.

[8] The alphas for these scales are .72, .50, and .74, respectively.

[9] The NELS coders use a five point scale from .5, indicating mostly below D, to 4 indicating mostly As.

[10] I present data from just one of the imputed data sets in the descriptive tables.

[11] Data limitations do not allow me to examine these youths by gender; therefore, I cannot speak to gender differences or similarities.

[12] As I discussed above, there are not enough cases to analyze paths of identificational assimilation multivariately by gender.

[13] Rumbaut (2009) argues that, along with the categories of Hispanic and Latino, all Latin American national origin identities are being racialized.

CHAPTER 4

Conclusion: Where the Paths Lead

The United States has always been a nation of immigrants. Currently, the proportion of the U.S. population that is of immigrant origin is close to its historical high, and the number of immigrants in the country is currently larger than at any previous time in history (Fix and Passel 2003). Taking into account immigrants' offspring reveals an even larger impact of immigration on the American population: almost a quarter of the U.S. population is made up of first and second generation immigrants (Portes and Fernández-Kelly 2008). As Portes and colleagues observe, it is unlikely that today's immigrants and their offspring, with their incredibly diverse ethnic and socioeconomic backgrounds, will follow the same trajectory of integration into U.S. society as previous waves of European immigrants. Segmented assimilation theory therefore proposes several alternative paths of immigrant incorporation.

This book examines these paths, as well as the factors associated with them, inter- and intragenerationally. This analysis focuses on starting point, gender, parental immigration status, and, in the case of intragenerational paths, life course stage to explore the multiplicity of incorporation experiences among children of immigrants. Segmented assimilation theory presents the assimilation experiences of the "new" immigration as varied but focuses on three paths: (1) an upward economic trajectory coupled with acculturation into middle-class forms; (2) a downward economic and cultural trajectory involving acculturation away from one's ethnic group of origin towards the cultural attributes of poor, inner-city minorities (and, more recently, the marginal working class); and (3) a more positive economic trajectory

173

associated with cultural retention. Previous segmented assimilation research has not explored a number of the possible variations in assimilation paths, including across the life course of individuals. Moreover, though the framework pays lip service to the importance of gender and starting points for shaping incorporation experiences, empirical research from these perspectives has been lacking. Finally, segmented assimilation researchers have either failed to include third and later generation youths for comparison or have incorrectly inferred intergenerational change from these comparisons. I found that paths of mobility and assimilation and the factors associated with them differed by starting point, gender, parental immigration status, and life course stage. The patterns of associations were very complicated; therefore, it is difficult to tell a coherent story from the varied associations. Below, I discuss how my results support my six criticisms of segmented assimilation theory and their implications for the theory.

First, as I stated in the introduction, segmented assimilation theory conflates pathways, trajectories of change, and segments, outcomes of assimilation or mobility. In this book, I focused on pathways of assimilation, examining the extent to which children of immigrants and other young adults experienced upward, stable, and downward patterns of economic mobility and classical, stable, and anti-classical paths of cultural assimilation. Regarding economic mobility, my results, as I discuss below, suggest that the downward path of mobility, upon which so much of segmented assimilation theory's attention has focused, is not all that common, although paths differed by the kind of mobility under examination (inter- vs. intra-generational), educational and occupational starting points, parental immigration status, and, to some extent, gender.

Turning to cultural factors, segmented assimilation theory refers to pathways of cultural assimilation but defines these pathways primarily by their endpoints: the (white) middle class and the underclass. However, many indicators of acculturation do not fall on a spectrum from underclass to middle class. Levels of language ability and use and ethnic identity, for example, are not linked specifically to either middle-class or underclass cultural forms. When considering immigrant acculturation, it makes more sense to envision the cultural spectrum from the immigrant's cultural origins[1] to more American cultural forms (whether or not one considers these forms to be middle class or underclass). I, then, defined pathways of acculturation differently, in relation to predictions of classical assimilation theory, as the following: (1) classical (taking on more American cultural characteristics), (2) stable, or (3) anti-classical (moving away from more American cultural characteristics towards more national origin cultural forms).

Second, I critiqued segmented assimilation theory for its lack of intergenerational focus. In chapter two, my results revealed that an intergenerational focus provided a much less negative view of children of immigrants' incorporation experiences than segmented assimilation theory suggests. Few youths experienced downward economic mobility, both educational and occupational, although the proportion of youths who did differed by their parents' educational and occupational status. Intergenerational mobility paths also differed by indicator of mobility: downward educational mobility was less common than downward occupational mobility. This result was due in part to the age of the sample. Because youths were in their mid-twenties by the time of the final data collection, many had reached their highest educational levels but far fewer had reached their highest occupational levels; therefore, occupational mobility experiences were generally more negative than educational mobility. Similarly, children of immigrants, who were younger on average than the third and later generation NELS respondents, had more negative intergenerational occupational mobility experiences than third and later generation youths. Children of immigrants, on the other hand, had statistically significantly better intergenerational educational mobility outcomes than third and later generation youths. In addition to age effects, differences in parental immigration status, which I will discuss more below, may explain this result.

Like economic mobility, the paths of intergenerational cultural assimilation differed greatly by the indicator under consideration. Classical intergenerational linguistic assimilation was very common among children of immigrants, while few experienced anti-classical assimilation. In contrast, anti-classical intergenerational identificational paths were much more common. These results suggest that the extent to which children of immigrants experience paths of mobility and assimilation in opposition to the claims of classical assimilation theory depends on the particular indicator of mobility or assimilation under consideration. Overall, children of immigrants and later generation youths do not seem to be falling behind their parents economically, including members of racial-ethnic groups for whom segmented assimilation theory predicts the most negative outcomes, and many follow classical paths of cultural assimilation, as well, particularly regarding language.

Third, segmented assimilation theory also fails to fully examine how starting points condition youths' mobility and acculturation experiences. I found that parents' and youths' initial economic and cultural characteristics were of the utmost importance for understanding their paths of assimilation and the characteristics influencing them. The paths that individuals can follow and the meanings of these paths depend upon their starting points. Youths from lower economic starting points were more likely to experience upward inter- and intragenerational mobility than other youths, while those from high economic starting points were more likely to experience downward mobility. Similarly, youths from less classically acculturated starting points were more likely to experience classical assimilation than youths who started off at a more "American" level of a particular cultural characteristic. Further research is required to examine what exactly are the lived experiences of these changes and where these paths will lead later in individuals' lives.

Some characteristics were consistently associated with paths of mobility and acculturation regardless of starting point. Among the demographic characteristics, higher parental economic status measures were consistently associated with more positive forms of inter- and intragenerational educational and occupational mobility. Some ethnic groups, particularly Cubans and Mexicans, appeared to have consistently lower odds of racialized and higher odds of resurgent inter- and intragenerational assimilation than "other" immigrants, regardless of starting point. Cubans and Mexicans also had lower odds of classical and higher odds of anti-classical intragenerational linguistic assimilation than "other" immigrants, regardless of their initial non-English ability and level of English use.

Of the downward leveling factors, having dropout friends was quite consistently associated with more negative intergenerational educational mobility patterns, regardless of parents' initial educational status. There was little consistency in the associations between downward leveling factors and cultural assimilation, however, except that having a larger proportion of Latino students in a school was associated with higher odds of anti-classical intragenerational English use assimilation.

Several protective factors were consistently associated with inter- and intragenerational mobility across different starting points. Most of these variables were related to school involvement or attitudes towards education, such as having friends with college plans, parent involvement in school, educational expectations, grades, and test scores. Parents' connections to youths' friends were also consistently associated with more positive intergenerational educational and occupational mobility. The following measures of cultural attachment were consistent predictors of intragenerational, but not intergenerational, assimilation across different starting points: the importance of relatives, language ability and use, the number of friends from abroad, and parent-child preferences for American ways.

While there was some consistency, I found a number of differences in associations across the different starting points. First, there were differences in associations between ethnic group and economic mobility patterns by starting points. For example, NELS Asians and CILS Southeast Asians had higher odds of more positive educational mobility than their respective reference groups from intermediate parental educational status starting points, while Filipinos with high educational status parents had higher odds of downward mobility. Second, there were differences in association between downward leveling factors and paths of mobility and assimilations by starting point. For example, school poverty was only associated with more negative intragenerational educational mobility in emerging adulthood among youths who had high educational expectations in eighth grade.

I found some inconsistencies for the protective factors, as well. Talking to parents was only protective of educational mobility for those youths with intermediate status parents, while neighborhood social capital and the importance of relatives were associated with more negative educational and occupational mobility among these youths. Of the twelve protective factors associated with paths of intragenerational educational mobility, only two (grades and test scores) were statistically significant for both youths who had intermediate expectations and those who had high educational expectations in eighth grade. While parent and youth cultural attachments were important for predicting inter- and intragenerational cultural assimilation, the exact measures associated with these paths of assimilation differed in most cases by the various linguistic and ethnic identity starting points.

Fourth, segmented assimilation theory also glosses over how incorporation experiences differ by gender. I found that gender was not statistically significantly associated with intragenerational educational mobility paths; however, it was associated with intergenerational mobility trajectories. Females had more positive educational mobility and more negative occupational mobility patterns than males. These findings are in line with previous research suggesting that women face more occupational than educational constraints. In contrast, inter- and intragenerational linguistic and intergenerational identificational assimilation paths did not differ statistically significantly by gender, and there were few statistically significant gender differences in terms of intragenerational identificational assimilation. These findings were somewhat unexpected, given that many scholars argue that females have greater cultural attachments than males (Portes and Rumbaut 2001a; Billson 1995; Waters 1996; Das Gupta 1997; Valenzuela 1999; Dion and Dion 2001; Espiritu 1999; Ginorio and Huston 2001; Williams et al. 2002; Suárez-Orozco and Qin 2006). Future research is required to tease out how acculturation may (or may not) differ by gender.

I found some gender similarities in the associations between paths of mobility and assimilation and my predictor variables. Parent economic status and family structure, again, were quite consistent predictors of educational mobility paths for both genders. There were some gender consistencies in associations between ethnic group and intragenerational linguistic assimilation paths. Having dropout friends had negative associations with intergenerational educational mobility for both young men and women. There were some consistent school composition associations with linguistic assimilation, also. A number of parent and friend characteristics were quite consistently protective of economic mobility for young men and women, while youths' own educational characteristics were associated with more positive mobility outcomes.

There were many cases, however, in which predictor variables were only statistically significant for one gender. For example, in many cases, associations between a particular ethnic origin group and mobility and assimilation held only for one gender. Only West Indian and Southeast Asian daughters of immigrants had higher odds of more positive intergenerational educational mobility from intermediate parental status than "other" daughters of immigrants. This finding suggests that incorporation experiences—particularly economic mobility—can differ substantially by gender, even within a particular ethnic group.

There were marked gender differences in the associations between downward leveling factors and inter- and intragenerational economic mobility. These differences largely reside among third and later generation youths because data limitations precluded examining children of immigrants separately by gender in some cases. These results reveal that, apart from the negative influence of dropout friends on young women's intergenerational educational success, downward leveling factors more often had statistically significant effects on young men's inter- and intragenerational economic mobility. As I discussed above, these findings can be best understood through a "doing gender" lens (West and Zimmerman 1987). Young men attempting to fit normative conceptions of masculinity may respond to challenges against them, take risks, and engage in other behaviors that are likely to lead to some kinds of disciplinary (and even legal) consequences, which may disrupt their educational and occupational successes (see for example, Kimmel and Mahler 2003). These same negative consequences do not hold for young women whose normative feminine performances may be more rewarded in schools (Burke 1989; Kimmel 2004). Overall, however, issues of masculinity and femininity play out differently in the arenas of school and work. While performances of femininity are more greatly rewarded in the school setting, work has largely been defined as a masculine enterprise (Acker 1990), and men's lesser educational successes have not translated into occupational disadvantages.

There were also some gender differences in associations between downward leveling factors and cultural assimilation. For example, the more youths believed there were racial problems in the United States, the higher the odds of classical-type patterns of non-English ability assimilation for females only, while having a larger proportion of black students in a school was associated with less classical patterns of non-English ability assimilation for males alone. Characteristics that segmented assimilation theory suggests are related to an adversarial subculture, then, may differ by gender. Males seemed to respond to large numbers of blacks in their schools by distancing themselves from the native minority group linguistically; while females' views that there were racial problems in the United States made them more likely to acculturate into mainstream language patterns. As Waters (1999) points out in her study of West Indian immigrants, West Indian young men often face worse, or at least more overt, discrimination than West Indian young women. Perhaps young immigrant men, then, are more motivated to distance themselves from native-born blacks in school than young women.

Finally, there were gender differences in associations with protective factors, as well. Some parent characteristics and activities were better predictors (more often statistically significant) of both inter- and intragenerational economic mobility for young women than young men. There was even evidence, in the case of intragenerational educational mobility from intermediate educational expectations in emerging adulthood, that parent characteristics, particularly strictness, functioned differently by gender. Parental strictness was associated with upward mobility for males and downward mobility for females. For young men, parents' strictness may indicate greater watchfulness, helping them attain and surpass their educational expectations, without limiting their successes. In the case of young women, parental strictness may restrict or constrain them so much that they are unable to attain their educational expectations. There were also some differences in the associations between protective factors and cultural assimilation by gender. Non-English use at home was a more important predictor of various forms of inter- and intragenerational linguistic assimilation for young women than young men. This finding suggests that cultural attachments in the home are important for influencing cultural attachments overall for young women but not young men. The overall results suggest that young men and young women experience incorporation differently. The nuances of these gendered experiences would be completely lost without performing separate analyses for males and females.

Fifth, along with its failure to fully incorporate gender, most segmented assimilation research also fails to incorporate data on U.S.-born individuals of U.S-born parents. In this book, I was able to compare economic mobility among children of immigrants to this group. Children of immigrants typically had more positive inter- and intragenerational educational but less positive intergenerational occupational trajectories than third and later generation youths. The educational results provided some support for the immigrant optimism hypothesis, which suggests that immigrant parents' selectivity and motivation help spur their children to greater success than children of non-immigrant parents. They also provide some support for segmented assimilation theory's claim that less assimilated youths will have more positive outcomes than more assimilated youths. However, the occupational results revealed that children of immigrants might have a more difficult time overcoming market constraints and making up for their parents' greater lack of connections and information about the labor market than third and later generation youths.

Third and later generation whites, the implicitly (and sometimes explicitly) understood mainstream group that supposedly marks the end result of assimilation and complete incorporation into American society, comprise the majority of the third and later generation group. My results suggest that even the (apparently) most assimilated group in the United States does not experience the level of inter- and intragenerational economic mobility as children of immigrants. Bivariate analyses comparing white third and later generation youths to children of immigrants bear out these results in terms of intergenerational educational and occupational and intragenerational educational mobility. The only exception is that there is no statistically significant difference between children of immigrants and third and later generation whites in terms of achieving their college expectations. These findings lead me to return to the question that many (segmented) assimilation researchers have asked, "Assimilation to what?" When the children of immigrants experience more positive mobility outcomes than the dominant group in the native-born population, we must consider whether the term "assimilation," at least in the economic sense, is a valid one.

Of course, within both children of immigrants and the third and later generation, not all racial-ethnic groups have the same experiences. The statistically significant results for individuals of Mexican origin support segmented assimilation theorists' and others' (Telles and Ortiz 2008) assertions that this group faces more challenges to economic advancement than other groups. However, these negative consequences were actually much more limited than segmented assimilation theory claims. They were limited to certain starting points, gender, and life course contexts. Also unexpected, consequences were not more negative (or less positive) for third and later generation Mexicans than their first and second generation counterparts.

Similarly I found evidence that third and later generation blacks had statistically significantly higher odds of positive intragenerational educational mobility outcomes than whites more often than West Indians did compared with "other" children of immigrants. These results suggest that native-born blacks are not models of negative mobility to immigrants, as segmented assimilation theory posits.

Instead, in some cases, their trajectories of mobility are even better than whites.

Although there were many differences between the two data sets in the downward leveling and protective factor variables, when there were equivalent variables, a few differences stood out between children of immigrants and the general population. For example, school poverty was only associated with more negative forms of mobility among third and later generation NELS youths (with high educational expectations in emerging adulthood). It is possible that the CILS youths had some protective factors that made up for the effects of school poverty that NELS youths lacked. Of the protective factors, parental involvement at school was associated with more positive mobility outcomes for NELS youths only. Perhaps immigrant parents, even when they are involved in their children's schools, lack the resources, information, or understanding of the U.S. school system to translate that involvement into more positive mobility outcomes for their children. I also might have had more similar results if I were able to control for the exact same characteristics in NELS and CILS. Nevertheless, this examination provided some basic comparison of mobility experiences of children of immigrants and later generation youths.

Sixth, segmented assimilation theory and research do not include a life course perspective. I focused on differences in mobility and assimilation paths in adolescence and the longer emerging adulthood period, which encompassed adolescence and early young adulthood. Positive forms of educational mobility were more common during adolescence than during the longer transition to emerging adulthood period in large part because adolescence involved only shifts in educational expectations while emerging adulthood involved attainment of expectations (or lack thereof). For non-English ability assimilation, the anti-classical path was more common over the longer period than the shorter adolescent period for both boys and girls. For English use assimilation, the opposite was the case: classical assimilation was more common during emerging adulthood than adolescence. The English use findings were in line with previous research, but the non-English ability results were more unexpected. Perhaps previous research has overstated language loss by not examining language ability over various stages in the life course. It is also possible that the period from twelfth grade to the mid-twenties is a time of linguistic ethnic renewal for many youths, who can join social groups based on their ethnic origin and take classes on their native language in college.

Patterns of identificational assimilation also differed across the life course. Youths with hyphenated identities in eighth grade were statistically significantly more likely to experience resurgent assimilation in adolescence than in emerging adulthood. In contrast, the stable path was statistically significantly more common among this group in emerging adulthood than adolescence. Among youths with national origin identities, the stable path was statistically significantly more common in adolescence than emerging adulthood while the linear path was more common in emerging adulthood than adolescence. These results suggest that youths were more likely to hold on to or come to adopt more national origin identities in the short term, while in the longer term, at least from national origin and hyphenated starting points, a somewhat more American identity (particularly a hyphenated identity) was more common. These results conflict with Portes and Rumbaut's (2001a) claims, based on the adolescent period only, that children of immigrants turn away from U.S.-based identities over time. As Portes and Rumbaut (2001a) point out, the passage of Proposition 187 in California in 1994, which denied social services to undocumented immigrants, may have reinvigorated some adolescents' national origin identities by the first follow-up interview in 1995-1996. By 1997, a federal judge found the major provisions of the proposition to be unconstitutional (McDonnell 1997). Therefore, over the longer emerging adulthood period, these effects may have diminished. The common practice of home-leaving by the end of the emerging adulthood period might have led to lesser connection to the national origin identities of one's parents and greater attachment to identities that showed both national origin and U.S. affiliation, as hyphenated identities at the endpoint of emerging adulthood were very common.

There were also differences in associations between demographic, downward leveling, and protective factors in adolescence and emerging adulthood. For intragenerational educational mobility, there were quite a few differences in associations between ethnic group and mobility path by life course stage. Some groups, such as Asians, had different (better) odds of maintaining (and increasing) their educational expectations, while others, such as Mexican women, had statistically significantly different (lower) odds of attaining their expectations by their mid-twenties. These findings suggest that greater maintenance of educational expectations for Asians does not necessarily translate into higher odds of attaining these expectations than other groups. There was somewhat more consistency across life course stages between ethnic group membership and paths of cultural assimilation. Among the downward leveling factors, school composition variables were associated with mobility and cultural assimilation in both adolescence and the longer emerging adulthood period, but the exact associations differed across the two life course stages. Of the protective factors, there was some evidence that parent characteristics mattered more in adolescence than in emerging adulthood, particularly for intragenerational educational mobility and non-English ability assimilation. Youths are less likely to live with their parents by the end of the emerging adulthood period; therefore, the parent-child relationship and parental characteristics may have less of an influence on youths' outcomes. This pattern was not apparent in terms of English use with friends, perhaps because parents have more of an impact on youths' language ability than their language use in friendship networks.

In addition to the general support of my initial criticisms, several unexpected findings challenged other claims of segmented assimilation theory. First, as I noted above, the results for blacks, and to some extent the results of Mexicans, were not as negative as segmented assimilation theory suggests. There were several cases in which blacks had statistically significantly more positive mobility results than whites. Portes and colleagues' claim that native-born minorities serve as a negative, downward leveling influence, pulling children of immigrants into the underclass, thus seems to be overstated, if not completely false.

Second, segmented assimilation theory suggests that immigrants who take on certain attitudes and characteristics of an "adversarial subculture" are at high risk for falling into the underclass. However, I rarely found statistically significant associations between these kinds of characteristics and economic mobility. The two statistically significant associations I found in the full models across the various analyses were actually more positive associations. For example, I found that youths who believed there were racial problems in the United States and those who had reported experiencing discrimination had higher odds of upward educational mobility (among third and later generation males with intermediate status parents) and lower odds of downward occupational mobility (among children of intermediate status immigrants). While Ogbu (1978, 1991) argues that this kind of oppositional subculture or reactive consciousness leads youths to give up on trying to succeed through education and other mainstream means, perhaps this kind of consciousness among youths who are not from the lowest status backgrounds actually better prepares them for challenges that lie ahead. Further research on this issue, particularly considering differences by youths' starting points, is necessary.

Third, Portes and colleagues emphasize the protective nature of cultural connections so much that they define one possible path of assimilation as involving economic mobility as a result of cultural retention. However, I found little evidence that cultural attachments were protective of youths' economic mobility. In fact, there were only two cases in which a culture attachment variable was statistically significantly associated with a more positive form of economic mobility: one for intragenerational educational mobility and one for intergenerational occupational mobility. In both cases, the association held only among youths from the highest status starting points, suggesting that high status may be necessary before cultural connections are useful for promoting more positive mobility outcomes. I also found that some cultural ties tended to have negative consequences for youths, especially the measure of importance of relatives, which was associated with more negative forms of intergenerational economic mobility.

This book has separated the idea of path from that of segment in segmented assimilation theory. I focused on the directions of mobility and assimilation that children of immigrants and third and later generation youths experienced. However, as I discussed in the first chapter, segmented assimilation theory claims that immigrants enter into different *segments* of American society, specifically, the underclass and middle class. Future research should attempt to examine the claim that immigrants and their offspring primarily enter these particular segments. Some immigrant groups clearly have more positive incorporation outcomes than others, but the extent to which these two segments capture the variety of immigrants' incorporation experiences has not yet been fully tested, although I have begun work in this area (Faulkner and Jakubowski 2007).

Segmented assimilation theory asserts that there is no one path of assimilation that immigrants follow. Instead, some experience upward mobility and acculturation into the middle class; others experience the opposite; and still others experience upward mobility with partial acculturation (mixed stable and classical acculturation). My results suggest that paths of mobility are even more complex. Different directions of assimilation are possible within both the economic and cultural dimensions of assimilation. Moreover, starting point, gender, generational status, and life course stage are all important for understanding these paths. Future research should tap into this complexity and attempt to draw out the different kinds of paths that are more and less common among immigrants.

Finally, as Neckerman, Carter, and Lee (1999) suggest, segmented assimilation theory discounts the idea of minority cultures of mobility. Instead, it suggests that connections to native minority groups, including their cultural attributes, are detrimental to immigrants' economic success and well-being. My findings indicate that some minority cultural attributes, particularly views of race in the United States and experiences of discrimination, are actually associated with more positive forms of economic mobility and classical forms of cultural assimilation in a number of cases. Future research should attempt to tease out native minorities' cultural and economic influences on immigrants' incorporation experiences.

In this book, I took one part of segmented assimilation theory—the idea that immigrants follow different *paths* of mobility and acculturation—and examined these paths in a simple, straightforward manner. In order to examine paths of mobility and assimilation more fully than the previous researchers, I performed true intergenerational analysis and examined pathways by starting point, gender, generational status, and, in the case of intragenerational assimilation, life course stage. My results have a number of implications for segmented assimilation theory as well as for the study of economic mobility, language ability, language use, and ethnic identity.

First, as I noted above, Portes and his colleagues (Portes, Fernández-Kelly, and Haller 2005) state that one way to "disprove" segmented assimilation theory is to show that downward assimilation does not occur or affects few immigrants. Segmented assimilation theorists' discussions of downward mobility suggest that an extreme form of downward mobility is one of three primary experiences of assimilation among recent immigrants and their children. The results of my analysis, which reveal that downward assimilation is not at all widespread, thus poses a serious challenge to segmented assimilation theory on its own terms. I found that downward mobility from lower starting points was very uncommon and stagnation from the lowest starting points was even rarer—particularly for intergenerational educational mobility. For example, even among youths with college educated parents (with, therefore, the most "room" for downward mobility), only about one-third of youths failed to attain their parents' levels of education by their mid-twenties.[2] This downward mobility, however, is not likely to be so extreme as to involve entry into the poorest stratum of American society. Among those for whom downward educational mobility would have more serious consequences, a much smaller proportion of youths with intermediate and low educational status parents experienced downward and stable mobility, respectively, than youths with high status parents. My results indicate that a path of downward mobility into the underclass is not a widespread enough experience to define one of three dominant patterns of immigrant incorporation.

Second, this book pioneers a new method of examining educational and occupational status over time—both inter- and intragenerationally—by examining a simple directional path of change in these characteristics. More importantly, I examined the factors associated with these paths of mobility by youths' and their parents' educational and occupational starting points. My results reveal that the factors influencing mobility differed depending on these starting points. There were, in fact, some surprising results—particularly regarding ethnic group—across the different starting points. Future research should consider how educational and occupational status conditions the mobility experiences of individuals.

My examination of indicators of acculturation also yielded insights for future research on language ability, language use, and ethnic identity. I found that the patterns of change in these characteristics differed markedly across life course stage. While some researchers claim that language acquisition is highly dependent on one's age (Lenneberg 1967; Laponce 1987; Bialystok and Hakuta 1994), none of the previous assimilation and acculturation literature has examined how patterns of linguistic assimilation may differ at different points in individuals' lives. My work suggests that shifts in non-English language ability do not follow the expected pattern: over the longer, transition-to-emerging-adulthood period, a larger proportion of youths increased their non-English ability than during the shorter, adolescent period alone. This result suggests that immigrants experience a bumpy path (Gans 1992) in terms of this form of linguistic assimilation. The patterns of assimilation in English use and ethnic identity followed a more consistent, classical trajectory across the time periods that I examined; however, there were many differences in the factors associated with these paths of linguistic and identificational assimilation across the life course stages—although ethnic origin was consistently associated with assimilation paths. Examining patterns of assimilation across various life course stages is the only way to uncover any of the bumps in the pathways of assimilation for immigrants intragenerationally.

While this book analyzes some of the claims of segmented assimilation theory more precisely than previous research, it, like all empirical research, suffers from a number of limitations. First, I attempted to strip down the idea of an assimilation path to its most basic sense. I examined directions of assimilation, then, but I did not measure amount of change. For example, youths experiencing upward educational mobility might have improved upon their parents' levels of education by one year or several. All such youths fell into the same category. It is likely that factors associated with these different kinds of upward mobility differ.

Future research can quite easily make up for this flaw, but data limitations create problems that are more difficult for this and future analyses. I was not able to examine changes in cultural factors, such as ethnic identity, among non-immigrants. I therefore could view cultural change only as an immigrant experience and not delve into it as a wider youth experience. The size and composition of the two data sets also led to a number of limitations. I was unable to examine all forms of mobility and assimilation because there were not enough cases of each kind. Similarly, I could not perform certain analyses by gender. In the CILS data, I was able to examine a wide variety of ethnic groups. However, in NELS, I had to make use of larger racial/ethnic groups for comparison because, even though the sample was large, there were not enough third and later generation members of other racial-ethnic groups. Finally, my examination of intergenerational assimilation was limited in the CILS data because only a subsample of CILS parents had surveys available.

In addition, the data I used for this analysis may not provide the best representation of immigrant incorporation experiences today. The CILS data provide a good representation of the most recent flows of immigration to the southern California region, which is still heavily dominated by Asians and Mexicans, although there have been some shifts in the flow, including an increase in Central American groups (Ramakrishnan and Johnson 2005). The recent CILS data represent southern Florida quite well. However, the growth of the Cuban population has slowed, and Mexicans are one of the fastest growing immigrant groups in Florida (Eisenhauer et al. 2007). These population changes suggest that fewer children of immigrants are likely to be of Cuban origin in the coming years. The NELS data, which I use primarily to represent third and later generation individuals, are somewhat more dated. In addition, neither data set allows us to examine the consequences on immigrants' and their children's documentation status. As Rumbaut and Komaie (2010) and many others have testified, lack of documentation status poses significant challenges to immigrants and their children—regardless of the children's own documentation status. Continued data collection across a wide variety of ethnic groups is necessary to improve our understanding of today's immigrants' incorporation experiences. But documentation status will likely continue to pose researchers a largely insurmountable challenge due to its sensitive nature.

New data would be useful to make up for some of these limitations as well as for further study of segmented and other theories of assimilation. One of the primary data sources of data for assimilation research, the U.S. Census, has dried up in recent years due to the discontinuation of survey items on parents' place of birth, although the March Current Population Survey helps fill some of this gap. Many nationally representative data sets lack immigrants (and children of immigrants) in sufficient numbers for analysis, especially by ethnic sub-group. Even data sets that have immigrants in sufficient numbers generally are deficient in appropriate cultural information for the study of multiple dimensions of assimilation, especially cultural information that is relevant to immigrants and non-immigrants alike. CILS data, on the other hand, suffer from their geographic specificity, lack of non-immigrant comparisons, and small parent interview subsample.

More widespread longitudinal data collection in the future on children of immigrants and the general youth population would provide for an even deeper examination of segmented assimilation theory. It would permit my claims regarding the general lack of downward mobility to be verified among a larger population. It would also permit more detailed examinations of intergenerational and intragenerational economic mobility and acculturation by starting point, gender, parental immigration status, and life course stage.

Finally, this book also has important policy implications. Economic mobility among immigrants does not seem to follow a process much different from the general population. There do not appear to be immigrant-specific characteristics that are associated with educational and occupational mobility. Policies that are aimed at reducing inequality and improving the lot of the poor across the board, then, will also be beneficial to poor immigrants.

Policy implications regarding the forms of cultural assimilation that I examined are less clear. While it may be beneficial for American society at large for all of its members to be able to communicate at least to a minimal degree in the same language, it is certainly not arguable that lacking skills in other languages is beneficial to society. As Portes and Rumbaut (2001a) suggest, non-English ability may be important for children of immigrants' economic success and integration into mainstream society because it may be necessary for communication between parents and children. Certainly, this book suggests that parents' involvement in the lives and activities of their children has important consequences for youths' economic well-being. It seems, then, that policies should be aimed at an additive form of language instruction—increasing youths' English ability—with as little subtraction as possible of youths' languages of origin. Apart from the importance of family relationships, non-English language ability is also likely to be useful in the increasingly global marketplace for young adults. Policy makers, then, should not attempt to hinder youths' learning of their non-English languages of origin and should, instead, promote non-English language acquisition among all youths—regardless of generational status.

In this book, English use and ethnic identity do not appear to have serious consequences for youths' economic well-being. Intergenerationally, there were no statistically significant associations between language use or ethnic identity and pathways of mobility. Intragenerationally, there were also no statistically significant associations between language use and educational mobility. Regarding ethnic identity, more "American" identities were associated with both positive and negative forms of intragenerational educational mobility. Youths with college expectations who had plain American identities had better odds of attaining these expectations than those with national origin identities, while their counterparts with racial/pan-ethnic identities had worse odds of attaining their college expectations. This book cannot speak to the idea that promoting greater use of English and acquisition of more "American" identities allows immigrants and their children to have a greater sense of belonging to American society;

however, it does suggest that these forms of assimilation do not have particularly positive consequences for their economic well-being.

___

NOTES

[1] Of course, different immigrant groups and immigrant group members' cultural characteristics may be closer or farther away from American cultural characteristics.

[2] I highlight intergenerational educational mobility because the intergenerational educational comparison of youths' and parents' educational levels was more valid than comparison of their occupational status. Moreover, as I noted above, discussions of assimilation generally focus on intergenerational change as the driving force of assimilation.

References

Acker, Joan. 1990. "Hierarchies, Jobs, Bodies: A Theory of Gendered Organizations." *Gender & Society* 4: 139-158.

Adler, Nancy E. and Katherine Newman. 2002. "Socioeconomic Disparities in Health: Pathways and Policies." *Health Affairs* 21: 60-76.

Ainsworth-Darnell, James W. and Douglas B. Downey. "Assessing the Oppositional Culture Explanation for Racial/Ethnic Differences in School Performance." *American Sociological Review* 63: 536-553.

Akresh, Ilana Redstone. 2007. "Contexts of English Language Use among Immigrants to the United States." *International Migration Review* 41: 930-955.

Alba, Richard. 1999. "Immigration and the American Realities of Assimilation and Multiculturalism." *Sociological Forum* 14: 3-25.

Alba, Richard and Reid M. Golden. 1986. "Patterns of Ethnic Marriage in the United States." *Social Forces* 65: 202-223.

Alba, Richard, John Logan, Amy Lutz, and Brian Stults. 2002. "Only English by the Third Generation? Loss and Preservation of the Mother Tongue among the Grandchildren of Contemporary Immigrants." *Demography* 39: 467-484.

Alba, Richard D., John R. Logan, Brian J. Stults, Gilbert Marzan, and Wenquan Zhang. 1999. "Immigrant Groups in the Suburbs: A Reexamination of

Suburbanization and Spatial Assimilation." *American Sociological Review* 64: 446-460.

Alba, Richard and Victor Nee. 1997. "Rethinking Assimilation Theory for a New Era of Immigration." *International Migration Review* 31: 826-874.

_____. 2003. *Remaking the American Mainstream: Assimilation and Contemporary Immigration*. Cambridge: Harvard University Press.

Alexander, Karl L., Bruce K. Eckland, and Larry J. Griffin. 1975. "The Wisconsin Model of Socioeconomic Achievement: A Replication." *American Journal of Sociology* 81: 324-342.

Allison, Paul D. 2000. "Multiple Imputation for Missing Data: A Cautionary Tale." *Sociological Methods and Research* 28: 301-309.

_____. 2002. *Missing Data*. Thousand Oaks, CA: Sage Publications.

American Association of University Women. 1992. *How Schools Shortchange Girls: A Study of Major Findings on Girls and Education*. Washington, DC: American Association of University of Women.

Anderson, Elijah. 1999. *Code of the Street: Decency, Violence, and the Moral Life of the Inner City*. New York: W.W. Norton & Company.

Anker, Richard. 1998. *Gender and Jobs: Sex Segregation of Occupations in the World*. Geneva: International Labour Office.

Arias, Elizabeth. 2001. "Change in Nuptiality Patterns Among Cuban Americans: Evidence of Cultural and Structural Assimilation?" *International Migration Review* 35: 525-556.

Arnett, Jeffrey Jensen. 2000. "Emerging Adulthood: A Theory of Development from the Late Teens through the Twenties." *American Psychologist* 55: 469-480.

_____. 2004. *Emerging Adulthood: The Winding Road from the Late Teens through the Twenties*. Oxford: Oxford University Press.

Arriagada, Paula A. 2005. "Family Context and Spanish-Language Use: A Study of Latino Children in the United States." *Social Science Quarterly* 86: 599-619.

Astone, Nan Marie and Sara S. McLanahan. 1991. "Family Structure, Parental Practices, and High School Completion." *American Sociological Review* 56: 309-320.

Bae, Yupin, Susan Choy, Claire Geddes, Jennifer Sable, and Thomas Snyder. 2000. *Educational Equity for Girls and Women.* Washington, D.C.: U.S. Government Printing Office.

Bankston, III, Carl L. 1995. "Gender Roles and Scholastic Performance among Adolescent Vietnamese Women: The Paradox of Ethnic Patriarchy." *Sociological Focus* 28: 161-176.

Bankston, III, Carl L. and Min Zhou. 1995. "Effects of Minority-Language Literacy on the Academic Achievement of Vietnamese Youths in New Orleans." *Sociology of Education* 68: 1-17.

Bean, Frank D., Susan K. Brown, and Rubén G. Rumbaut. 2006. "Mexican Immigrant Political and Economic Incorporation." *Perspectives on Politics* 4: 309-313.

Beller, Andrea and Kee-Ok Kim Han. 1984. "Occupational Sex Segregation: Prospects for the 1980s." Pp. 91-114 in *Sex Segregation in the Workplace: Trends, Explanations, and Remedies,* edited by Barbara F. Reskin. Washington, DC: National Academy Press.

Bialystok, Ellen. 1997. "The Structure of Age: In Search of Barriers to Second Language Acquisition." *Second Language Research* 13: 116-137.

Bialystok, Ellen and Kenji Hakuta. 1994. *In Other Words: The Science and Psychology of Second-Language Acquisition.* New York: Basic Books.

Bianchi, Suzanne M. and Daphne Spain. 1996. "Women, Work, and Family in America." *Population Bulletin* 51: 2-48.

Billson, Janet Mancini. 1995. *Keepers of the Culture: The Power of Tradition in Women's Lives.* New York: Lexington Books.

Blake, Judith. 1989. *Family Size and Achievement*. Berkeley: University of California Press.

Blau, Francine D., Marianne A. Ferber, and Anne E. Winkler. 1998. *The Economics of Women, Men, and Work*. 3rd ed. Upper Saddle River, NJ: Prentice Hall.

Blau, Francine D., Patricia A. Simpson, and Deborah Anderson. 1998. "Trends in Occupational Segregation in the United States Over the 1970s and 1980s." NBER Working Paper No. W6716.

Borjas, George. 1990. *Friends of Strangers: The Impact of Immigration in the U.S. Economy*. New York: Basic Books.

Bourgois, Philippe. 1996. *In Search of Respect: Selling Crack in El Barrio*. Cambridge: Cambridge University Press.

Boyd, Monica. 2002. "Educational Attainments of Immigrant Offspring: Success or Segmented Assimilation." *International Migration Review* 36: 1037-1060.

Brandon, Peter David. 2002. "The Living Arrangements of Children in Immigrant Families in the United States." *International Migration Review* 36: 416-436.

Brubaker, Rogers. 2001. "The Return of Assimilation? Changing Perspectives on Immigration and Its Sequels in France, Germany, and the United States." *Ethnic and Racial Studies* 24: 531-548.

Buckley, John E. 2002. Rankings of Full-Time Occupations, by Earnings, 2000. *Monthly Labor Review* 125: 46-57.

Burke, Peter J. 1989. "Gender Identity, Sex, and School Performance." *Social Psychology Quarterly* 52: 159-169.

Cameron, Stephen V. and James J. Heckman. 2001. "The Dynamics of Educational Attainment for Black, Hispanic, and White Males." *The Journal of Political Economy* 109: 455-499.

Caplan, Nathan, Marcella H. Choy, and John K. Whitmore. 1991. *Children of the Boat People: A Study of Educational Success.* Ann Arbor: University of Michigan Press.

Carter, Prudence. 2005. *Keepin' It Real: School Success Beyond Black and White.* New York: Oxford University Press.

_____. 2006. "Intersection Identities: 'Acting White,' Gender, and Academic Achievement." Pp. 111-132 in *Beyond Acting White: Reframing the Debate on Black Student Achievement,* edited by Erin McNamara Horvat and Carla O'Connor. Lanham, MD: Rowman and Littlefield Publishers.

Cerulo, Karen A. 1997. "Identity Construction: New Issues, New Directions." *Annual Review of Sociology* 23" 385-409.

Cerrutti, Marcela and Douglas S. Massey. 2001. "On the Auspices of Female Migration from Mexico to the United States." *Demography* 38: 187-200.

Chambliss, William J. 1973. "The Saints and the Roughnecks." *Society* 11: 24-31.

Chiswick, Barry. 1979. "The Economic Progress of Immigrants: Some Apparently Universal Patterns." Pp. 357-399 in *Contemporary Economic Problems 1979,* edited by William Fellner. Washington, DC: American Enterprise Institute.

Coleman, James. 1988. "Social Capital in the Creation of Human Capital." *American Journal of Sociology* 94: S95-S120.

Conzen, Kathleen Neils, David A. Gerber, Ewa Morawska, George E. Pozzetta, and Rudolph J. Vecoli. 1992. "The Invention of Ethnicity: A Perspective from the U.S.A." *Journal of American Ethnic History* 12: 3-41.

Cook, Philip J. and Jens Ludwig. 1998. "The Burden of 'Acting White': Do Black Adolescents Disparage Academic Achievement?" Pp. 375-401 in *The Black-White Test Score Gap,* edited by Christopher Jencks and Meredith Phillips. Washington, DC: Brookings Institution.

Côté, James E. and Anton L. Allahar. 1996. *Generation on Hold: Coming of Age in the Late Twentieth Century.* 2nd edition. New York: New York University Press.

Crowley, J.E. and D. Shapiro. 1982. "Aspirations and Expectations of Youth in the U.S." *Youth and Society* 13: 391-422.

Crul, Maurice and Jens Schneider. 2010. "Comparative Integration Context Theory: Participation and Belonging in New Diverse European Cities." *Ethnic and Racial Studies* 33: 1249-1268.

Curtin, Thomas R., Steven J. Ingels, Shiying Wu, and Ruth Heuer. 2002. *National Education Longitudinal Study of 1988: Base-Year to Fourth Follow-up Data File User's Manual* (NCES 2002-323). Washington, DC: U.S. Department of Education, National Center for Education Statistics.

Dahl, Espen. 1994. "Social Inequalities in Ill-Health: The Significance of Occupational Status, Education and Income-Results from a Norwegian Survey." *Sociology of Health & Illness* 16: 644-667.

Das Gupta, Monisha. 1997. "'What Is Indian About You?': A Gendered, Transnational Approach to Ethnicity." *Gender and Society* 11: 572-596.

Dion, Karen K. and Kenneth L. Dion. 2001. "Gender and Cultural Adaptation in Immigrant Families." *Journal of Social Issues* 57: 511-521.

Donato, Katharine M. 2010. "U.S. Migration from Latin America: Gendered Patterns and Shifts." *The Annals of the American Academy of Political and Social Science* 630: 78-92.

Donato, Katharine M., Donna Cabaccia, Jennifer Holdaway, Martin Manalansan, IV, and Patricia R. Pessar. 2006. "A Glass Half Full? Gender in Migration Studies." *International Migration Review* 40: 3-26.

Downey, Douglas B. 1995. "When Bigger Is Not Better: Family Size, Parental Resources, and Children's Educational Performance." *American Sociological Review* 60: 746-761.

Downey, Douglas B. and Anastasia S. Vogt Yuan. 2005. "Sex Differences in School Performance During High School: Puzzling Patterns and Possible Explanations." *The Sociological Quarterly* 46: 299-321.

Duckwork, Angela Lee and Martin E.P. Seligman. 2006. "Self-Discipline Gives Girls the Edge: Gender in Self-Discipline, Grades, and Achievement Test Scores." *Journal of Educational Psychology* 98: 198-208.

Dumais, Susan A. 2002. "Cultural Capital, Gender, and School Success: The Role of Habitus." *Sociology of Education* 75: 44-68.

Eisenhauer, Emily, Yue Zhang, Cynthia S. Hernandez, and Alex Angee. 2007. "Immigrants in Florida: Characteristics and Contributions." A report issued by the Research Institute for Social and Economic Policy of the Center for Labor Research and Studies at Florida International University.

England, Paula. 1992. *Comparable Worth: Theories and Evidence*. New York: Aldine De Gruyter.

Erikson, Erik H. 1950. *Childhood and Society*. New York: Norton.

_____. 1968. *Identity: Youth and Crisis*. New York: Norton.

Espiritu, Yen Le. 1999. "Gender and Labor in Asian Immigrant Families." *American Behavioral Scientist* 42: 628-647.

Farkas, George, Daniel Sheehan, and Robert P. Grobe. 1990. "Coursework Mastery and School Success: Gender, Ethnicity, and Poverty Groups within an Urban School District." *American Educational Research Journal* 27: 807-827.

Farley, Reynolds and Richard Alba. 2002. "The New Second Generation in the United States." *International Migration Review* 36: 669-701.

Faulkner, Caroline L. and Jessica Jakubowski. 2007. "Predicting Segmented Outcomes: Young Adult Assimilation in the United States." Presented at the annual meeting of the American Sociological Association, New York, New York.

Feliciano, Cynthia and Rubén G. Rumbaut. 2005. "Gendered Paths: Educational and Occupational Expectations and Outcomes among Adult Children of Immigrants." *Ethnic and Racial Studies* 28: 1087-1118.

Ferguson, Ann Arnett. 2000. *Bad Boys: Public Schools in the Making of Black Masculinity.* Ann Arbor, MI: University of Michigan Press.

Fernández-Kelly, M. Patricia. 2008. "The Back Pocket Map: Social Class and Cultural Capital as Transferable Assets in the Advancement of Second-Generation Immigrants." *The Annals of the American Academy of Political and Social Science* 620(1): 116-137.

Fernández-Kelly, M. Patricia and Richard Schauffler. 1994. "Divided Fates: Immigrant Children in a Restructured U.S. Economy." *International Migration Review* 28: 662-689.

Ferree, Myra Marx and Elaine J. Hall. 1996. "Rethinking Stratification from a Feminist Perspective: Gender, Race, and Class in Mainstream Textbooks." *American Sociological Review* 61: 929-950.

Fix, Michael and Jeffrey S. Passel. 2003. "U.S. Immigration—Trends and Implications for Schools." Presentation to the National Association for Bilingual Education, New Orleans, LA.

Fodor, Éva. 2006. " A Different Type of Gender Gap: How Women and Men Experience Poverty." *East European Politics and Societies* 20: 14-39.

Foner, Nancy. 2000. *From Ellis Island to JFK: New York's Two Great Waves of Immigration.* New Haven: Yale University Press.

_____. 2009. "Gender and Migration: West Indians in Comparative Perspective." *International Migration* 47: 3-29.

Frase, Mary J. 1989. *Dropout Rates in the United States 1988.* National Center for Education Statistics Analysis Report (NCES 89-609). Washington, DC: U.S. Department of Education Office of Educational Research and Improvement

Freese, Jeremy and Brian Powell. 1999. Sociobiology, Status, and Parental Investment in Sons and Daughters: Testing the Trivers-Willard Hypothesis." *American Journal of Sociology* 104: 1704-1743.

Fuligni, Andrew J. 1997. "The Academic Achievement of Adolescents from Immigrant Families: The Roles of Family Background, Attitudes, and Behavior." *Child Development* 68: 351-363.

_____. 2001. "A Comparative Longitudinal Approach to Acculturation among Children from Immigrant Families." *Harvard Educational Review* 71: 566-578.

Fuligni, Andrew J. and Melissa Witkow. 2004. "The Postsecondary Educational Progress of Youth from Immigrant Families." *Journal of Research on Adolescence* 14: 159-183.

Gager, Constance T., Teresa M. Cooney, and Kathleen Thiede Call. 1999. "The Effects of Family Characteristics and Time Use on Teenagers' Household Labor." *Journal of Marriage and the Family* 61: 982-994.

Gans, Herbert J. 1979. "Symbolic Ethnicity: The Future of Ethnic Groups and Cultures in America." *Ethnic and Racial Studies* 2: 1-20.

_____. 1990. "Deconstructing the Underclass: The Term's Dangers as a Planning Concept." *Journal of the American Planning Association* 56: 271-277.

_____. 1992. "Second-Generation Decline: Scenarios for the Economic and Ethnic Futures of the Post-1965 American Immigrants." *Ethnic and Racial Studies* 15: 173-192.

García-Vázquez, Enedina, Luis A. Vázquez, Isabel C. López, and Wendy Ward. 1997. "Language Proficiency and Academic Success: Relationships between Proficiency in Two Languages and Achievement among Mexican American Students." *Bilingual Research Journal* 21: 395-439.

Gee, Ellen M., Barbara A. Mitchell, and Andrew V. Wister. 2003. "Home Leaving Trajectories in Canada: Exploring Cultural and Gendered Dimensions." *Canadian Studies in Population* 30: 245-270.

Gibson, Margaret A. 1988. *Accommodation without Assimilation: Sikh Immigrants in an American High School*. Ithaca: Cornell University Press.

Gilligan, Carol. 1982. *In a Different Voice: Psychological Theory and Women's Development*. Cambridge: Harvard University Press.

Ginorio, Angela and Michelle Huston. 2001. *¡Sí, Se Puede! Yes We Can: Latinas in School*. Washington, DC: American Association of University Women Educational Foundation.

Glenn, Evelyn Nakano. 1992. "From Servitude to Service Work: Historical Continuities in the Racial Division of Labor." *Signs* 18: 1-43.

_____. 2000. "The Social Construction and Institutionalization of Gender and Race: An Integrative Framework." Pp. 3-43 in *Revisioning Gender*, edited by Myra Marx Ferree, Judith Lorber, and Beth B. Hess. Walnut Creek, CA: Alta Mira Press.

Glick, Jennifer E. and Michael J. White. 2003. "The Academic Trajectories of Immigrant Youths: Analysis Within and Across Cohorts." *Demography* 40: 759-783.

Golash-Boza, Tanya. 2006. "Dropping the Hyphen? Becoming Latino(a)-American through Racialized Assimilation." *Social Forces* 85: 27-55.

Gordon, Milton. 1964. *Assimilation in American Life: The Role of Race, Religion, and National Origins*. New York: Oxford University Press.

Gottman, John M. and Regina H. Rushe. 1993. "The Analysis of Change: Issues, Fallacies, and New Ideas." *Journal of Consulting and Clinical Psychology* 61: 907-910.

Gratton, Brian. 2002. "Race, the Children of Immigrants, and Social Science Theory." *Journal of American Ethnic History* 21: 74-84.

Gregory, James F. 1995. "The Crime of Punishment: Racial and Gender Disparities in the Use of Corporal Punishment in U.S. Public Schools." *The Journal of Negro Education* 64: 454-462.

Haggstrom, Gus, David Kanouse, and Peter Morrison. 1986. "Accounting for the Educational Shortfall of Mothers." *Journal of Marriage and the Family* 48: 175-186.

Haller, William. 2006. Personal communication.

Hanson, Sandra L. 1994. "Lost Talent: Unrealized Educational Aspirations and Expectations among U.S. Youths." *Sociology of Education* 67: 159-183.

Hao, Lingxin and Melissa Bonstead-Bruns. 1998. "Parent-Child Differences in Educational Expectations and the Academic Achievement of Immigrant and Native Students." *Sociology of Education* 71: 175-198.

Hao, Lingxin and Suet-Ling Pong. 2008. "The Role of School in the Upward Mobility of Disadvantaged Immigrants' Children." *The Annals of the American Academy of Political and Social Science* 620: 62-89.

Harris, Kathleen Mullan. 1999. "The Health Status and Risk Behaviors of Adolescents in Immigrant Families." Pp. 286-347 in *Children of Immigrants: Health, Adjustment, and Public Assistance*, edited by Donald J. Hernández. Washington, D.C.: National Academy Press.

Hauser, Robert M. and John Robert Warren. 1997. "Socioeconomic Indexes for Occupations: A Review, Update, and Critique." *Sociological Methodology* 27: 177-298.

Hauser, Robert M., John Robert Warren, Min-Hsiung Huang, and Wendy Y. Carter. 2000. "Occupational Status, Education, and Social Mobility in the Meritocracy." Pp. 179-229 in *Meritocracy and Economic Inequality*, edited by Kenneth Arrow, Samuel Bowles, and Steven Durlauf. Princeton, NJ: Princeton University Press.

Hirschman, Charles. 1994. "Problems and Prospects of Studying Immigrant Adaptation from the 1990 Population Census: From Generational Comparisons to the Process of 'Becoming American.'" *International Migration Review* 28: 690-713.

_____. 2001. "The Educational Enrollment of Immigrant Youth: A Test of the Segmented Assimilation Hypothesis." *Demography* 38: 317-336.

Hirschman, Charles and Ellen Kraly. 1988. "Immigrants, Minorities, and Earnings in the United States in 1950." *Ethnic and Racial Studies* 11: 332-365.

_____. 1990. "Racial and Ethnic Inequality in the United States, 1940 and 1950: The Impact of Geographic Location and Human Capital." *International Migration Review* 24: 4-33.

Hondagneu-Sotelo, Pierrette. 1994. *Gendered Transitions: Mexican Experiences of Immigration.* Berkeley: University of California Press.

Hondagneu-Sotelo, Pierrette (editor). 2003. "Gender and Immigration: A Retrospective and Introduction." Pp. 3-19 in *Gender and U.S. Immigration: Contemporary Trends.* Los Angeles: University of California Press.

Ingels, Steven J., Kathryn L. Dowd, John D. Baldridge, James L. Stipe, Virginia H. Bartot, and Martin R. Frankel. 1994. "NELS:88 Second Follow-Up: Student Component Data File User's Manual." (NCES 94-374). U.S. Department of Education. Washington, D.C.: National Center for Education Statistics.

Jacob, Brian A. 2002. "Where the Boys Aren't: Non-Cognitive Skills, Returns to School, and the Gender Gap in Higher Education." National Bureau of Economic Research Working Paper 8964.

Jacobs, Jerry A. 1996. "Gender Inequality and Higher Education." *Annual Review of Sociology* 22: 153-185.

Jacobs, J.A. and M.E. Greene. 1994. "Race and Ethnicity, Social Class, and Schooling in 1910." Pp. 209-256 in *After Ellis Island: Newcomers and Natives in the 1910 Census*, edited by Susan Cotts Watkins. New York: Russell Sage Foundation.

Jencks, Christopher. 1992. *Rethinking Social Policy: Race, Poverty, and the Underclass.* Cambridge: Harvard University Press.

Jung, Moon-Kie. 2009. "The Racial Unconscious of Assimilation Theory." *Du Bois Review* 6: 375-395.

Kao, Grace. 1999. "Psychological Well-Being and Educational Achievement among Immigrant Youth." Pp. 410-477 in *Children of Immigrants: Health, Adjustment, and Public Assistance*, edited by Donald J. Hernández. Washington, D.C.: National Academy Press.

Kao, Grace and Marta Tienda. 1995. "Optimism and Achievement: The Educational Performance of Immigrant Youth." *Social Science Quarterly* 76: 1-19.

Kasinitz, Philip, John Mollenkopf, and Mary C. Waters. 2002. "Becoming American/ Becoming New Yorkers: Immigrant Incorporation in a Majority Minority City." *International Migration Review* 36: 1020-1036.

Kasinitz, Philip, John H. Mollenkopf, Mary C. Waters, and Jennifer Holdaway. 2008. *Inheriting the City: The Children of Immigrants Come of Age*. Cambridge and New York: Harvard University Press and Russell Sage Foundation.

Katz, Michael B. 1993. *The "Underclass" Debate: Views from History.* Princeton, NJ: Princeton University Press.

Keating, Daniel P. and Lawrence V. Clark. 1980. "Development of Physical and Social Reasoning in Adolescence." *Developmental Psychology* 16: 23-30.

Kessler, S., D.J. Ashenden, R.W. Connell, R.W. and G.W. Dowsett. 1985. "Gender Relations in Secondary Schooling." *Sociology of Education* 58: 34-48.

Kimmel, Michael S. 2004. *The Gendered Society*. New York: Oxford University Press.

Kimmel, Michael S. and Matthew Mahler. 2003. "Adolescent Masculinity, Homophobia, and Violence: Random School Shootings, 1982-2001." *American Behavioral Scientist* 46: 1439-1458.

Kingston, Paul W., Ryan Hubbard, Brent Lapp, Paul Schroeder, and Julia Wilson. 2003. "Why Education Matters." *Sociology of Education* 76: 53-70.

Kleinfeld, Judith. 1999. "Student Performance: Males versus Females." *Public Interest* 134: 3-20.

Konczal, Lisa and William Haller. 2008. "Fit to Miss, but Matched to Hatch: Success Factors among the Second Generation's Disadvantaged in South Florida." *The Annals of the American academy of Political and Social Science* 620: 161-176.

Kroneberg, Clemens. 2008. "Ethnic Communities and School Performance among the New Second Generation in the United States: Testing the Theory of Segmented Assimilation." *The Annals of the American Academy of Political and Social Science* 620(1): 138-160.

Laponce, J.A. 1987. *Languages and Their Territories*. Translated from French by Anthony Martin-Sperry. Toronto: University of Toronto Press.

Lenneberg, Eric. 1967. *Biological Foundations of Language*. New York: Wiley.

Lieberson, Stanley. 1980. *A Piece of the Pie: Blacks and White Immigrants Since 1880*. Berkeley: University of California Press.

Lieberson, Stanley and Mary C. Waters. 1988. *From Many Strands: Ethnic and Racial Groups in Contemporary America*. New York: Russell Sage Foundation.

Lietz, Jeremy J. and Mary K. Gregory. 1978. "Pupil Race and Sex Determinants of Office and Exceptional Educational Referrals." *Educational Research Quarterly* 3: 61-66.

Lopez, Nancy. 2002. *Hopeful Girls, Troubled Boys: Race and Gender Disparity in Urban Education*. New York: Routledge.

Lutz, Amy. 2006. "Spanish Maintenance among English-Speaking Latino Youth: The Role of Individual and Social Characteristics." *Social Forces* 84: 1417-1433.

Lutz, Amy and Stephanie Crist. 2008. "Why Do Bilingual Boys Get Better Grades in English-Only America? The Impacts of Gender, Language, and

Family Interaction on Academic Achievement of Latino/a Children of Immigrants." *Ethnic and Racial Studies* iFirst: 1-23.

Marcia, James. 1980. "Identity in Adolescence." Pp. 159-187 in *Handbook of Adolescent Psychology*, edited by Joseph Adelson. New York: Wiley.

Mare, Robert D. 1997. "Differential Fertility, Intergenerational Educational Mobility, and Racial Inequality." *Social Science Research* 26: 263-291.

Marini, Margaret Mooney. 1978. "The Transition to Adulthood: Sex Differences in Educational Attainment and Age at Marriage." *American Sociological Review* 43: 483-507.

_____. 1980. "Sex Differences in the Process of Occupational Attainment: A Closer Look." *Social Science Research* 9: 307-361.

_____. 1984. "The Order of Events in the Transition to Adulthood." *Sociology of Education* 57: 63-84.

_____. 1989. "Sex Differences in Earnings in the United States." *Annual Review of Sociology* 15: 343-380.

Marini, Margaret Mooney and Ellen Greenberger. 1978. "Sex Differences in Educational Aspirations and Expectations." *American Educational Research* Journal 15: 67-79.

Marmot, Michael G., Carol D. Ryff, Larry L. Bumpass, Martin Shipley, and Nadine F. Marks. 1997. "Social Inequalities in Health: Next Questions and Converging Evidence." *Social Science Medicine* 44: 901-910.

Martinez, Jr., Ramiro, Matthew T. Lee, and Amie L. Nielsen. 2004. "Segmented Assimilation, Local Context, and Determinants of Drug Violence in Miami and San Diego: Does Ethnicity and Immigration Matter?" *International Migration Review* 38: 131-157.

Martorano, Suzanne C. 1977. "A Developmental Analysis of Performance on Piaget's Formal Operations Tasks." *Developmental Psychology* 13: 666-672.

Massey, Douglas S. 2009. "Racial Formation in Theory and Practice: The Case of Mexicans in the United States." *Race and Social Problems* 1: 12-26.

Matute-Bianchi, Maria Eugenia. 1986. "Ethnic Identities and Patterns of School Success and Failure among Mexican-Descent and Japanese-American Students in a California High School: An Ethnographic Analysis." *American Journal of Education* 95: 233-255.

Mauldin, Teresa and Carol B. Meeks. 1990. "Sex Differences in Children's Time Use." *Sex Roles* 22: 537-554.

McDonnell, Patrick J. 1997. "Prop. 187 Found Unconstitutional by Federal Judge." *Los Angeles Times*, November 15, 1997.

McFadden, Anna C., George E. Marsh, Barrie Jo Price, and Yunhan Hwang. 1992. "A Study of Race and Gender Bias in the Punishment of Handicapped School Children." *The Urban Review* 24: 239-251.

Messerschmidt, James W. 1993. *Masculinities and Crime: Critique and Reconceptualization of Theory.* Lanham, MD: Rowman & Littlefield.

Mickelson, Roslyn Arlin. 1989. "Why Does Jane Read and Write So Well? The Anomaly of Women's Achievement." *Sociology of Education* 62: 47-63.

_____. 1990. "The Attitude-Achievement Paradox among Black Adolescents." *Sociology of Education* 63: 44-61.

Morgan, Stephen L. 1996. "Trends in Black-White Differences in Educational Expectations, 1980-1992." *Sociology of Education* 69: 308-319.

_____. 1998. "Adolescent Educational Expectations: Rationalized, Fantasized, or Both?" *Rationality and Society* 10: 131-162.

_____. 2005. *On the Edge of Commitment: Educational Attainment and Race in the United States.* Stanford: Stanford University Press.

Mouw, Ted and Yu Xie. 1999. "Bilingualism and the Academic Achievement of First- and Second-Generation Asian Americans: Accommodation with or without Assimilation?" *American Sociological Review* 64: 232-252.

Muller, Chandra. 1993. "Parent Involvement and Academic Achievement: An Analysis of Family Resources Available to the Child." Pp. 77-113 in *Parents, Their Children, and Schools*, edited by Barbara Schneider and James S. Coleman, Boulder, CO: Westview.

_____. 1995. "Maternal Employment, Parental Involvement, and Mathematics Achievement among Adolescents." *Journal of Marriage and the Family* 57: 85-100.

_____. 1998. "Gender Differences in Parental Involvement and Adolescents' Mathematics Achievement." *Sociology of Education* 71: 336-356.

Neckerman, Kathryn, Prudence Carter, and Jennifer Lee. 1999. "Segmented Assimilation and Minority Cultures of Mobility." *Ethnic and Racial Studies* 22: 945-965.

Newman, Katherine. 1999. *No Shame in My Game: The Working Poor in the Inner City.* New York: Knopf and the Russell Sage Foundation.

Noh, Marianne S. 2008. "Contextualizing Ethnic/Racial Identity: Nationalized and Gendered Experiences of Segmented Assimilation among Second Generation Korean Immigrants in Canada and the United States." Ph.D. dissertation, Graduate Faculty of The University of Akron.

Nonn, Timothy. 1995. "Hitting Bottom: Homelessness, Poverty, and Masculinity." Pp. 225-234 in *Men's Lives*, 3rd edition, edited by Michael S. Kimmel and Michael A. Messner. Boston: Allyn and Bacon.

Ogbu, John U. 1978. *Minority Education and Caste: The American System in Cross-Cultural Perspective.* New York: Academic Press.

_____. 1991. "Immigrant and Involuntary Minorities in Comparative Perspective." Pp. 3-33 in *Minority Status and Schooling: A Comparative Study of Immigrant and Involuntary Minorities*, edited by Margaret A. Gibson and John U. Ogbu. New York: Garland.

Omi, Michael and Howard Winant. 1994. *Racial Formation in the United States*. New York: Routledge.

Ontai-Grzebik, Lenna L. and Marcela Raffaelli. 2004. "Individual and Social Influences on Ethnic Identity among Latino Young Adults." *Journal of Adolescent Research* 19: 559-575.

Padavic, Irene and Barbara Reskin. 2002. *Women and Men at Work*. Thousand Oaks, CA: Pine Forge Press.

Park, Robert. 1928. "Human Migration and the Marginal Man." *American Journal of Sociology* 33: 881-893.

_____. 1950. *Race and Culture*. Glencoe, IL: The Free Press.

Park, Robert and Ernest W. Burgess. [1921] 1924. *Introduction to the Science of Sociology*. Chicago: University of Chicago Press.

Pérez, Lisandro. 2001. "Growing Up in Cuban Miami: Immigration, the Enclave, and New Generations." Pp. 91-125 in *Ethnicities: Children of Immigrants in America*, edited by Rubén G. Rumbaut and Alejandro Portes. Berkeley: University of California Press.

Perlmann, Joel. 2001. "Young Mexican Americans, Blacks, and Whites in Recent Years: Schooling and Teen Motherhood as Indicators of Strengths and Risks." Levy Economics Institute Working Paper No. 335.

Perlmann, Joel and Roger Waldinger. 1997. "Second Generation Decline? Children of Immigrants, Past and Present—A Reconsideration." *International Migration Review* 31: 893-922.

Perreira, Krista M., Kathleen Mullan Harris, and Dohoon Lee. 2006. "Making It in America: High School Completion by Immigrant and Native Youth." *Demography* 43: 511-536.

Pessar, Patricia R. 1999a. "Engendering Migration Studies: The Case of New Immigrants in the United States." *American Behavioral Scientist* 42: 577-600.

_____. 1999b. "The Role of Gender, Households, and Social Networks in the Migration Process: A Review and Appraisal." Pp. 53-70 in *Handbook of International Migration: The American Experience*, edited by Charles Hirschman, Philip Kasinitz, and Josh DeWind. New York: Russell Sage Foundation.

Petersen, Anne C. 1983. "Adolescent Development." *Annual Review of Psychology*, 39: 583-607.

Phinney, Jean S. 1990. "Ethnic Identity in Adolescents and Adults: Review of Research." *Psychological Bulletin* 108: 499-514.

_____. 1992. "The Multigroup Ethnic Identity Measure: A New Scale for Use with Diverse Groups." *Journal of Adolescent Research* 7: 156-176.

Planty, Michael, William Hussar, Thomas Snyder, Stephen Provasnik, Grace Kena, Rachel Dinkes, Angelina KewalRamani, and Jana Kemp. 2008. *The Condition of Education 2008*. Washington, DC: National Center for Education Statistics, Institute of Education Sciences, U.S. Department of Education.

Portes, Alejandro. 1995. "Children of Immigrants: Segmented Assimilation and Its Determinants." Pp. 248-279 in *Economic Sociology of Immigration: Essays on Networks, Ethnicity, and Entrepreneurship*, edited by Alejandro Portes. New York: Russell Sage Foundation.

_____. 1998. "Social Capital: Its Origins and Applications in Modern Sociology." *Annual Review of Sociology* 24: 1-12.

_____. 2007. "Migration, Development, and Segmented Assimilation: A Conceptual Review of the Evidence." *The Annals of the American Academy of Political and Social Science* 610: 73-97.

Portes, Alejandro and M. Patricia Fernández-Kelly. 2008. "Educational and Occupational Achievement among Disadvantaged Children of Immigrants." *Annals of the American Academy of Political and Social Science* 620: 12-36.

Portes, Alejandro, M. Patricia Fernández-Kelly, and William Haller. 2005. "Segmented Assimilation on the Ground: The New Second Generation in Early Adulthood." *Ethnic and Racial Studies* 28: 1000-1040.

_____. 2009. "The Adaptation of the Immigrant Second Generation in America: A Theoretical Overview and Recent Evidence." *Journal of Ethnic and Migration Studies* 35: 1077-1104.

Portes, Alejandro and Lingxin Hao. 2002. "The Price of Uniformity: Language, Family and Personality Adjustment in the Immigrant Second Generation." *Ethnic and Racial Studies* 25: 889-912

Portes, Alejandro and Rubén G. Rumbaut. 1996. *Immigrant America: A Portrait*. Second edition. Berkeley: University of California Press.

_____. 2001a. *Legacies: The Story of the Immigrant Second Generation.* Berkeley: University of California Press.

_____. 2001b. "Conclusion: The Forging of a New America: Lessons for Theory and Policy." Pp. 301-317 in *Ethnicities: Children of Immigrants in America*, edited by Rubén G. Rumbaut and Alejandro Portes. Berkeley: University of California Press.

_____. 2005. "Introduction: The Second Generation and the Children of Immigrants Longitudinal Study." *Ethnic and Racial Studies* 28: 983-999.

Portes, Alejandro and Richard Schauffler. 1994. "Language and the Second Generation: Bilingualism Yesterday and Today." *International Migration Review* 28: 640-661.

Portes, Alejandro and Min Zhou. 1993. "The New Second Generation: Segmented Assimilation and Its Variants." *Annals of the American Academy of Political and Social Science* 530: 74-96.

Ramakrishnan, S. Karthick and Hans P. Johnson. 2005. "Second-Generation Immigrants in California." *California Counts: Population Trends and Profiles* 6 (4). San Francisco: Public Policy Institute of California.

Randour, M.L., G.L. Strasburg, G.L. and J. Lipman-Blumen. 1982. "Women in Higher Education: Trends in Enrollments and Degrees Earned." *Harvard Educational Review* 52: 189-202.

Reskin, Barbara. 1988. "Bringing the Men Back In: Sex Differentiation and the Devaluation of Women's Work." *Gender and Society* 2: 58-81.

_____. 1993. "Sex Segregation in the Workplace." *Annual Review of Sociology* 19: 241-270.

Rolison, Garry L. 1991. "An Exploration of the Term Underclass as It Relates to African-Americans." *Journal of Black Studies* 21: 287-301.

Rosen, Bernard C. and Carol S. Aneshensel. 1978. "Sex Differences in the Educational-Occupational Expectation Process." *Social Forces* 57: 164-186.

Royston, Patrick. 2005. "Multiple Imputation of Missing Values: Update." *The Stata Journal* 5: 1-14.

Rubin, Donald B. 1996. "Multiple Imputation After 18+ Years." *Journal of the American Statistical Association* 91: 473-489.

Rumbaut, Rubén G. 1994. "The Crucible Within: Ethnic Identity, Self Esteem, and Segmented Assimilation among Children of Immigrants." *International Migration Review* 28: 748-794.

_____. 1995. "The New Californians: Comparative Research Findings on the Educational Progress of Immigrant Children." In Rubén G. Rumbaut and Wayne A. Cornelius, eds., *California's Immigrant Children: Theory, Research, and Implications for Educational Policy.* La Jolla: Center for U.S.-Mexican Studies, University of California, San Diego.

_____. 1997a. "Assimilation and Its Discontents: Between Rhetoric and Reality." *International Migration Review* 31: 923-960.

_____. 1997b. "Paradoxes (and Orthodoxies) of Assimilation." *Sociological Perspectives* 40: 483-511.

_____. 2004. "Ages, Life Stages, and Generational Cohorts: Decomposing the Immigrant First and Second Generations in the United States." *International Migration Review* 38: 1160-1205.

_____. 2005. "Turning Point in the Transition to Adulthood: Determinants of Educational Attainment, Incarceration, and Early Childbearing among Children of Immigrants." *Ethnic and Racial Studies* 28: 1041-1086.

_____. 2008. "The Coming of the Second Generation: Immigration and Ethnic Mobility in Southern California." *The Annals of the American Academy of Political and Social Science* 620: 196-236.

_____. 2009. "Pigments of Our Imagination: On the Racialization and Racial Identities of 'Hispanics' and 'Latinos.'" Pp. 15-36 in *How the U.S. Racializes Latinos: White Hegemony and Its Consequences*, edited by José A. Cabas, Jorge Duany, and Joe R. Feagin. Boulder, CO: Paradigm Publishers.

Rumbaut, Rubén G. and Golnaz Komaie. 2010. "Immigration and Adult Transitions." *The Future of Children* 20: 39-63.

Sayer, Liana C. 2005. "Gender, Time and Inequality: Trends in Women's and Men's Paid Work, Unpaid Work and Free Time." *Social Forces* 84: 285-303.

Schneider, Barbara L. and David Stevenson. 2000. *The Ambitious Generation: America's Teenagers, Motivated But Directionless*. New Haven: Yale University Press.

Sewell, William H. and Robert M. Hauser. 1975. *Education, Occupation, and Earnings: Achievement in the Early Career*. New York: Academic Press.

Sewell, William H., Robert M. Hauser, and Wendy C. Wolf. 1980. "Sex, Schooling, and Occupational Status." *American Journal of Sociology* 86: 551-583.

Shaw, Steven R. and Jeffery B. Braden. 1990. "Race and Gender Bias in the Administration of Corporal Punishment." *School Psychology Review* 19: 378-383.

Silverman, Irwin W. 2003. "Gender Differences in Delay of Gratification: A Meta-Analysis." *Sex Roles* 49: 451-463.

Simons, Sarah E. 1901. "Social Assimilation. I." *American Journal of Sociology* 6: 790-822.

Singleton, David and Lisa Ryan. 2004. *Language Acquisition: The Age Factor.* Towanda, NY: Multilingual Matters Ltd.

Skelton, Christine. 2001. *Schooling the Boys: Masculinities and Primary Education.* Buckingham, UK, and Philadelphia: Open University Press.

Skiba, Russell J., Reece L. Peterson, and Tara Williams. 1997. "Office Referrals and Suspension: Disciplinary Intervention in Middle Schools." *Education and Treatment of Children* 20: 295-315.

Smith, James P. 2003. "Assimilation across the Latino Generations." *American Economic Review* 93: 315-319.

_____. 2006. "Immigrants and the Labor Market." *Journal of Labor Economics* 24: 203-233.

St-Hilaire, Aonghas. 2002. "The Social Adaptation of Children of Mexican Immigrants: Educational Aspirations Beyond Junior High School." *Social Science Quarterly* 83: 1026-1043.

Steelman, Lala Carr and Brian Powell. 1991. "Sponsoring the Next Generation: Parental Willingness to Pay for Higher Education." *American Journal of Sociology* 96: 1505-1529.

Stepick, Alex, Carol Dutton Stepick, Emmanuel Eugene, Deborah Teed, and Yves Labissiere. 2001. "Shifting Identities and Intergenerational Conflict: Growing up Haitian in Miami." Pp. 229-266 in *Ethnicities: Children of Immigrants in America*, edited by Rubén G. Rumbaut and Alejandro Portes. Berkeley: University of California Press.

Stevens, Gillian. 1985. "Nativity, Intermarriage, and Mother-Tongue Shift." *American Sociological Review* 50: 74-83.

_____. 1986. "Sex Differences in Language Shift in the United States." *Sociology and Social Research* 71: 31-36.

_____. 1992. "The Social and Demographic Context of Language Use in the United States." *American Sociological Review* 57: 171-185.

_____. 1999. "Age at Immigration and Second Language Proficiency among Foreign-Born Adults." *Language in Society* 28: 555-578.

Stromquist, Nelly P. 1989. "Determinants of Educational Participation and Achievement of Women in the Third World: A Review of the Evidence and a Theoretical Critique." *Review of Educational Research* 59: 143-183.

Suárez-Orozco, Carola and Desirée Baolian Qin. 2006. "Gendered Perspectives in Psychology: Immigrant Origin Youth." *International Migration Review* 40: 165-198.

Suárez-Orozco, Carola and Marcelo Suárez-Orozco. 2001. *Children of Immigration.* Cambridge, MA: Harvard University Press.

Sui-Chu, Esther Ho and J. Douglas Willms. 1996. "Effects of Parental Involvement on Eighth-Grade Achievement." *Sociology of Education* 69: 126-141.

Tajfel, Henri. 1981. *Human Groups and Social Categories: Studies in Social Psychology.* New York: Cambridge University Press.

Taylor, Maurice C. and Gerald A. Foster. 1986. "Bad Boys and School Suspensions: Public Policy Implications for Black Males." *Sociological Inquiry* 56: 498-506.

Teachman, Jay D., Kathleen Paasch, and Karen Carver. 1997. "Social Capital and the Generation of Human Capital." *Social Forces* 75: 1343-1359.

Telles, Edward E. and Vilma Ortiz. 2008. *Generations of Exclusion: Mexican Americans, Assimilation, and Race.* New York: Russell Sage Foundation.

Thorne, Barrie. 1993. *Gender Play: Girls and Boys in School.* New Brunswick, New Jersey, and London: Rutgers University Press.

Trusty, Jerry, and Morag B. Colvin Harris. 1999. "Lost Talent: Predictors of the Stability of Educational Expectations Across Adolescence." *Journal of Adolescent Research* 14: 359-382.

Tyson, Karolyn, William Darity, Jr., and Domini R. Castellino. 2005. "It's Not 'a Black Thing': Understanding the Burden of Acting White and Other Dilemmas of High Achievement." *American Sociological Review* 70: 582-605.

Urciuoli, Bonnie. 1991. "The Political Topography of Spanish and English: The View from a New York Puerto Rican Neighborhood." *American Ethnologist* 18: 295-310.

U.S. Bureau of the Census. 1995. "American Women: A Profile." *Statistical Brief,* SB/95-19. Washington, DC: U.S. Bureau of the Census.

U.S. Department of Homeland Security. 2007. *Yearbook of Immigration Statistics: 2006.* Washington, DC: U.S. Department of Homeland Security Office of Immigration Statistics.

Valde, Gregory A. 1996. "Identity Closure: A Fifth Identity Status." *Journal of Genetic Psychology* 157: 242-254.

Valdez, Zulema. 2006. "Segmented Assimilation Among Mexicans in the Southwest." *The Sociological Quarterly* 47: 397-424.

Valenzuela, Jr., Abel. 1999. "Gender Roles and Settlement Activities Among Children and Their Immigrant Families." *American Behavioral Scientist* 42: 720-742.

Van Hook, Jennifer and Kelly Stamper Balistreri. 2002. "Diversity and Change in the Institutional Context of Immigrant Adaptation: California Schools 1985-2000." *Demography* 39: 639-654.

Veltman, Calvin. 1981. "Anglicization in the United States: The Importance of Parental Nativity and Language Practice." *International Journal of the Sociology of Language* 32: 65-84.

_____. 1988. "Modeling the Language Shift Process of Hispanic Immigrants." *International Migration Review* 22: 545-562.

_____. 1990. "The Status of Spanish Language in the United States at the Beginning of the 21st Century." *International Migration Review* 24: 108-123.

Vermeulen, Hans. 2010. "Segmented Assimilation and Cross-National Comparative Research on the Integration of Immigrants and the Their Children." *Ethnic and Racial Studies* 33: 1214-1230.

Waldinger, Roger and Cynthia Feliciano. 2004. "Will the New Second Generation Experience 'Downward Assimilation'? Segmented Assimilation Re-Assessed." *Ethnic and Racial Studies* 27: 376-402.

Waldinger, Roger and Renee Reichl. 2007. "Today's New Second Generation: Getting Ahead or Falling Behind." Pp. 17-41 in *Securing the Future: U.S. Immigrant Integration Policy, A Reader*, edited by Michael Fix. Washington, DC: Migration Policy Institute.

Warikoo, Natasha. 2005. "Gender and Ethnic Identity among Second-Generation Indo-Caribbeans." *Ethnic and Racial Studies* 28: 803-831.

Warner, W. Lloyd and Leo Srole. 1945. *The Social Systems of American Ethnic Groups*. New Haven: Yale University Press.

Warren, John Robert, Jennifer T. Sheridan, and Robert M. Hauser. 2002. "Occupational Stratification across the Life Course: Evidence from the Wisconsin Longitudinal Study." *American Sociological Review* 67: 432-455.

Waterman, Alan S. 1982. "Identity Development from Adolescence to Adulthood: An Extension of Theory and a Review of Research." *Developmental Psychology* 18: 341-358.

Waters, Mary C. 1990. *Ethnic Options: Choosing Identities in America.* Berkeley: University of California Press.

_____. 1996. "The Intersection of Gender, Race, and Ethnicity in Identity Development of Caribbean American Teens." Pp. 65-81 in *Urban Girls: Resisting Stereotypes, Creating Identities*, edited by Bonnie J. Ross Leadbeater and Niobe Way. New York: NYU Press.

_____. 1999. *Black Identities: West Indian Immigrant Dreams and American Realities.* New York: Russell Sage Foundation.

_____. 2004. "Race, Ethnicity, and Immigration in the United States." Pp. 20-38 in *Social Inequalities in Comparative Perspective*, edited by Fiona Devine and Mary C. Waters. Malden, MA: Blackwell Publishing.

West, Candace and Don H. Zimmerman. 1987. "Doing Gender." *Gender and Society* 1: 125-151.

Whitbourne, Susan K. and Stephanie A. Tesch. 1985. "A Comparison of Identity and Intimacy Statuses in College Students and Alumni." *Development Psychology* 21: 1039-1044.

Wildsmith, Elizabeth. 2004. "Race/Ethnic Differences in Female Headship: Exploring the Assumptions of Assimilation Theory." *Social Science Quarterly* 85: 89-106.

Williams, David R. and Chiquita Collins. 1995. "U.S. Socioeconomic and Racial Differences in Health: Patterns and Explanations". *Annual Review of Sociology*, 21: 349-386.

Williams, L. Susan, Sandra D. Alvarez, and Kevin S. Andrade Hauch. 2002. "My Name Is Not Maria: Young Latinas Seeking Home in the Heartland." *Social Problems* 49: 563-584.

Willis, Paul E. 1977. *Learning to Labour: How Working Class Kids Get Working Class Jobs.* Farnborough, England: Saxon House.

Wilson, William Julius. 1987. *The Truly Disadvantaged: The Inner City, the Underclass, and Public Policy.* Chicago: University of Chicago Press.

Xie, Yu and Emily Greenman. 2005. "Segmented Assimilation Theory: A Reformulation and Empirical Test." *Population Studies Center Research Report 05-581.*

Zhou, Min. 1997. "Segmented Assimilation: Issues, Controversies, and Recent Research on the New Second Generation." *International Migration Review* 31: 975-1008.

Zhou, Min and Carl L. Bankston, III. 1994. "Social Capital and the Adaptation of the 2nd Generation: The Case of Vietnamese Youth in New Orleans." *International Migration Review* 28: 821-845.

_____. 1998. *Growing Up American: How Vietnamese Children Adapt to Life in the United States.* New York: Russell Sage Foundation.

_____. 2001. "Family Pressure and the Educational Experience of the Daughters of Vietnamese Refugees." *International Migration* 39: 133-151.

Zhou, Min, Jennifer Lee, Jody Agius Vallejo, Rosaura Tafoya-Estrada, and Yang Sao Xiong. 2008. "Success Attained, Deterred, and Denied: Divergent Pathways to Social Mobility in Los Angeles's New Second Generation." *The Annals of the American Academy of Political and Social Science* 620: 37-61.

Zhou, Min and Yang Sao Xiong. 2005. "The Multifaceted American Experiences of the Children of Asian Immigrants: Lessons for Segmented Assimilation." *Ethnic and Racial Studies* 28: 1119-1152.

Index

THE HOME POTTER